The Conquest of the Missouri

Grant Marsh

The Conquest of the Missouri

Captain Grant Marsh, and the Riverboats of the American Civil War and Plains Indian Wars

Joseph Mills Hansom

The Conquest of the Missouri
Captain Grant Marsh, and the Riverboats of the American Civil War and Plains Indian Wars
by Joseph Mills Hansom

First published under the title
The Conquest of the Missouri

Leonaur is an imprint of Oakpast Ltd
Copyright in this form © 2011 Oakpast Ltd

ISBN: 978-0-85706-751-7 (hardcover)
ISBN: 978-0-85706-752-4 (softcover)

http://www.leonaur.com

Publisher's Notes

The opinions of the authors represent a view of events in which he was a participant related from his own perspective, as such the text is relevant as an historical document.

The views expressed in this book are not necessarily those of the publisher.

Contents

Preface	9
Westward by the Main Channel	13
The Ice Gorge of '56	18
Old-Time Packets and the Men Who Ruled Them	22
"Mark Twain" at the Rudder	27
Cupid at the Apple-Butter Stirring	32
The Battle Morn of Shiloh	35
Barbarism at Bay	44
With Sully Into the Sioux Lands	47
Three Roads to El Dorado	53
The "Luella" at Fort Benton in Vigilante Days	59
The Troubles of a Treasure Ship	66
The Captain Encounters a "Bad Man"	72
Blockaded by Buffalo	75
A Game of Strategy	79
Ice-Bound on the Nile	83
Wood Hawks	90
The Vegetable Trip of the "North Alabama"	94
The Hare and the Tortoise	100
A Three Thousand Mile Race	104
The Railroad Comes	109
With Forsyth of Beecher's Island	113

"Yellowstone" Kelly guides the "Key West"	120
Campaigning With the Seventh Cavalry	129
Pioneer Paths	142
Bound for the Mountains	145
Breasting Unknown Waters	152
Lonesome Charlie	157
By Line and Spar to the Head of Navigation	160
First Blood For Crazy Horse	169
Custer to the Front	175
The Heroine of the Upper River	178
Strong Men and True	184
The Last Council of War	188
The Seventh Marches Into the Shadow	196
The Messenger of Disaster	200
The Squadron That Perished	208
The Aftermath of Battle	215
The "Far West" Races With Death	224
The Battle at Powder River	237
Terry Takes the Field	248
Patrol Duty With Miles and "Buffalo Bill"	253
The Fruits of Struggle	264
The "Rosebud" Carries the General of the Army	273
The Bones of Heroes	279
Rustlers	285
With Kendrick to the Musselshell	294
The Sioux Bend to Fate	301
Turned Turtle	311
The Garden Out of the Wilderness	315

To My
Mother

Preface

In preparing the following narrative of the principal events in the life of Captain Grant Marsh, the author has naturally been furnished by the latter with much the larger part of the material set forth. Captain Marsh was an actor in events of great historic moment, covering almost the entire period of the conquest of the upper Missouri River Valley, the subjugation of the Sioux Indians and the opening to civilization of the vast territory which they had occupied. But the direct observations of a man in his position were generally and necessarily limited to his immediate surroundings, and the recital of his experiences alone during his years of activity in the Northwest would give to the reader but an indistinct impression of the conditions prevailing there and of their underlying causes. Hence it has been deemed best to amplify the story of the captain's adventures with as much general history as is essential to a clear understanding of the period and of the part which he played in it. Such a course is rendered more imperative by the fact that many of the events treated have never received more than passing attention from historians, and remain today practically unknown save to those who participated in them.

The author has endeavoured, whenever possible, to verify Captain Marsh's recollections of events possessing any historical significance, by reference to official or other reliable documents, and very rarely has the captain's memory been found at fault, even in details. In cases where documentary evidence was unobtainable, verification has been sought from other sources, chiefly by correspondence with persons intimately acquainted with the facts, either through historical research or by reason of personal experience. Most of the latter to whom the author has applied have been associated with Captain Marsh at one time or another during his years on the rivers of the West. The correspondence with them has been undertaken for the double purpose of securing evidence on historical facts, and of obtaining from them their personal recollections of the captain. All of them have responded most generously to requests for information and the author's thanks are particularly due to those mentioned below.

The late Major-General James W. Forsyth, U.S.A., and the late Brigadier-General Samuel B. Holabird, U.S.A., both of whom have died since their kind assistance was rendered.

The late Mary Louise Dalton, Librarian of the Missouri Historical Society, St. Louis, Mo., for placing the collections of the Society at the author's disposal, and for critical reading of his entire manuscript.

Miss May Simonds, Reference Librarian of the Mercantile Library, St. Louis, Mo., for assistance in obtaining works of reference.

Mrs. Laura E. Howey, Secretary and Librarian of the Montana State Library, Helena, Mont., for researches among the records of the Historical Society of Montana.

Doctor W. J. McGee, Director of the St. Louis Public Museum, formerly Ethnologist in Charge, Bureau of American Ethnology, for assistance in determining the proper spelling and use of Indian names.

Brigadier-General Edward S. Godfrey, U.S.A., Commandant of the Special Service School of Application for Cavalry and Field Artillery, Fort Riley, Kansas, for painstaking assistance in the preparation of many chapters.

The following other officers and non-commissioned officers of the United States Army, all retired, for written communications or for the critical reading of portions of the manuscript:

Lieutenant-General Nelson A. Miles, Lieutenant-Colonel and Brevet Brigadier-General George A. Forsyth, Major William H. H. Crowell, Major Frederick M. H. Kendrick, Major Luther R. Hare, Lieutenant Charles Braden, Sergeant M. C. Caddie.

The following steamboat men, for communications or for the loan of photographs:

Horace Bixby, Alexander Lamont, Nicholas Buesen, George Foulk, William H. Gould, Grant C. Marsh.

The following other persons, for critical reading of portions of the manuscript, for communications, or for the loan of photographs:

Colonel William F. Cody, James M. Sipes, John H. Fouch, Major Luther S. Kelly, Walter H. Carr, Major Joseph R. Hanson, Samuel L. Clemens, Peter Koch, George W. Kingsbury, Sr., Joseph H. Taylor, Colonel C. A. Lounsberry, A. C. Leighton, J. R. Mann, Olin D. Wheeler, Major Martin Maginnis and the late Robert E. McDowell.

The following institutions for the loan of photographs: The Historical Society of Montana, the Carnegie Public Library, Miles City, Montana.

Many of the chapters have been submitted to competent authorities for critical reading. Such errors as existed have thus been found and corrected, while, in a number of instances, additional facts have been inserted. Mrs. Laura E. Howey and Major Martin Maginnis have read the chapters relating to the first trip of the steamer *Luella* to Fort Benton, in 1866; Major-General Samuel B. Holabird, those on the trip of the *Ida Stockdale;* Brigadier-General George A. Forsyth, those on the exploration of the lower Yellowstone River by the *Key West*; Lieutenant Charles Braden, that on the Stanley Expedition; Major William H. H. Crowell, those on the exploration of the upper Yellowstone by the *Josephine;* Brigadier-General E. S. Godfrey, those on the Little Big Horn campaign; General Godfrey and Colonel C. A. Lounsberry, that on the run of the *Far West* with the wounded from the battlefield of the Little Big Horn; and Lieutenant-General Nelson A. Miles, those on the campaigns immediately succeeding the battle of the Little Big Horn.

Joseph Mills Hanson.

CHAPTER 1

Westward by the Main Channel

Since the days when the first far-scattered Spanish and French and English adventurers forced their slow way into the untamed North American wilderness, striving mightily against savage foes and more savage nature, the rivers of the continent have marked the lines of warfare and the boundaries of conquest. The natural avenues of communication between one region and another, it has been beside and upon their waters that the pioneers have ever pushed their persistent way through dangers and difficulties until the whole land lay open at their feet. It was but yesterday that the last strongholds of barbarism along the Rio Grande del Norte, and the Colorado of the Southwest, and the Missouri with its fretful tributaries of the Northwest, still stood locked and defiant against the besieging hosts of civilization. Today they are fallen, never to rise again.

But amid the regions traversed by those historic streams, where the echo of the war whoop and the sharp crack of the cavalry carbine have scarce died away, still linger many of the men who helped to bring to submission those final citadels of savagery. Gray-haired they may be, feeble, perhaps, some of them. But in their carriage is a manner of self-reliant freedom and in their eyes a light of power which men bred to milder modes of life cannot know. For they have looked upon Nature in her unconquered strength and majesty; they have grappled with her creatures in equal combat, and have come off victors. The continent will not know their like again.

Though for the most part these survivors of a vanished era have retired into the peaceful old age which their years of effort have earned for them, a few are still living and working in the fields of their earlier activities. So, if one should walk down to the river front of the little town of Washburn, North Dakota, on almost any day during the summer season, he would be apt to encounter there, busied about the loading or unloading of one of the small, stern-wheel steamboats which still ply the upper waters of the Missouri, a man whose whole appearance and manner would at once call to mind the history and romance of the days when the Big Muddy ran far beyond the confines of civilization and was the scene of military activity and frontier adventure. Nor does the truth belie his appearance. Tall, broad-shouldered and powerful of frame, clear-eyed and gentle of voice, this veteran navigator of the Missouri has lived and worked, shoulder to shoulder, with many men famous in history, and passed through as many strange and rugged experiences as would stock the biography of an adventurer of the Spanish Main.

Though the river traffic of the Missouri is generally held to have died out many years ago, Grant Prince Marsh, steamboat captain and pilot, still finds on its tawny waters the home and the congenial occupation to which he has been devoted since the long-ago day in 1846 when, as a small lad of twelve years, bent upon seeing the world, he applied for a position to Captain Alfred Reno, of the steamer *Dover*, lying at the levee of Pittsburg, Pa., and was shipped as cabin-boy for the first of his hundreds of voyages on the waterways of the West.

The impulse which sent him to seek the life of the river at so tender an age was as natural as that which impels many a boy born within sound of the ocean's breakers to seek a home on the face of the deep as soon as he can contrive to slip away from the paternal roof. Since his baby eyes had first learned to see, this child of the freshwater regions had known steamboats. When scarcely more than old enough to talk, he and his playmates in his little native town of Rochester, thirty miles below Pittsburg, had been accustomed to rush to the river bank whenever a packet came by, watching her in awe and admiration until she passed beyond view.

Sometimes, impelled by a childish impulse of mischief, they would throw stones at the labouring monsters. The veteran boatman remembers with amusement an afternoon when the big side-wheeler *Isaac Newton*, Captain Mason, came puffing up from Cincinnati, and he and his playmates began their pastime of throwing stones at her. The *Newton* was a short, wide boat, very difficult to handle, and as she passed she suddenly *ran away* with her pilot and came straight toward the shore where the boys were assembled. Smitten with terror, and thinking that she was in pursuit of them, they fled precipitately up the hill, never stopping until safe in their homes.

But young Marsh had learned a larger respect for the puissant steamboat when, a few years later, he proudly took his place as a member of the crew of the *Dover* and heard the paddles churn as she swung out into the current, bearing him away upon his first voyage. The *Dover* was an Allegheny River boat, plying between Pittsburg and Freeport, Pa., and her trade was heavy and continuous, as was that of her numerous consorts on the Ohio and its tributaries. West of the Allegheny Mountains no railroads had penetrated at that date, and the steamboats controlled all the commerce of the teeming river towns as well as the immense volume of immigration which was rolling constantly westward into the great, undeveloped regions of the Mississippi Valley and the fertile vastnesses beyond. It was a time when men's thoughts turned westward irresistibly, drawn by the fascination of unknown but alluring lands. The prairies of Iowa and the wooded hills of Missouri were as attractive to thousands of home-seekers as was the lure of the far-off California gold-fields to other thousands.

Young Marsh, being of a disposition to follow where fortune might lead, with increasing years gradually drifted westward on the universal tide, leaving the Allegheny to work on the boats running between Pittsburg and Ohio River points, and finally catching his first glimpse of the Mississippi when, in the early spring of 1852, he found employment as a deckhand on board the Pittsburg-St. Louis packet *Beaver,* commanded by Captain Sharp Hemphill, and went on her to St. Louis. This city, the metropolis of the Mississippi Valley then as now, presented a very different aspect to its present one when young Marsh first beheld it from the deck of the *Beaver.* Spread along the river bank was a city of 95,000 people, containing many great business establishments and commanding the commerce of a vast territory.

But not a foot of railroad was then in operation out of the city, nor, indeed, was there a foot in operation anywhere west of the Mississippi. On the other hand, her levee was lined with scores of steamboats whose trade routes radiated to the four points of the compass and brought to her merchants produce to the value of over $10,000,000.00 annually. The arrivals of steamboats in the port of St. Louis at this time averaged 3,000 yearly, and the total rated capacity of these was about 50,000 tons, making St. Louis the third port in the Union in amount of enrolled steam tonnage, New York and New Orleans alone exceeding her.[1]

The young boatman's first recollections of the western city carry

---

1. J. Thomas Scharf, *History of St. Louis City and County.*

The old Post Trader's store at Fort Buford, Dakota

(This building stood from 1856 t0 1872, when it was torn down by the firm of Leighton & Jordan and replaced by a new structure. The building shown, with its log walls and dirt roof, is typical of the architecture employed in constructing all of the early military posts along the upper Missouri.)

with them something of gloom, for 1852 was one of the years when Asiatic cholera was scourging the country; and St. Louis suffered heavily from the plague. Just as Marsh first stepped on the levee from the deck of the *Beaver*, he met a man leaving another boat with two babies in his arms. This gentleman accosted him and stated that the parents of the children he was carrying had both died of cholera on the boat and he, in pity, had taken charge of the helpless orphans in the hope of finding them a home.

Having attained the Mississippi, for two years Grant Marsh contented himself with remaining in the Louisville and St. Louis trade. Then once more the restless desire for new lands took possession of him, and in the spring of 1854 he shipped as a deck hand on the Missouri River steamer *F. X. Aubrey*, commanded by Captain Ambrose Reeder, and running in the open season between St. Louis and St. Joseph, Mo. Thus the boy of nineteen, already familiar with the intricate duties and versed in the peculiar kinds of knowledge demanded by western river navigation, first came upon the waters of that greatest and most erratic of American streams where most of his life was to be spent. For one year he remained with the *Aubrey* and then changed to the *A. B. Chambers*, Captain Bowman.

There was plenty of business to do, for until the summer of 1855, when the Missouri Pacific was completed to Jefferson City, no railroad extended westward along the Missouri from St. Louis. All the commerce of the prosperous agricultural country lying between the Mississippi and the Kansas line was handled by steamers, and a particularly heavy business was always done in the autumn, when the great crops of tobacco, hemp, and small grain, produced by slave labour on the plantations of the valley, began to pour into the steamboat landings for shipment to the St. Louis markets. Kansas City did not yet exist and Westport was the northern terminus of the historic old Santa Fé Trail, and also the distributing point for the section of country of which the former city is now the centre. Goods for Sedalia, Marshall, Warrensburg, Holden and other important towns in the interior were put ashore at the nearest river landing and hauled thence to their destinations in large freight wagons, drawn by several span of oxen or horses.

CHAPTER 2

The Ice Gorge of '56

During the winter of 1855-1856, the *A. B. Chambers* lay in ice-harbour at the St. Louis levee and Grant Marsh remained on board her as watchman. The winter was an unusually severe one, and the river, which does not often freeze over at St. Louis, closed hard and fast on New Year's Day, 1856, the ice continuing to grow thicker for some time after that. The river front, says Captain Marsh, was so solidly lined with steamboats that without stepping ashore one could walk upon their decks from Belcher's sugar refinery to Almond (now Valentine) Street, a distance of twenty blocks.

Late in February a period of warm weather set in on the upper rivers, causing a rise of water at St. Louis before the heavy ice had begun to thaw there. The result was terrible. On the day following, February 28th, a local newspaper[1] published an account of the disaster which is so graphic that it may well be reproduced here:

> The ice at first moved slowly, (says the chronicle), and without perceptible shock. The boats above Chestnut Street were merely shoved ashore, and for five minutes sustained no damage. Messrs. Eads' and Nelson's *Submarine Number* 4, which had just finished her work at the wreck of the *Parthenia*, was almost immediately capsized, and became herself a hopeless wreck. The *Submarine* floated down, lying broadside against the *Federal Arch*, which boat was being wrecked and of little value. Here the destruction commenced. The *Federal Arch* parted her fastenings and became at once a total wreck. Lying below were the steamers *Australia, Adriatic, Brunette, Paul Jones, Falls City, Altoona,*

---

1. *The Missouri Republican*, after the editor of which the steamer *A. B. Chambers* was named.

A. B. Chambers and *Challenge,* all of which were torn away from the shore and in company with the *Submarine* and *Federal Arch,* floated down with the immense field of ice.

The fleet of ten boats were more or less damaged at starting by crowding against one another. All the upper works of the *Brunette* and *Australia* were torn to pieces and the *Altoona* was badly damaged. The shock and the crushing of these boats when they were driven together can be better imagined than described. All their ample fastenings were as nothing against the enormous flood of ice, and they were carried down apparently fastened and wedged together. The first obstacles with which they came in contact were a large fleet of wood boats, barges and canal boats. These small fry were either broken in pieces or forced out of the water upon the levee in a very damaged condition.

We are not able to state the number, but there could not have been short of fifty in all, which were either sunk, broken or carried away with the descending boats. About twenty of them met with the latter fate, and the whole fleet lodged about one mile below, against the point of the island at the Lower Dyke. The *Adriatic* lost one of her wheels by swinging against the *Falls City* after they landed upon the bar below. The *Falls City* and the *Paul Jones* are very badly damaged, the *A. B. Chambers* but slightly. The *Challenge* is also badly injured.

After these boats had passed down, the *Bon Accord* and *Highland Mary,* lying together, were carried off and are both a total loss. The new *St. Paul,* on the docks, was slightly damaged, and part of the docks swept away from under her. The *Highland Mary* struck against the *Die Vernon,* damaging the latter boat considerably. The *Louisville* was also torn away from her moorings, and at last accounts was lying broadside and across the current with the other boats below. She is probably a total loss. The *Lamartine* was carried away in the same manner and will doubtless be lost. The *Westerner* broke her fastenings and swung against the *Jeanie Deans,* injuring the latter considerably.

Some of the boats lying above Chestnut Street fared badly in the meantime. The *F. X. Aubrey* was forced into the bank and had her larboard wheel broken. The noble *Nebraska,* which everyone thought in a most perilous situation, lost her larboard wheel and was not otherwise much injured. The *Gossamer, Luella, Alice* and *Badger State* were forced ashore and slightly damaged. Both the Alton wharf boats were sunk and broken to pieces. The old *Shenandoah,* being wrecked, and the *Sam Cloon* were forced away from shore and floated down together against the steamer *Clara.* The latter did not part her fastenings, and she and the *Shenandoah* lodged, when they were soon torn to pieces and sunk by the ice and one of the ferryboats, which came down alone.

The ferryboat floated on to the foot of Market Street, carrying part of the *Shenandoah* with her. The steamers *Clara* and *Ben Bolt* were both badly damaged by the ice and forced partly ashore. The *C. W. Sparhawk* was sunk, and looked as if broken in two lying at the shore. The Keokuk wharf boat maintained its position against the flood and saved three boats below, the *Polar Star, J. S. Pringle* and *Forest Rose,* none of which were up to this time materially injured.

After running about one hour, the character of ice was changed and came down in frothy, crumbled condition, with now and then a heavy piece. At the end of two hours it ran very slowly, and finally stopped about half-past five o'clock. During this interval a number of persons crossed it from the ferry landing on Bloody Island. They were chiefly passengers by a train just arrived, anxious to reach the city. The experiment was daring, but they landed safely on this side.

Just before the river gorged, huge piles of ice twenty and thirty feet in height were forced up by the current on every hand, both on the shore and at the Lower Dyke, where so many boats had come to a halt. In fact, these boats seemed to be literally buried in ice. It had not been broken below Cahokia Bend, and all the drift thus far had gorged between the city and that point; hence its sudden stop. At six o'clock p. m. the river had risen at least ten feet. At dark the people went home.

The terrible sweep of waters with its burden of ice, the mashing to pieces of boats, the hurrying to and fro of the excited crowd, was one of the most awful and at the same time most imposing scenes we have ever witnessed. The officers and crews of many of the boats went down the river with them; the lookers-on became alarmed and sprang from boat to boat in a rush for the shores. The captains and owners of canal, flatboats and barges fled, leaving their property to the mercy of circumstances. At seven p. m. the gorge below broke and the ice began running again. The current was now much more swift and the night very dark, a heavy and steady rain having set in.

That night and the next day the escaping ice completed the demolition of several boats already damaged, but the second day's destruction was not so great nor so unexpected as that of the first, whose record will always remain one of the most appalling of those in the history of the Mississippi. The *A. B. Chambers* came through with less injury than many of her consorts, though Watchman Marsh, floating upon her alone and helpless through the splintering wreckage along the levee, expected nothing less than to be killed, until she finally lodged against the wall of the United States Arsenal, three miles from her starting point, and he found himself once more safe.

CHAPTER 3

Old-Time Packets and the Men Who Ruled Them

Even such a wholesale loss of boats as that just described could not more than temporarily injure the vast floating traffic of the western rivers, for in those long years "before the War" steamboating was in the zenith of its prosperity, and the majestic packet had no rival to contest its right to commercial supremacy. Vast sums of money were expended in fitting up palatial vessels, and passengers paid well for the privilege of travelling upon them, as, indeed, would have been necessary in any case, for the expense of running the boats by the imperfect methods then in vogue was very great. Certain mechanical features of these old steamers which would seem curious indeed to the present-day marine engineer, are remembered by Captain Marsh.

At that time the size of a boat was determined by the number of boilers she carried, and in describing any vessel a riverman would term her "a two-boiler boat," or "four-boiler boat," without reference to her length or breadth of beam. The reason for this was that every vessel was obliged to carry as many boilers as could be crowded upon her in order to make her go at all. The waste of steam and fuel was enormous, for the practice of exhausting in the chimneys had not yet been thought of nor had that of heating the water before it went into the boilers. The big steamer *Eclipse,* Captain Sturgeon, built in the '50s, had a battery of fifteen boilers, eight large and seven small, and to keep them heated required wood by the car load. Captain Marsh tells a story, once current along the river, of the old *Nebraska,* a boat of the same class as the *Eclipse.*

It is to the effect that once on a trip to New Orleans she landed at a yard and took on one hundred cords of wood. As there were no snubbing posts at the landing to tie to during the progress of the work, Captain Jolly held her up to the bank by the outside wheel, which made it necessary to keep the engines going. When the fuel was loaded and the boat ready to start, it was discovered that all the wood taken aboard had been used up in holding her to the bank!

While this same steamer *Nebraska* was being built at Cincinnati, her mate, a man named Bassett, ordered for her a hawser eight inches in diameter. The rope manufacturers were dazed on receiving an order for a rope of such extraordinary size, but they rigged up special machinery and made it. When finished it required two freight cars to carry the cable to the steamboat. The captain saw at once that it was too large and unwieldy for service and sent it back to the factory where, after enough ropes for the *Nebraska's* use had been made from it, the remainder was still sufficient to equip several other steamers.

Asbestos and spring packing were unknown in the '50s and the engines were packed with cotton rope and cedar blocks, materials which served their purpose but indifferently. When it came to the control and navigation of a steamer, the methods then in force also differed greatly from those of later years. For example, it was customary to have a speaking trumpet extending from the hurricane deck down to the fire-doors on the main deck. When making a landing, the captain, standing on the upper deck, would use this trumpet to direct the firemen. At such times the engineer had nothing to say; the captain engineered her from the roof, shouting through the tube: "Open the quarter doors!" "Fill up the wing doors!" "Fill up clear across!" or whatever other orders he chose to give.

But the captain was by no means the most important individual on the ante-bellum steamboat. In point of authority, of prestige and of general indispensability, he loomed exceedingly small beside that truly despotic lord of the old-time river, the pilot. Upon the pilot depended absolutely the safety of vessel, passengers and cargo, and when the boat was under way, his word was a law before which every one bowed. His profession was a very difficult one to learn, requiring years of apprenticeship, and as the pilots themselves were the only ones who could train new men for places in their ranks, they took good care that their numbers were kept down to small and select proportions in order that neither their power nor the princely salaries which they commanded should be diminished. Every pilot was, as he is today, licensed by the government and no boat could move without him, but as the profits of steamboating were great then, he could demand almost any wages he chose, and Captain Marsh relates several amusing anecdotes in this connection of pilots whom he knew and worked with.

One of these was Joe Oldham, a man famous in his time for three things; his skill as a pilot, his independence and his extravagance in personal adornment. His was the distinction of possessing the largest, heaviest and most expensive gold watch on the river. Its stem contained a diamond worth five hundred dollars, and he wore it suspended about his neck by a massive gold chain. In the winter he wore huge fur mittens reaching to his elbows, and in the summer kid gloves of the most delicate hue.

One day a small, side-wheel packet, the *Moses Greenwood,* on her way up from the Ohio bound for Weston, Mo., came into St. Louis looking for a Missouri River pilot. It happened that Oldham was the only one in town and when the captain came to him, he blandly stated that he would take the *Moses Greenwood* to Weston and back, about a week's trip, for one thousand dollars. The captain demurred, but after several days, during which no other pilots appeared, and being in a hurry, he went to Oldham and said that he would pay the price.

"Well, I can't accept now, captain," answered the pilot, nonchalantly. "I'm going to a picnic this afternoon."

Pleadings were of no avail, and to the picnic he went.

On another occasion the steamer *Post Boy,* Captain Rider, came into St. Louis on her way to Leavenworth. Captain Rider sent for Oldham, who was again the only member of the craft in town, and he came down to the levee, bedecked with diamonds as usual, wearing a silk hat and patent-leather shoes, and shielding himself from the summer sun with a gold-handled, silk umbrella.

"How much will you charge to take my boat to Leavenworth and back, Mr. Oldham?" asked the captain.

"Fifteen hundred dollars," answered the pilot, gently.

"What?" shouted Captain Rider. "Man, that's more than the boat will make."

Oldham shrugged his shoulders.

"Well, talk fast, captain," he said. "I won't stand here in the hot sun fifteen minutes for fifteen hundred dollars."

The captain ground his teeth, but there was nothing to be done save pay the price or lie in port. So at length he said:

"All right, I'll consent to be robbed this time. We're all ready to start. Come aboard."

"But I'm not ready," quoth the pilot. "Just call a carriage and send me up to my rooms for my baggage."

Nevertheless, once aboard he did his work well, making the round trip in the excellent time of nine days and with no mishaps from the pitfalls of the treacherous Big Muddy. Despite all the money he earned during the years of the river's prosperity, when it was over, poor, improvident Oldham found himself penniless, and when he died, years after, it was in abject poverty, in a wretched hovel near the river bank at Yankton, South Dakota.

It was fortunate for Captain Rider in his transaction with Oldham, that the latter was not of as sensitive a disposition as was the pilot in another similar case. This man's name was Bob Burton and one day when the steamer *Aleonia,* Captain Miller, appeared at St. Louis, Bob demanded one thousand dollars for taking her to Weston, with the result that Captain Miller called him a robber and ordered him off the boat. As usual, the captain could secure no one else, and after several days, sent for Bob and told him that he would pay the thousand dollars.

"I won't go for less than fifteen hundred," replied Bob.

"What?" growled the captain. "You said you'd go for a thousand."

"Yes," said Bob, "but you insulted me, sir, and I charge you five hundred dollars for that."

Whatever the wages they could command, the pilots were not always entirely successful in navigating the difficult Missouri, but they seldom permitted themselves to be criticised or to appear disconcerted even in the face of repeated mishaps for which they were responsible. This was aptly demonstrated in the case of a certain member of the craft who once, in steering a boat up from St. Louis, met with so many accidents such as running aground, breaking the wheel and otherwise mutilating the vessel, that at last the captain came to him angrily and demanded:

"Look here, how many times have you been up the Missouri River, anyway?"

"Twice," responded the navigator unabashed. "Once in a skiff and once on horseback."

Another of Captain Marsh's brother pilots of early days was Jim Gunsalis, who almost rivalled Oldham in the barbaric splendour of his apparel. When he was pilot of the *A. B. Chambers No. 2,* his regular salary was eight hundred dollars per month. His particular weakness was for diamonds. Though the cabin was always so filled with passengers that the officers of the boat were accustomed to take their meals in the Texas,[1] Gunsalis positively refused to do so, insisting on a seat at the saloon table, where his jewellery might receive its due meed of admiration. He, like Oldham, died in poverty, his last occupation being that of tender for a dump boat at Carondelet, below St. Louis, and his funeral expenses were paid by subscription.

Next to the pilot, the most important individual on the old-time steamboat was the barkeeper. No sooner would the papers announce that a contract had been let for a new packet than everyone would begin speculating as to who would be selected for barkeeper. On a first-class boat, the barkeeper's dignity would not permit him to descend to the vulgarity of mixing drinks. He employed help for that purpose and himself mingled with the passengers and assisted the professional gamblers, who infested every boat, in fleecing them, receiving for his services a handsome commission. The gamblers never took long trips, but after making a *winning*, would disembark before they should be suspected. But the barkeeper, like the poor, the passengers had always with them.

---

1. It is said that in early days, when steamboats were small and their cabins few, it was customary to name the cabins after the States of the Union, and the cabin which was superimposed upon the others, being much the largest, was called the "Texas" cabin, after the largest state. In course of time the custom died out with respect to the other cabins, but the *Texas* has always retained its name.—J. M. H.

CHAPTER 4

"Mark Twain" at the Rudder

In the year following the disastrous St. Louis ice gorge, young Marsh once more extended the horizon of his experiences by going to Omaha on the large side-wheel packet *Alonzo Child,* of which he was enrolled as mate under Captain Joe Holland. The young man had passed the stage of apprenticeship and entered upon that of command.

In Omaha he found a town of the old frontier in the truest sense. It was a veritable mud-hole, consisting of two wretched streets straggling along the river bank and lined with the flimsy frame and log structures of a people too eagerly bent upon the pursuit of success to squander time or expense on the niceties of civilization. It was the outfitting place for the thousands of emigrants preparing to take the long trail across the desert and mountains for the California goldfields, and as such its squalid thoroughfares were thronged with every type of man, from the earnest home-seeker to the desperado, all drawn forth by dazzling dreams of wealth to be gathered in that far El Dorado beyond the Rockies.

Fifteen miles above Omaha lay Florence Landing, and forty miles below that of Wyoming, which points were then the places of rendezvous for the caravans of Mormons moving westward to their newly established Promised Land of Deseret, beside the dead waters of the Great Salt Lake. In some sense outcasts from their kind, these peculiar people would not mingle with the *Gentiles* in Omaha, preferring to make preparations for their long journey at the more secluded if less convenient landings mentioned.

In the autumn of this year, Marsh changed from the *Alonzo Child* to the *Hesperian,* Captain F. B. Kercheval, and went out with her on a late trip to Omaha, carrying freight for that place and intermediate points. The whole country was in the throes of a financial panic at that time, due to the deplorable system which permitted the issue of *wildcat* currency by irresponsible banks. When the *Hesperian* got beyond St. Joseph, it was found that the merchants had nothing with which to pay the freight charges on their goods except paper money. At some of the good steamboat landings, speculators were found who had come out from the East with a bale of *wild-cat* money and, going into camp, had opened a *bank*. Captain Kercheval refused to accept the worthless stuff, and as a consequence the *Hesperian* returned to St. Louis with her cargo nearly intact. At only two places, Council Bluffs, Ia., and Forest City, Mo., was gold or silver offered in payment of freight charges, and at those places the merchants received their goods.

When cold weather put an end to navigation on the Missouri, it was usual for many of the boats regularly engaged there to enter the St. Louis and New Orleans trade during the winter months. At that season the cold weather of the North and Northwest locks the headwaters of the Missouri and Mississippi in an icy grip and the latter stream falls to a very low stage below St. Louis, compelling many of the deeper draught steamers to lie up and wait for the spring freshets to raise the channel. But to the light-draught Missouri River boats, built for service on waters normally shoal and full of shifting sandbars, the low stage of the Mississippi furnished an opportunity. Most of the regular packets being out of commission, freight rates rose high and the small steamers would wait until they could demand a dollar a barrel for transporting flour to New Orleans and proportionate rates on other merchandise, and then load for the metropolis of the Gulf, certain of making a modest fortune on each trip.

During the winter of 1858-1859, the Missouri River boat of which Marsh was then mate, the *A. B. Chambers No. 2*, commanded by Captain George W. Bowman, thus became engaged in the New Orleans trade. Before setting out from St. Louis, two Mississippi River pilots were hired to take her down to New Orleans. One of these, James C. Delancey, proved unfortunate, frequently running the boat aground, and his services were dispensed with at the end of the trip.[1] But the second pilot of the *A. B. Chambers,* a smooth-faced young

---

1. Whatever his errors as a pilot on this voyage, however, James Delancey proved himself a hero a few years later, when, as captain of the Confederate River Defence ram, *Colonel Lovell,* in the naval battle before Memphis, he fought his vessel until she went down with colours flying, carrying seventy of her eighty-five men to watery graves.

STEAMER *NELLIE PECK*
AT THE FORT BENTON LEVEE, 1872
The piles of freight on the bank give some
idea of the commercial importance of
Fort Benton in its steamboating days.

STEAMER *WASHBURN*. LANDED WITH SACKED WHEAT AT THE
LEVEE, WASHBURN, NORTH DAKOTA, 1901

fellow, whose quiet and retiring manner did not prevent his being very popular with all his associates, proved a most excellent, navigator, knowing his river thoroughly and possessing the judgement to make the best use of his knowledge. This young man was familiarly known as Sam Clemens, who has since become the most famous and beloved of American humorists, *Mark Twain*. An incident showing his almost instinctive familiarity with the snares of the big river occurred while the *A. B. Chambers* was making her second trip to New Orleans, and is narrated by Captain Marsh with enjoyment.

The weather had been very cold and on the day that the *Chambers* set out from St. Louis, masses of floating ice filled the channel, rendering progress difficult. The next afternoon, when about 165 miles from St. Louis and two miles below the town of Commerce, Mo., the boat was hugging the shore of Power's Island to avoid the grinding pack of the mid-channel, when she went hard aground on the foot of the island. No efforts availed to get her off and soon the fuel gave out. The cabin was full of passengers and the lower deck laden with live stock, so it was imperative that she should be floated as soon as possible.

In common with all the boats of her day, the *Chambers* burned wood in her furnaces. To supply the demands of traffic, hundreds of wood-yards and scores of flatboats were scattered along the banks of all navigable streams, but it so happened that no yard was near the point where the *Chambers* had come to grief. Therefore Captain Bowman instructed the mate to take a crew in the yawl, return to Commerce and float a wood-flat down, Clemens going with him to navigate.

To keep out of the ice-filled channel, Clemens crossed to the Illinois shore and then turned upstream through a narrow cut-off between Burnham's Island and the main bank. This cut-off the yawl followed to the head of the island, near the town of Thebes, Ill., across the river from and slightly above, Commerce. The river, wide above and below, was here very narrow, flowing swiftly between high banks. The drifting ice frequently jammed in the cut, leaving a space of open water in front, until the volume of cakes piling up behind would break the gorge and the whole mass come sweeping down resistlessly. To cross a small boat through one of those spaces of open water, into which at any moment the grinding cakes might rush, was an exceedingly hazardous undertaking, but there was no other way of reaching Commerce.

With anxious eyes the little party in the yawl scanned the menacing waters. When the ice lodged above, no man could tell whether it would remain stationary long enough for them to cross, or break and overwhelm them in mid-channel. At length a favourable opportunity seemed to come and the pilot ordered the men to pull for the Missouri shore. They had gone but a few yards when the jam broke and surged down upon them.

"Turn back quick, Sam!" shouted Marsh to Clemens. "We'll be crushed."

"No," answered the pilot quietly, watching the river and continuing to hold his rudder square. "Go ahead, as fast as you can."

Putting every ounce of muscle into their arms the crew rowed on, the ice seeming to open before them, while between them and the shore they had left, it closed in a seething cauldron. Almost miraculously they slipped through and reached Commerce in safety, though, but for Clemens, Captain Marsh declares the lives of all would undoubtedly have been lost. The incident occurred many years before *Mark Twain* became world-famous, but he still remembers it well today[2] as one of the exciting episodes of the times when his chief ambition was to become an expert steamboat pilot. He and Grant Marsh grew to be fast friends during their association on the *A. B. Chambers No. 2*, and for a long time after he had left the river and entered upon his literary career, they maintained a more or less regular correspondence.

---

2. In response to a letter requesting his recollection of this incident, Mr. Clemens kindly communicated with the author regarding it. His remembrance of it agrees in every particular with that of Captain Marsh, related above.—J. M. H.

Chapter 5

Cupid at the Apple-Butter Stirring

Among the shipmates of Grant Marsh during the season of 1860 was a young *striker* engineer[1] who may be referred to here as Jonathan Poore, though that was not the name by which his friends knew him. He was an industrious lad and allowed nothing to deter him from a diligent application to his work, but when moments of idleness overtook him he could think clearly and converse fluently upon but one subject. This subject was a certain young lady residing in St. Louis, and it was evident from his glowing descriptions of her that he thought her nothing less than the one ideal representative of her sex.

Realizing his condition of mind, his comrades on the boat for a time patiently submitted to his interminable monologues on this favourite topic, but at length the endurance of all became exhausted and they turned upon the love-sick swain in open protest. That is, all excepting Marsh, who, being perhaps of a more tolerant disposition than the average, still allowed himself to be used as an escape-valve for the young engineer's pent-up emotions. The result of this generosity was that Poore attached himself closely to his sympathetic listener and became more communicative than ever. Now and then Marsh, to relieve himself, would laughingly express doubt as to the young lady possessing all the perfections attributed to her by her admirer, and at such times Poore would exclaim earnestly:

"All right, Grant, believe it or not, but it's so, and I wish some evening when we're in St. Louis you would go up with me to see her and judge for yourself."

The family of which the young lady was a member belonged to a colony of Pennsylvanians which had moved to St. Louis a few years

---

1. An engineer's apprentice, in river parlance.

before, bringing with them all the manners and customs of their native region. Poore and Marsh were both from the same section, but Marsh had not mingled much with the colonists in St. Louis, who naturally maintained close social intercourse with one another. But at length, late in the autumn, he was prevailed upon by Poore to accompany him to his lady's home. The mate's curiosity had at last been aroused and he desired to see the girl who had stirred such a tempest of emotion in the bosom of his friend.

Poore sent word in advance of their coming, and she prepared to entertain them pleasantly by summoning a few of her friends to an *apple-butter stirring*. This was a form of entertainment very popular among the young people of Pennsylvania at that time, combining work with pleasure in a manner similar to the *husking bees* and *quilting parties* of other sections. It was, moreover, as easily to be arranged in St. Louis as in Pennsylvania. A quantity of apples would be prepared beforehand, and when the guests arrived they would find the apple-butter, which had already been cooking for a long time, in a large kettle over the fire, just approaching its final stage of preparation. By that time it was thick and heavy and required frequent stirrings with a large ladle to keep it from burning. Here was where the fun came in, for the ladle was too large, in theory, at least, to be handled by one person, and it was customary for the girls and boys in pairs to take turns in stirring. The lady always had the choice of a partner to assist her when her turn came, and whichever swain she selected was regarded by the others as her favourite *beau*, he and she both being subjected to all the good-natured banter that the wits of the assemblage could devise. When the work was completed, the guests partook of as much of the fresh apple-butter as they cared for, while the remainder went to replenish the home larder of the hostess.

On the evening set for the entertainment in their honour, the young steamboat men carefully arrayed themselves in their best apparel and set forth to the lady's home, Jonathan in an ecstasy of anticipation, Grant possessed merely by a mild curiosity. They found the other guests already gathered, but the hostess met them at the door with a gracious welcome, and the engineer, after partially recovering his equilibrium, introduced his companion. But upon looking into the smiling face before him, the lord of the lower deck found himself all at once bereft of that easy flow of language which he commanded when addressing the roustabouts. A wave of admiration and embarrassment swept over him which left him almost speechless, and as he took his seat among the others and furtively watched his hostess chatting with Poore, he could only repeat to himself in a helpless way:

"Well, Jonathan certainly has good taste."

Never before had the thought of marriage entered his mind, but now there was borne in upon him suddenly a conviction that he needed a wife more than anything else on earth.

At length the time came for stirring and Poore proudly walked up to the kettle with his hostess. As he watched them talking and laughing confidentially, their hands very close together on the big ladle, Grant could bear the sight no longer. Mustering up his courage with a more desperate effort than he ever found necessary in later years when facing the bullets of Indians, he stepped to her side and while Jonathan frowned at him across the kettle, tremblingly whispered in her ear:

"Let's you and I stir this apple-butter next time."

Instantly she turned and looked searchingly into his eyes. And then, with a dazzling smile, she said simply:

"All right."

It did not seem, on the surface, a very portentous exchange of words, but it was one of those moments which come in life when words count for little and unspoken thoughts for much. At all events, it marked the end to the hopes of poor Jonathan, for a few months later Grant moved into a cosy little home of his own, a married man. And the wife who accompanied him there and who for forty-six long years was to walk at his side, faithfully and lovingly sharing his joys and sorrows, his triumphs and disappointments, was the girl he had met and won at an old-fashioned, Pennsylvania *apple-butter stirring*.

CHAPTER 6

The Battle Morn of Shiloh

In the spring following Grant Marsh's marriage, the terrible tragedy of the Civil War burst upon the country. For many years the political controversies between North and South had been growing more bitter until a resort to arms became inevitable. The men who made their living on the rivers of the West found themselves in a position much resembling that of the people of the border States. The latter were torn by conflicting emotions of loyalty to the Union and love for the ideals and institutions of the South, and so it was with the steamboat men. Their vocation called them to all the regions reached by the Mississippi, from St. Paul to New Orleans. Among their friends and business associates most of them numbered as many cotton and tobacco planters of Tennessee or Louisiana as they did lumbermen and farmers of Wisconsin or Illinois. On the outbreak of hostilities it was not surprising, therefore, that as many steamboat men cast in their lot with the young Confederacy as remained true to the Union.

It was with deep regret that a man so given to warm attachments as Grant Marsh saw many of his dearest friends thus turn their faces from the old flag and become its enemies. But despite his sorrow that they should go, his own loyalty to the Government did not for a moment waver. Though he dreaded the effects of the fratricidal war on those of the South who were dear to him, he held himself ready to serve the Union whenever opportunity should arise. The call did not come at once, but in the early spring of 1862 General Grant began preparations for moving his army from Fort Donelson, Tenn., which he had recently captured, southward to Pittsburg Landing, on the Tennessee River, in an offensive campaign against General Beauregard's army at Corinth, Miss. For the transportation of Grant's forces, an immense flotilla of steamboats was gathered at St. Louis. The fleet consisted of eighty-two steamers, among them being the *John J. Roe,* a St. Louis and New Orleans packet, one of the largest on the river, of which Grant Marsh was mate.

Before leaving St. Louis the *Roe* was loaded with army supplies, and on arriving at Fort Donelson she took on board the 8th Missouri Infantry, Colonel Morgan L. Smith, and the 11th Indiana Infantry, Colonel G. F. McGinnis. Both of these regiments, which had done heroic service in the fighting about Donelson, belonged to the division of Major-General Lew Wallace, who accompanied them up the river on the *Roe*. When the two regiments came aboard, they filled the vessel so completely that it became necessary for Captain Simmons, the commissary officer in charge of the supplies brought from St. Louis, to remove his goods to the hold, that the troops might have room. The shifting of cargo was quickly accomplished, and with General Wallace in military command, the steamer proceeded on her way up the Tennessee. The *John J. Roe* was an old boat and had long borne the reputation of being a slow one. *Mark Twain*, who saw service on her before the outbreak of the war, has made some characteristically witty observations in his *Life on the Mississippi* concerning the vessel's lack of speed. He says:

> For a long time I was on a boat that was so slow we used to forget what year it was we left port in. But, of course, this was at rare intervals. Ferryboats used to lose valuable trips because their passengers grew old and died, waiting for us to get by. This was at still rarer intervals. I had the documents for these occurrences, but through carelessness they have been mislaid. This boat, the *John J. Roe,* was so slow that when she finally sank in Madrid Bend, it was five years before the owners heard of it. That was always a confusing fact to me, but it is according to the record, anyway. She was dismally slow; still, we often had pretty exciting times racing with islands, and rafts, and such things. One trip, however, we did rather well. We went to St. Louis in sixteen days. But even at this rattling gait I think we changed watches three times in Fort Adams reach, which is five miles long. A *reach* is a piece of straight river, and of course the current drives through such a place in a pretty lively way.

It is evident from the above that the crew and the numerous passengers of the *John J. Roe* had plenty of time for enjoying the scenery while sailing up the Tennessee from Fort Donelson. But the voyage was not devoid of redeeming features. The 8th Missouri was composed almost entirely of St. Louis steamboat men, and its officers were in great part gentlemen who had been passenger agents of some of the principal packet lines doing business there before the war. Among these were Colonel Smith, his brother, Lieutenant-Colonel Giles A. Smith, and Major John McDonald. In the organization, therefore, Mate Marsh found many old friends whose presence served to make the journey a pleasant one. At Crump's Landing, a point about four miles below Pittsburg, General Wallace debarked with his troops. The General took up his headquarters on the stern-wheel packet *Jesse K. Bell,* which was lying there at the bank. A number of other regiments of his division had already arrived and were encamping, and the scene about the landing as the *Roe* came in was one of lively martial interest. After clearing her crowded decks she went on to Pittsburg Landing, near which the greater part of Grant's forces were in position, and Captain Baxter, the commissary officer having in charge all the water transportation of the army, assumed control of the boat and moved his office and clerks on board.

It was now late in March. For several days life ran smoothly on the many steamers gathered there along the shores of the Tennessee, and the dangers of battle seemed far away. Though Beauregard and Albert Sidney Johnston were concentrating their forces at Corinth, eighteen miles distant, preparatory to their momentous advance upon Shiloh Church and Pittsburg, inside the Union lines nothing was known of their movements and apparently no preparations were being made for receiving them. At length one day there came up from Cincinnati to join the fleet the side-wheel steamer *Madison,* having in tow a large model barge loaded with new army wagons. The *Madison* made her charge fast to the bank at Savannah, a small town seven miles below Pittsburg and on the eastern side of the river, where the main commissary depot of the army of the Tennessee was located. Here one night the water fell and left the barge high and dry on the shore. She was a valuable craft and Captain Baxter instructed Mate Marsh and Carpenter Frank Borden, of the *John J. Roe,* to go down and work her off the bank, detailing a detachment of the 14th Wisconsin Infantry under Lieutenant Fox to assist them.

The release of the barge proved a rather difficult task, and a number of days were consumed in the work. Meanwhile the party thus engaged had frequent opportunity for seeing General Grant, the quiet, self-possessed man who was in chief command of the army, and whose name was already famous throughout the country by reason of his brilliant victory at Fort Donelson. The general's headquarters were in the Cherry mansion, a large brick house in Savannah standing within sight of the stranded barge, and he often appeared on the river bank, going to or returning from the private boat on which he made his daily visits to the army at Pittsburg. This boat was a small, sidewheel, Ohio River packet named the *Tigress,* and was commanded by Captain Perkins. Before the war she had been accustomed to go to the lower Mississippi during the winter months and there engage in the cotton trade, and she was regarded as a speedy boat for her class.

On the evening of Saturday, the 5th day of April, the work of restoring the barge to the water had been nearly completed, and Mate Marsh and his assistants retired that night expecting to complete their labours next day. No news had come of a disturbing nature and all was quiet along the wide front of the army. But when they awoke at dawn it was to hear the morning air throbbing with sounds which drove all thought of the barge from their minds. It was the roar of artillery beating down from Pittsburg Landing, seven miles away, while in the clustered infantry camps about Savannah arose a turmoil of excited preparation. Marsh and Borden threw on their clothes and ran to the river bank, where in the first dim flush of dawn the *Tigress,* with steam up, lay fretting at the landing. Just as they arrived, General Grant and his staff and orderlies, all mounted, came clattering down the bank and rode aboard. The two steamboat men, considering, simply and loyally, that at such a time their place was with the *John J. Roe,* scrambled aboard also, and in a moment the lines were cast off, and the *Tigress,* trembling in every timber, was rushing away up the river.

General Grant had dismounted from his big buckskin horse and seated himself in a chair on the boiler deck near the front stairs. Here, surrounded by his staff, he calmly listened to the roar of battle. The boat had proceeded but a mile or two when she met the steamer *John Warner* racing downstream. The *Warner* hailed, and on both boats slowing down, a lieutenant hurried on board the *Tigress,* bearing a dispatch from General Stephen A. Hurlbut to General Grant. Hurlbut was in command of one of the five hard-pressed divisions now hotly engaged near Shiloh Church with Hardee's and Bragg's advance. Marsh was standing near Grant when the staff-officer handed the latter his dispatch and verbally reported that the enemy were massed in great numbers all along the front and were driving the army back on the river. With perfect composure Grant read Hurlbut's message and listened to the remarks of the bearer. He did not move from his chair, and his only comment was to the effect that when he arrived he would surround the enemy.

Leaving the *Warner* behind, the *Tigress* resumed her headlong course, but at Crump's Landing, in obedience to an order from the General, she again slowed down and went to the bank alongside the *Jesse K. Bell,* where Grant and Wallace, standing on their respective boats, held a short conversation. Wallace inquired what Grant's orders were for him. The commander replied that he should remain at Crump's, holding his division ready to march, and would receive his orders from the field. Mate Marsh did not note the exact hour at which this brief exchange of words occurred, but Grant has stated it at about eight o'clock a. m., while Wallace placed it at about nine. The events following it gave rise to one of the most celebrated controversies of the war, for when Wallace did receive his orders he marched for the front by the wrong road, had to be recalled and did not arrive on the field in time for his division to be of any service in the first day's fighting. Grant blamed him for mistaking his road, while Wallace contended that he took the only road he had been expected to take and the disputed point was not settled between the two noted soldiers for many years.[1]

The delay was but for a moment or two, and the *Tigress* then backed out into the stream and did not again halt until Pittsburg Landing was reached. Here General Grant and his party hurriedly mounted and took their departure. It was the last time that Grant Marsh ever saw the distinguished commander, and the scene was indelibly impressed upon his memory as the General rode away up the smoke-shrouded hill into the turmoil of battle to rescue his disorganized army from impending destruction.

About the landing everything was in an uproar as the *Tigress* came in. The fight seemed to be raging just beyond the brow of the hill, and shells were bursting over the woods and river. A little way upstream lay the wooden gunboats *Lexington* and *Tyler,* impatiently waiting an opportunity to open fire with their deadly 64-pounders which later in the day did so much to repulse the last desperate assaults of the Confederate columns. The river bank was crowded with a confusion of wounded soldiers, stragglers and commissary guards, staff-officers and steamboat men, for this was the rear of the army, the base of am-

---

1. For a more extended discussion of the matter, by General Grant and others, see Vol. 1, *Battles and Leaders of the Civil War.*

munition supply, and the furthest point to which the waves of panic could roll, here finding a barrier which proved insurmountable. On the morning of April 6th, the army of the Tennessee was truly in a perilous position, with an exultant enemy pounding along its front, and the river in its rear. But help was near at hand. The advance of General Don Carlos Buell's army of the Ohio, marching from Nashville, had already reached Savannah the day before, and if these fresh troops could be brought upon the field in time, defeat might yet be turned to victory.

Marsh and Borden found the *John J. Roe* lying at the landing with steam up, and immediately after their arrival she received orders to go up to Savannah after troops. All that long, bloody Sunday, while the waves of battle surged to and fro through the scrub-oak thickets about Shiloh, she continued this work, making several round trips between Savannah and Pittsburg. After one of these trips, and while she was debarking a load of troops at Pittsburg, the steamer *Fort Wayne* came in to the landing near her, bringing a cargo of pontoon boats from Cincinnati. At the moment of her arrival, Mate Marsh noticed an officer of General Buell's army standing on the bank, whose nerve had been badly shaken by the events of the day. This officer no sooner caught sight of the *Fort Wayne* than he shouted excitedly to her commander:

"For God's sake, captain, land and get those pontoons in position so that the army can cross the river!"

Such an action at that critical time would have been a disastrous blunder, but it fortunately happened that General Rawlins, of Grant's staff, was also on the bank, directing the arriving troops to their positions on the field. He heard the appeal of the frightened officer of Buell's command, and shaking his finger at the captain of the *Fort Wayne*, cried:

"You take your boat away from the landing and keep her away or I will burn her up. Do you understand?"

It was obvious that Rawlins was by no means whipped, and his peremptory order was promptly obeyed. He was at the landing through most of that eventful day, and did much to maintain order there. Another instance of his cool courage was witnessed by Mate Marsh a few moments after the *Fort Wayne*, with her undesirable cargo, had retired from the bank. There was lying at the landing a small stern-wheel boat named the *Rocket*, Captain John Wolf, having in tow two barges loaded with ammunition. A line of army wagons was engaged in hauling these from the river up to the battle field. Presently a shell swooped down and burst close to one of the barges. This was too much for Captain Wolf. He yelled to his mate to cut the lines and commenced backing the *Rocket* out. General Rawlins saw her going and, hurrying over, shouted to the captain to come back or he would shoot every man on the boat. The *Rocket* came back very expeditiously, and made no further attempt to run away.

Another man who aroused the lively admiration of Grant Marsh on that day was a young private on board the *Roe* named E. P. Wilcox, one of Captain Baxter's commissary clerks. Once during the afternoon, as the *Roe* lay at Pittsburg, young Wilcox was standing on the bank with a manifest in hand, checking a pile of commissary goods. While thus engaged, a shell came down and decapitated a cavalryman within a few feet of him. Wilcox scarcely even glanced up, but, undisturbed, continued his work as if the perils of battle were a thousand miles away. After the fight, Marsh did not see the plucky private again during the war.

But one day nearly ten years later, his Missouri River packet steamed up to the landing at Sioux City, Iowa, and the captain saw, standing on the levee, a man, at sight of whose face there swept over him in a rush of recollection all the fierce excitement of that long-past battle Sunday at Shiloh. He hastened to the bank and grasped the hand of Wilcox. The latter was surprised at the warmth of his greeting, for he did not at first recognize the captain, but his memory was soon refreshed, and they enjoyed a long talk over old times. When the captain's boat pulled out up river, Wilcox was aboard and went with her to Yankton, Dakota, then Marsh's home. There he concluded to establish himself, and there today he still resides, one of the town's most respected citizens, (as at time of first publication).

By Sunday evening a large number of troops had arrived on the river bank opposite Pittsburg, and all that night and next morning the *John J. Roe* and her consorts spent in ferrying the divisions of Nelson and Crittenden to the west shore. Throughout the night a rain was falling so heavily as to amount almost to a cloudburst, adding much to the difficulty of the movement, and the river rose eight feet before dawn. Nevertheless, the work went on without interruption, on one trip the capacious *Roe* carrying over an entire brigade at a single crossing. General Thomas L. Crittenden himself went on this trip. It was the first time Marsh had ever seen the well-known commander, but they were destined to come into frequent intercourse in after years on the upper Missouri, where Crittenden, as colonel of the 17th United States Infantry, was for a long time stationed during the Indian wars. His only son, Lieutenant J. J. Crittenden, fell with Custer's ill-fated command at the Little Big Horn, where Captain Marsh also rendered such conspicuous service.

With the superiority of numbers established by Buell's providential arrival, Grant was able to assume the offensive on Monday, April 7th, and speedily drove the Confederates from the field. The steamboats continued bringing up additional reinforcements during most of the day, the *Roe* taking, along with others, from Savannah to Pittsburg, Colonel Hassendeubel's famous 17th Missouri Infantry, one of the many regiments raised during the war from among the loyal Germans of St. Louis. By afternoon the Confederate forces had all withdrawn in the direction of Corinth, and the great battle was over.

Early next morning Mate Marsh and some of his shipmates set out through the woods to find the 8th Missouri, and learn how their friends in that regiment had fared. They had walked a mile or more from the river, finding the way strewn with many dead and wounded men to remind them of the dreadful struggle just over, when to their consternation a volley of musketry suddenly crashed out close at hand. The officers of the regiment through whose bivouac they were passing, sprang to their feet, shouting to their men;

"Fall in, boys! Fall in!"

For a few moments, while the troops were forming, confusion reigned, for every one believed the enemy had returned to the attack. Then word was passed that the volley had been fired by an adjacent command merely to empty their muskets of wet cartridges, and amid a chorus of relieved laughter and jokes, the battle-line dissolved again.

That night the *John J. Roe* started down river with 600 wounded men on board, principally Indianians, who were conveyed to Evansville. The remainder, being Missouri troops, were taken on to St. Louis. The next summer Grant Marsh participated in some of the operations of the army in Arkansas, and for a time his boat again had on board the 17th Missouri, whose gallant commander, Colonel Hassendeubel, was mortally wounded a few months later before Vicksburg. Marsh's vessel was present at the mouth of the Yazoo River when, on July 1st, 1862, the Gulf Squadron under Flag-Officer David G. Farragut, and the Mississippi Flotilla commanded by Flag-Officer Charles H. Davis, were united there by the action of the Gulf Squadron in running the Vicksburg batteries. But he was soon ordered North, and missed by a few days the spectacular engagement which occurred when the Confederate ram *Arkansas,* defiantly steamed out of the Yazoo and, passing through the entire Union fleet at anchor, made her way safely to Vicksburg.

CHAPTER 7

Barbarism at Bay

Grant Marsh's interesting experiences in the Civil War were now over, but the spring of 1864 found him serving his country quite as effectively in a territory far removed from the battle grounds of Dixie, for it was then that he first ascended to the regions of the upper Missouri, where he was to remain for so long and be identified with so many stirring and momentous events. In the year 1864 the government was engaged in prosecuting a vigorous campaign against the hostile Indian tribes of the Northwest who, since the Minnesota massacres of 1862, had united in a desperate effort to prevent the people of the United States from encroaching further upon their hunting grounds. Up to the commencement of the gold rush to California in 1849, both the Comanche and Arapahoe Indians of the South and the numerous tribes comprised in the great Sioux Nation of the North, had remained practically at peace with the whites, for the reason that they were left in undisturbed possession of their vast domains, stretching from the Mississippi and the western borders of Missouri on the east to the Rocky Mountains on the west, and from the British border to the Rio Grande, north and south.

Previous to that time these Indians of the plains had maintained no intercourse with the white race save along the frontiers of settlement and with those few and scattering adventurers who came among them as peaceful and conciliatory traders and trappers. But when the flood of emigration to California set in, cutting its resistless way up the valley of the Platte and across what is now Wyoming, through the very heart of their ancestral empire, it was like the thrust of a lance into their vitals, and they commenced relentless warfare upon the emigrants.

Their conduct caused the government to exert its power, and military posts were established along the line of travel. At Fort Laramie, in 1851, a treaty was made with most of the principal tribes which was so skilfully drawn that for a few years the animosity of the Indians was lulled and they permitted the emigrant trains to pass through their territory with comparatively little interference. Then a trifling incident led to the massacre of Lieutenant Grattan and his detachment near Fort Laramie, in 1854, and the speedy punishment of the murderers by General Harney, who inflicted a crushing defeat upon them at Ash Hollow, Nebraska, in the following year.

After the battle, General Harney moved with his troops to Fort Pierre, on the Missouri River, a fur trading post which the Government had recently purchased from the American Fur Company. Here he spent the winter of 1855-56, pacifying and making new treaties with the disturbed tribes, and the next spring moved 194 miles down the river and established Fort Randall, which continued for some time to be occupied as the most advanced military post of the Missouri Valley.

Faith in General Harney's treaties and the presence of the troops at Fort Randall combined for several years to keep the Sioux on their good behaviour. But in 1862 several causes operated to produce an outbreak which in extent and ferocity exceeded anything in the history of Indian warfare. The first and most potent cause was the growing dissatisfaction of the Indians with the manner in which their treaty annuities were distributed. These consisted of goods, such as clothing and food, a certain quantity of which were to be distributed to them annually for a stated number of years as payment for the great tracts of land which from time to time they had ceded to the government. The distribution of the annuity goods was put in the charge of agents who, in many instances, shamefully abused their trust. The Indians, seldom receiving more than a fraction of the supplies to which by treaty they were justly entitled, year by year became more incensed and more distrustful of the government, until a time came when they waited only a favourable opportunity for venting their anger in open hostility.

With the commencement of the Civil War in the United States the opportunity seemed to arise. Stories of the imminent overthrow of the government and of the weakness of frontier settlements due to the dispatch of volunteers to the south, were industriously circulated among the Indians by interested parties, some, perhaps, from the Southern Confederacy, many, certainly, from the British settlements and trading posts in the valley of the Red River of the North. The

Indians of the Minnesota Valley, after much hesitation, finally took the warpath in August, 1862, and immediately all the tribes of Minnesota and Dakota Territory, with a few exceptions, blazed forth into fierce revolt. A thousand settlers, men, women, and children, were massacred in Minnesota before the savages were checked. They were then driven north to the vicinity of Devil's Lake by General H. H. Sibley, and would doubtless have been pursued even farther had not the advent of winter put an end to military operations for that year.

During the cold season the Indians prepared for the next summer by recruiting and solidifying their forces, and when spring opened they presented a strong and united opposition to the columns sent against them. From the valley of the Minnesota General Sibley again moved toward Devil's Lake and the upper Dakota River, with the purpose of driving them westward to the Missouri, while General Alfred Sully with another force ascended the latter stream to intercept their retreat. Sibley defeated them in three successive engagements between the Dakota and the Missouri, but owing to the fact that low water detained the steamboats on which his supplies were embarked, Sully was unable to accomplish his part of the plan. The Indians made good their retreat to the west bank of the Missouri, and it was a month later before Sully reached their crossing place.

Meantime the Minnesota expedition had begun retiring toward its starting point, and the Indians, still unbroken in spirit, had recrossed the Missouri and followed it. Sully, ascertaining their movements, pursued them in turn, defeating them in a pitched battle at Whitestone Hill, Dakota, though he and Sibley were unable to make such dispositions as to catch and crush their elusive enemy. Again the approach of cold weather compelled the abandonment of field operations, and General Sully moved down the Missouri to a point on the east bank some four miles below the present city of Pierre, South Dakota, where he established Fort Sully and maintained a garrison through the winter. Fort Randall thus ceased to be the most advanced post of the valley.

CHAPTER 8

With Sully Into the Sioux Lands

With the advent of warm weather in 1864 it was determined to send another strong expedition under General Sully into the hostile country, in an endeavour to bring the Indians to final subjection. A number of steamboats were required for the transportation of supplies, and it was as mate of one of these, the *Marcella,* commanded by Captain Sousley, that Grant Marsh made his first trip to the upper river. The boats were gathered at St. Louis and included, beside the *Marcella,* the *Sam Gaty,* Captain Silver; the *Chippewa Falls,* Captain Hutchison; the *General Grant,* Captain Packard; the *Isabella,* Captain Dozier; the *Tempest;* the *Alone,* Captain Rea; and the *Island City,* Captain Lamont;[1] eight steamers in all.

The Missouri River habitually has two seasons of high water during the year; the first in April, occasioned by the melting snows and spring rains of the lower valley; the second in June, to which the breaking of winter in the Rocky Mountains contributes, flooding the sources of the stream. Sometimes a late spring in the lower valley or an early one in the mountains will release their accumulations of surplus water simultaneously, and then floods of greater or less magnitude are the usual result. Sometimes, on the contrary, light snow-falls during the cold season prevent the water attaining great height during either period. It was the latter condition which obtained in the spring of 1864. The river remained low through April, and the *Marcella* and her

---

1. No history seems ever to have been written of this campaign, even in the form of official reports, which makes more than the most casual reference to the part played by the steamboats. In addition to the information derived from Captain Marsh, the author has received much assistance from Captain Alexander Lamont, formerly commander of the *Island City,* in preparing the present chapter and especially in ascertaining the names of the boats and their captains.—J. M. H.

consorts were unable to reach Sioux City, Iowa, until June.

By the time this point was attained the river had again fallen, and owing to the dangers of snags and sandbars, slow progress was made to Fort Sully. Early in July, however, the fort was reached, and a number of troops who had wintered there were taken on board. The fleet then proceeded about 240 miles farther to a point on the right, or west, bank of the Missouri above the mouth of Cannon Ball River, where Fort Rice was established as a base of operations.

Leaving a garrison of five companies here, General Sully with the remainder of his troops started westward in search of the hostiles, who were reported to be assembled in one great camp somewhere near the headwaters of Heart River. He took with him supplies enough for only about three weeks, his intention being, after attacking the Indians, to march across to the old trading post at the Brasseau Houses on the Yellowstone River, fifty miles above the mouth, where he instructed some of his steamers to meet him with supplies.[2] The force with which General Sully started consisted of about 2,200 men, chiefly cavalry, divided into two brigades, and under their escort there marched also an emigrant train of about 150 persons headed by Captain Fisk, and bound for the newly discovered Wind River goldfields of Western Montana.

The expedition moved up the Cannon Ball to its sources and thence across to the headwaters of the Heart, where the scouts learned that the Indian camp lay to the north-westward, near the Little Missouri. Parking the emigrant and supply trains under a heavy guard, the main body advanced by forced marches, and on the early morning of July 28th, came in contact with the enemy on the edge of a region of precipitous and heavily-wooded hills called Tahkahokuty, or Killdeer, Mountain. The Indians were in great force, there being some 1,600 lodges in the camps among the hills and fully 6,000 warriors to offer battle;[3] these were from the Uncpapa, Sans Arcs, Blackfoot, Minneconjoux, Yanktonais and Santee tribes. But notwithstanding the fact that they had ample warning of his approach and even attacked him on the open prairie while still several miles from their main positions, Sully completely defeated and routed them, capturing nearly all their camp equipage and great stores of food. From the battle ground he

---

2. Official report of General Sully.
3. Sully's estimate. Doane Robinson, in his *History of the Dakota or Sioux Indians*, declares it to be ridiculously high and that there were not above 1,600 warriors present.—J. M. H.

hastened back to his trains on Heart River and immediately set out for the Yellowstone, as his supplies were already running perilously low.

The march of the column through the Bad-Lands of the Little Missouri proved extremely slow and arduous and was attended with more strange and unusual hardships of savage warfare and inhospitable Nature than often fall to the lot of military expeditions even in a wilderness land. The region was of volcanic origin, covered with blackened scoria and wastes of broken rock. When General Sully, standing upon its brink, beheld that forbidding sweep of jagged hills and naked valleys extending away to the horizon, confused and tumbled as a stormy sea, he is said to have turned to his staff and exclaimed, with characteristic vigour:

"Gentlemen, there is Hell with the lights put out!"

He would gladly have turned back, but his depleted supplies and the exhausted condition of his animals forbade the long return march to Fort Rice. Of all his Indian scouts, there was only one who professed to the General any familiarity with the gloomy region or who would undertake to pilot the troops through it. Under this man's guidance they reluctantly moved forward, at once to find themselves involved in extreme difficulties.

In order to bring the wagons through, it became necessary to grade hills and to span ravines. In the semi-arid waste the grass grew but sparsely, and what little water could be found was bitter with alkali, so that along the way scores of horses and mules died of exhaustion and starvation. It was courting certain death for a man to stray even a short distance from the main body, for the Indians recently defeated at Tahkahokuty had followed them and, hovering among the hills, harassed the troops day and night by incessant attacks, while they were also at pains to burn the grass off in advance of the column, leaving no forage. The progress made day by day was painfully slow, and the command was reduced to half rations. For a time it seemed that the tragedy of Kabul Pass was about to be re-enacted there in the Bad Lands of Dakota, 500 miles beyond the frontiers of civilization.

But at length the Little Missouri, where the hills ended and the plains began, was reached and crossed. Here the Indian attacks ceased, since the open country did not admit of their near approach, but new afflictions took their place.

It was hoped that when the plains were reached there would be grazing for the animals, but the country was found to be suffering under a scourge of grasshoppers which had eaten off all vegetation, leaving the ground as naked as a desert. When to this was added the heat of the cloudless midsummer sun and the fervid breath of the south gales, driving before them clouds of dust across the parching waste, the sufferings of the troops as they struggled forward became intense. They had almost reached the limit of endurance when at last, on the 12th of August, their eyes were gladdened by the sight of the swift-rolling Yellowstone, and the memorable march came to an end at the appointed rendezvous.

Here some of the boats were found awaiting them, as instructed, with sufficient provisions to relieve their immediate necessities. But misfortune had fallen upon the steamer bearing the greater portion of the supplies, and General Sully was therefore obliged to forego that part of his plan of campaign which contemplated the establishment of a permanent military post on the Yellowstone—a design which was to be cherished by the government for many years before it would become practicable of realization. The boats which Sully had ordered to the Yellowstone were the *Island City*, on board which he had carried his headquarters previous to the beginning of the overland march, the *Alone*, and the *Chippewa Falls*. These vessels were selected on account of their extremely light draft, the *Chippewa Falls* drawing only about twelve inches, light.

When they left Fort Rice, several of the other steamers accompanied them but did not go as far as the Yellowstone. Among these was the *Marcella*, with Grant Marsh on board. He relates that immediately above the site of the present city of Bismarck, the crests of the high bluffs bordering the left bank of the stream were noticed to be littered with pieces of bent and twisted iron. Its presence in that wild country excited wonder, and Marsh and some of his companions landed to investigate.

They found the iron to be the tires and other metal parts of a number of wagons which had belonged to the Minnesota Indians when they retreated before General Sibley the previous year. Finding themselves unable to take the wagons with them in their flight across the Missouri, they had abandoned and burned them. Owing to this circumstance the steamboat men called the eminence Wagon-wheel Bluff, by which name it is still known.

The *Island City* and her consorts proceeded on their way to the Yellowstone, and at about sunset on the evening when they expected to enter it, the *Island City* struck a snag which tore a large hole in her

Mandan Village at Fort Berthold, about 1870

Fort Thompson, Crow Creek Indian Reservation

bottom.[4] The crew were at supper when the crash came and were obliged to make a quick escape, as she sank rapidly, settling, however, in shallow water. The hold of the *Island City* was filled with corn for Sully's animals and with barrelled pork for the troops, as well as with materials for the contemplated fort on the Yellowstone. All of these supplies were lost, and those which the other steamers carried up were barely sufficient to subsist the troops on their return to Fort Rice. The machinery of the *Island City* was shortly afterwards removed and taken away by the *Belle of Peoria,* a steamer downward bound from Fort Benton, Montana. After vicissitudes which in themselves would make a stirring romance, Captain Lamont finally succeeded in conveying it safely to St. Louis, where it was placed in a new boat and did good service for many years.

When Sully's troops reached the Yellowstone, the *Alone* and the *Chippewa Falls* ferried them across that stream, after which they marched down to Fort Union, at its mouth. The river was very low when the boats came to the rendezvous, but it fell still more before they left there. Despite their shallow draft, it seemed for a time that they would have to be abandoned. But by removing all the cargoes to the army wagons and then hitching the horses to the boats with long ropes and dragging them over the shallowest bars and rapids, they were at last brought safely into the Missouri. Here they again ferried the soldiers across to Fort Union, where a garrison of one company was left for the winter. The troops then marched down the north bank of the Missouri, past Fort Berthold, where another garrison was posted, arriving at Fort Rice on September 8th, thus successfully terminating one of the most unusual Indian campaigns on record. The posts established by General Sully all continued to be garrisoned for a number of years, until the Indian wars of the Northwest were brought to an end.[5]

---

4. Captain Lamont states that the accident occurred about four miles below the fur-trading post of Fort Union and directly opposite the point where Fort Buford now stands.
5. The *Official Records of the War of the Rebellion,* Part 1, Vol. 41, Series 1, contain the military reports of this campaign.

CHAPTER 9

Three Roads to El Dorado

But causes other than Indian disturbances were at work bringing life and activity to the lonely waters of the Missouri during and immediately following those years in which the great military struggle between South and North was absorbing nearly all the energy and interest of the Nation. Gold, that most potent magnet to the adventurous in all times and lands, was the chief of these causes. The precious metal had been discovered in the regions now embraced in Idaho and Montana as early as 1852, but it was not until ten years later that the findings became sufficiently rich to attract widespread attention. The first important discoveries were made around Bannack, Dakota Territory, in the summer of 1862.

During the following year the exceedingly rich placer deposits in Alder Gulch came to light and a city of 10,000 people sprang up where but a few weeks before the wolves had howled. Last Chance Gulch being discovered late in the autumn of 1864, by the next spring the infant city of Helena covered its rugged hillsides and for several years thereafter immigration poured into the whole country in a ceaseless stream.[1] At the time of their settlement all of these places lay in Dakota or Idaho, for the territory of Montana had not yet been erected.

The torrent of white invasion, coming suddenly into the primeval regions of which the Indians had hitherto held undisturbed possession, aroused them to a frenzy of resistance. The fortune-seekers chose three main routes of travel for reaching the gold-fields. The first of these, and the one by which the original discoverers had entered, came from the Pacific regions across the western slopes of the Continental

---

1. Contributions to the Historical Society of Montana.

Divide. It was the most convenient route from California, but inaccessible to immigration from the Eastern states. The second was by way of the Missouri River to Fort Benton, at the head of navigation, and thence by a comparatively short overland journey into the mines. The third, and most menacing from the Indian point of view, left the great trans-continental road to California at Fort Laramie on the North Platte River, and extended from that point north-westward, skirting the base of the Big Horn Mountains, to the valley of the Yellowstone and Bozeman, near the headwaters of that stream.

The last route, which came to be called the Montana or Bozeman Road, traversed the very heart of the region where ranged the vast herds of buffalo upon which the Indians chiefly depended for their supply of both food and clothing. They naturally regarded the invasion of this country by white men with great indignation and alarm, but regardless of the protests of the rightful owners, the emigrants presumed upon right of highway across it and soon established a well-defined thoroughfare.[2] In 1865 the government sought to justify the action of its citizens and to insure them in continued possession of the road, by making a treaty at Fort Sully in which the Indians consented to its existence. But it was noticeable that the Indians who signed this treaty on behalf of the Sioux Nation were of those tribes which dwelt close to the river and that the Ogalalla, the most powerful tribe of the Sioux and the one actually in occupation of the buffalo country, not only did not sign but protested against the provisions of the treaty and flatly repudiated it.[3]

In the early summer of 1866 the government again attempted to arrange a treaty, at Fort Laramie, with the Northern Cheyenne and the Ogalalla tribes, by which they would consent to the use of the road, but it ended in failure, and Red Cloud, a leading Ogalalla chief, left the fort with his followers after declaring open war against the United States. Troops were then sent out along the Montana Road, establishing military posts at Forts Reno, Phil Kearney and C. F. Smith. But Red Cloud, whose military ability had seldom been excelled by men of his race, immediately concentrated his forces about the new posts in such numbers that their garrisons had great difficulty in even maintaining themselves, let alone assisting emigrants to keep the road open. For many months all the forts, and especially Phil Kearney, were in a state of investment, while bloody engagements were of frequent occurrence.

---

2. Contributions to the Historical Society of Montana.
3. *History of the Sioux Indians*, by Doane Robinson.

Finally, in 1868, the government reluctantly decided to abandon the road entirely, and arranged a treaty with Red Cloud to this effect, he in return consenting to the construction of any desired roads south of the North Platte River, a matter in which he was little interested, since the vital point for which he and his people had been contending was conceded to them, and their victory was virtually complete.

The practical abandonment of the Montana Road by emigration, in 1866, left the Missouri River as the only avenue of ingress to the mining regions from the East. Parties following this route took steamboats at St. Louis or some other point on the lower river, and travelled by them to Fort Benton, 2,300 miles above the mouth of the Missouri, whence an overland journey of about 200 miles brought them to the heart of the ore-producing district. Fort Benton, which for many years had been an obscure trading-post of the American, and later of the North-western Fur Company, thus became the rendezvous and outfitting point for the whole mining region and immediately leaped to a position of great commercial importance.

Where, previous to 1866, only about a half-dozen steamers had arrived at the Fort Benton levee annually, carrying freight to a total of perhaps 1,500 tons, in 1866 there were thirty-one arrivals and in 1867, thirty-nine.[4] During the latter year these boats transported 8,061 tons of freight to Fort Benton, and carried some 10,000 passengers to and from that point. The average fare of each of these passengers was $150, or $1,500,000 total receipts for passengers alone. Of the freight carried, 2,095 tons belonged to the government, the remainder being provisions, dry goods, and mining machinery owned by private parties.[5] On the long stretch of 1,306 miles between Fort Benton and Fort Randall, where the settlements began, the only ports in 1867 were the military and fur-trading posts of Crow Creek (Fort Thompson), Fort Sully,[6] Fort Rice, Fort Stevenson, Fort Berthold, Fort Buford, Fort Hawley and Camp Cooke. To them during the season of 1867, twenty-eight cargoes were consigned from St. Louis, aggregating 8,094 tons, of which 5,832 tons was government freight and 2,262 tons, private.[7]

---

4. Contributions to the Historical Society of Montana.
5. Report of Captain C. W. Howell, U. S. A., in Report of the Secretary of War, 1867-1868.
6. The new post, established in 1866 when the old one was abandoned, and located about thirty-three miles farther up the river than the latter.— *South Dakota Historical Collections*, Vol. 1.
7. Report of Captain C. W. Howell.

Although from the above figures it may readily be imagined that the upper river presented an animated appearance during these years of prosperity, the route was none the less beset with many perils. Rocks and snags, especially the latter, were scattered all along the channel, and the steamboat pilot was obliged to be ever on the alert to guard his vessel against injury or destruction by these menacing obstacles. The numberless sandbars, constantly being shifted in form and even location by the restless current, offered obstructions less dangerous, it is true, but none the less annoying, for hours and often days were consumed in forcing a boat across them. But the greatest danger to be feared in the passage to Fort Benton was from the Indians. Though Red Cloud had gathered about him for his warfare along the Montana Road a majority of the malcontents of all the Northern tribes, there were still hovering along the banks of the Missouri a great many hostiles whose attacks upon passing steamers and even upon the military posts of the region were frequent and annoying.

That the Indian war was not confined to Fort Phil Kearney and its vicinity in these years may be appreciated when it is said that on July 31, 1866, the garrison of Fort Rice fought an engagement with Indians near the post, and on December 24th and 25th, the troops at Fort Buford had a similar action. On July 9, August 8, and October 10, 1867, Fort Stevenson's garrison was engaged, and on November 6th, Fort Buford again received attention from the red men.[8] It was in 1868, however, after the Montana Road had been closed, that Indian activity along the Missouri became really menacing. A great many warriors of Red Cloud's following, not content to be guided by the example of their illustrious leader and remain at peace, turned their attention to the river posts and floating traffic.

On May 13th of that year, two men were killed, scalped, and their bodies shot full of arrows near Fort Buford by an Uncpapa war party, and on the 15th of the same month two Government mail-carriers were waylaid and massacred between Fort Stevenson and Fort Totten, at the eastern end of Devil's Lake.[9] On May 17th, Camp Cooke, near the mouth of the Judith River, Montana, was attacked, and again, on May 19th, at the mouth of Musselshell River, a detachment of the garrison from that post, under Lieutenant Edwards, fought an engagement with a party of seventy-five Sioux. Detachments of the Camp Cooke garrison fought on May 24th, on the Musselshell, and also near

---
8. Historical Register and Dictionary of the United States Army.
9. Report of the Secretary of War, 1868-69.

the Yellowstone, and on June 13th they were engaged at Twenty-Five Yard Creek.

On July 28th, near old Fort Sully, August 20th, at Fort Buford, and September 26th, near Fort Rice, the hostiles approached in sufficient force to precipitate action.[10] Captain Howell, U. S. A., who ascended the river as far as Dauphin's Rapids on the steamer *Miner,* in 1868, reported on reaching Fort Buford, August 3rd, that the Sioux had raided the cattle herd the previous day but had done little harm. On August 20th, however, they succeeded in stampeding the herd of 250 head and escaping with all but fifty-seven. The soldiers in the fort were erecting *adobe* post-buildings when the savages swooped down, and they seized their arms and rushed out, but too late, though they lost two men killed and five wounded in the futile pursuit. On August 9th the steamer *Leni Leoti* was fired into near Fort Berthold and one passenger killed, and during the summer two hay cutters lost their lives near Fort Stevenson.[11]

But despite the dangers of navigation, the profits of the upper river commerce were too great to be ignored, for five-sixths of all the precious metals from the mines came to the States by this route.[12] The value of a cargo of gold dust often amounted to hundreds of thousands of dollars. Many lower river boats of deep draft were tempted by the enormous profits to engage in the "mountain trade," as it was called, and they frequently came to grief in the shoal waters of the upper river if their return was delayed until after the spring freshets had passed down. But the light-draft steamers built especially for this region could often navigate throughout the summer. The boats generally left St. Louis early in April, or as soon as the ice was out, and consumed two months or more in reaching Fort Benton. With the aid of the rapid current, the return trip took a much shorter time, between two and four weeks being sufficient if no accidents befell; and some of the light-draft boats were able to make two round trips in a season, though the feat was an unusual one.

---

10. Historical Register and Dictionary of the United States Army.
11. Report of the Secretary of War, 1868-69.
12. Report of Captain C. W. Howell.

SIOUX WAR-DANCE

CHAPTER 10

The "Luella" at Fort Benton in Vigilante Days

Among the large fleet which drew out from St. Louis in the early spring days of 1866 and, turning westward past Mobile Point into the swelling tide of the Missouri, started on the long, up-hill climb toward the mountains, was the stanch packet *Luella,* Captain Grant Marsh, master. She was the first boat of which he had ever been in chief command, but the owners who had placed her in his charge felt that his work with the Sully Expedition had well qualified him for the responsible position, and the sequel proved the wisdom of their choice. There were none too many steamboat men familiar with the hitherto untraveled waters of the Northwest to meet the sudden demands caused by the *gold rush,* and the younger men in the business who had been on the upper river and had profited by their experiences, thus found ready opportunities for promotion.

On this his first trip with the *Luella,* Captain Marsh, as has been his practice ever since, acted as both master and chief pilot, thus not only saving the expense of an extra navigator but also holding the boat at all times much more absolutely under his personal control. As has been pointed out, pilots, especially in the old days, were an independent and assertive race who frequently preferred to ignore the captain's authority entirely, and fortunate indeed was the commanding officer who could himself stand a watch at the wheel and dispense with the services of one of the haughty clan. The partner who alternated watches with Captain Marsh on this trip was Rube McDaniel, skilful as a pilot and modest as a man and much less given than some of his professional brethren to the arrogation of authority.

The *Luella* left St. Louis on the 18th of April with a cabin-full of passengers and 113 tons of freight, chiefly mining machinery and staple groceries. She had started promptly as soon as the ice was out of the river because her speed was less than that of many of the boats engaged in the Fort Benton trade, and time was precious. After Fort Randall had been left behind, downward-bound boats brought news of the extreme hostility of the Indians above, and passengers and crew began to grow uneasy over the prospect. There was really little cause for apprehension, since nearly everyone on board was well armed and the boat itself had been especially prepared to withstand Indian attacks. But it was difficult for the captain to calm the fears of the more timid. In those years everyone had heard of the frequent assaults on passing steamers by bands of Sioux, and the still more frequent ones on the small parties of miners who now and then attempted the perilous trip from Fort Benton to the States in mackinaw boats or canoes.

The captain and Rube McDaniel, when on duty at the wheel, could breathe freely whatever happened, for the pilot-house of the *Luella,* like that of every upper-river boat was sheathed with boiler iron against which the bullets of the savages might patter harmlessly. The people in the cabins below were not quite so well protected, but among them all there was only one who so completely lost his nerve that he could not bring himself to go through to Fort Benton. This was the boat's clerk, a young fellow named Mellon. So panic-stricken did he become that he was on the verge of nervous collapse when the *Luella* reached Milk River, Montana, 350 miles below her destination. Here was encountered the deep-draft steamer *Rubicon,* Captain Horace Bixby, which, finding herself unable to proceed farther upstream, was preparing to return to St. Louis.

Regardless of protests and ridicule, Mellon immediately left the *Luella* and took passage on the *Rubicon* for home. Captain Bixby, who was thus perhaps the means of saving the youth from an untimely end by nervous prostration, was the famous Mississippi River navigator who had been confidential pilot to Flag-Officers Foote and Davis, of the Mississippi Flotilla, in the days of the Civil War, who had *learned* Mark Twain the river at an earlier day, and who, in return for this service, was ere long to be immortalized by the genial humorist in his *Life on the Mississippi.* Captain Bixby's experiences among the sandbars of the upper Missouri did not arouse in him any admiration for the region, and since the voyage of the *Rubicon* he has confined himself to the deeper channels of the Father of Waters, which he knows so well. A few years since, a gentleman from Montana, voyaging through

Louisiana with Captain Bixby and observing the deference paid to the veteran by all other steamboat men, dubbed him "the Grant Marsh of the lower Mississippi."

"And by the Lord, sir," says Captain Bixby, in recounting the incident, "it was a high compliment, for any man who can run a boat for twenty years in that rainwater creek above Bismarck is surely the king of pilots."

Although above Wagonwheel Bluffs the river was entirely strange to Captain Marsh, he threaded his way through its difficulties successfully, and on June 17th, having encountered no Indians, reached his destination safely, just sixty days out from St. Louis. It was a strange scene upon which he looked forth from the pilothouse after he had rung the last landing bell and the boat lay snubbed to the bank. Before him on the open prairie stretched a straggling hamlet of rude log cabins and rutted wagon tracks, containing but 500 people, yet the commercial centre of a vast territory. Before the doorways of the trading establishments stood the huge freight wagons drawn by a half-dozen span of oxen or mules, ready to start out on their toilsome journeys to Alder Gulch, Last Chance Gulch, Deer Lodge or other mining camps back among the mountains. In shabby huts where villainous whiskey sold for forty cents a glass and in tawdry dance-halls presided over by women whose records had driven them from older settlements, men jostled one another to spend in an hour's debauchery the fruits of toilsome months.

Here were swarthy sons of Mexico, dressed in the gaudy fashion popular south of the Rio Grande; here were soft-spoken Southerners in plenty, flotsam of the wrecked Confederacy, some from the far-flung "left wing of Price's army," some from more distant regions of Dixie, but all bent upon wringing from Montana's golden valleys the wealth they had lost in their stricken native land. Here were many ex-soldiers of the Union armies, slaking a thirst for adventure which the battlefield had not satisfied, and gladly giving the hand of fellowship to their erstwhile foes. Here were miners from the Pacific slope, farmers from the Atlantic seaboard, fur-traders and hunters of the vanishing North-western wilderness, clergymen, ex-convicts, hardened desperadoes, and heroes of law and order; every type and condition of man that the continent could produce, gathered together by one common aim and impulse, the pursuit of wealth.

From the naked hills whose summits over-topped the infant community, the untamed Indians looked down sullenly upon its fevered industry, seeing in every freight wagon that left its streets for the distant mines another contribution to the forces which were slowly dispossessing them of their native land, hearing in every whistle-blast from the crawling steamboats before the levee, the hoarse challenge of civilization to barbarism. A short distance along the river bank from the new town loomed the massive but crumbling walls of old Fort Benton, the American Fur Company's post, which for twenty years had stood guard over the troubled waters, the habitation of men who came as suppliants for trade into the empire of the nomads. Its days of usefulness had already passed, for at its base stood now a settlement of white men strong enough in numbers to defy the unskilled Indians without the aid of adobe walls and bastions.

Less than two years had elapsed since Montana had been erected into a territory, and only a few months since the new territorial officials had reached Bannack from their distant homes in the East, removing soon after to the new capital at Alder Gulch, which had been renamed the City of Virginia.[1] During all the interval between the opening of the mining settlements and the arrival of these officials, a state of anarchy had existed in Montana. There was no legislature, no executive, no judiciary, no militia. Though most of the region was nominally a part of Madison County, Idaho, nothing approaching enforcement of law was undertaken by the Idaho government, and virtually every settler was a law unto himself. In a country whose only wealth consisted of gold and where every inhabitant possessed more or less of the precious metal, such a state of affairs was an irresistible temptation to crime. Highway robberies, accompanied more often than not by cold-blooded murders, became alarmingly frequent.

No traveller's life was safe if he was suspected by the highwaymen, or *road agents*, of having gold in his possession. The robbers grew so bold and numerous that they banded themselves together and, working in parties, did not even hesitate to waylay stage-coaches filled with well-armed passengers, and before long, more than one hundred innocent men had fallen victims to their rapacity. But at length the anger of the long-suffering community was aroused, and during the winter of 1863-64, the Vigilance Committee was organized, a crude but mighty engine of stern justice for the protection of life and property. In its ranks were found the best and most law-respecting men

---

1. All the facts in this chapter relating to the early history of Montana, except those of a nature personal to Captain Marsh, are based upon articles contained in the published volumes of contributions to the *Historical Society of Montana*.—J. M. H.

of every settlement; men who desired peace and order and safety of person and were determined to have it at any price. With heroic courage, for they were dealing with desperate criminals, they proceeded against the road agents, pursuing, capturing and hanging them wherever found.

Among the very first who, upon ample evidence, they convicted and executed, was Henry Plummer, the leader of the cut-throat gang. It was a grimly humorous evidence of the sort of law prevailing before the reign of the vigilantes commenced that this man during his whole career of crime had been the duly appointed sheriff of Madison County, Idaho. His official position he had skillfully used as a cloak to hide his true character and an aid in discovering the most profitable victims for murder. But the keen eyes of the Vigilance Committee penetrated the disguise, and he with four of his accomplices gave up their lives on the same gibbet at Virginia City one day in January, 1864, sacrifices to their mediaeval methods of acquiring wealth.

At the time of Captain Marsh's first arrival, the feeble arm of the new territorial government had not yet gained strength to reach from Virginia City to Fort Benton, and here the Vigilance Committee still ruled supreme. The men composing it did not meet in formal conclave to debate the punishment of a suspected offender. A few low words spoken in passing as they met each other on their daily business, a vote taken in the same manner, and perhaps the next morning a still figure would be found hanging by the neck before one of the stores, or some hulking individual would have disappeared from his familiar haunts never to return, fled in the night from a grim warning he did not dare question or resist. The law of the Vigilance Committee was stern and uncompromising, but it was seldom unjust, for even the extremity of its punishments found excuse in the chaotic conditions of frontier society.

In Fort Benton so great had become the terror inspired by its constant menace of swift vengeance upon evil doing, that Captain Marsh saw men ride in from the mines, fling down their saddles, with sacks of gold dust tied to the cantles, upon the floor of Baker, Carroll and Steele's store and go away for a week's spree, to find when they sobered up and returned that their property had not been touched. While the *Luella* was unloading, one of her deck hands stole from the cargo a box of patent medicine, doubtless because the nostrum contained a large percentage of alcohol. In some way the vigilantes learned of the theft. The miscreant was tried by one of their mysterious tribunals and the next night was seized and borne away to a secluded spot where he was whipped until nearly dead. The captain afterwards was informed that the Vigilance Committee had come within three votes of returning a verdict for hanging the thief, but the punishment accorded was sufficient, and no more petty pilfering occurred on board the *Luella*.

A few days after this experience with the vigilantes, there appeared at Fort Benton a representative of the firm of Smith, Hubbell & Hawley, who, in the previous year, had bought out all the interests of the long-established American Fur Company. The new firm had determined to abandon the post at Fort Union, opposite the mouth of the Yellowstone, and their representative was looking for a steamer to convey the goods from it to Fort Benton. He selected the *Luella*, and Captain Marsh thereupon ran down, loaded everything on board, and brought it to its destination without mishap. Probably no one thought of it at the time, but when the *Luella* dropped away from the bank that day, leaving the stout walls of the deserted fort, which had withstood the storms of thirty-seven years, to crumble into dust, she had turned the last leaf on the closing chapter of an epoch which for thrilling romance has seldom been equalled in the history of the continent. Fort Union had been the greatest of the Indian trading-posts within the boundaries of the United States, and in its prime was a centre of much commercial importance.

For years the most powerful tribes of the Northwest had congregated there for purposes of trade; there had come the factors of the Company's other posts from all over the vast watershed of the upper Missouri; there had assembled the bold *voyageurs* of the wilderness from the Great Slave Lake and the Platte, from the Rocky Mountains and the Red River of the North; there had visited at one time and another some of the world's most famous scientists and explorers, among others, George Catlin, Prince Maximilian and Audubon. When Fort Union passed away, there passed with it the last vestige of the fur trade as an independent commercial institution, and the steamer *Luella,* industriously engaged in the laudable work of building up civilization in western Montana, was the visible agent of its passing.

The Fort Union cargo had scarcely been unloaded when Captain Marsh was called upon to make another short trip. The shallow water of midsummer made it dangerous for the lower-river boats to delay their departure from Fort Benton after the June rise began to decline. But one of these, the *Marion,* Captain Abe Wolf, had done this, and on at last starting with a heavy load of passengers, she had gone aground at Pablos Rapids, seventy miles below Benton, where the rapidly falling river had left her hopelessly stranded. Captain Marsh went down, rescued the passengers and bought the *Marion's* machinery, which he took back to Fort Benton and sold.

It was now late in August and the *Luella* was the only boat left at Benton, for never before had one dared stay until so late in the season. But the captain was confident of his ability to get out of the upper river safely and advertised in the Helena papers that the *Luella* would leave for St. Louis during the first week in September. Since, after disposing of the *Marion's* machinery, he had still a number of days remaining before he could leave according to schedule, he organized a party from among the officers and crew and prospective passengers of the boat, and went on a hunting expedition into the Highwood Mountains, about thirty miles south from the river. In this region of abundant game which had never been disturbed by hunters they spent a delightful week, returning to Fort Benton on September 1st, ready to commence the tedious journey to the States.

CHAPTER 11

The Troubles of a Treasure Ship

As the *Luella* offered the last opportunity of the year for leaving the country, there was naturally a great rush of applications for passage, and when she departed on September 2nd, she had on board 230 miners and $1,250,000 in gold dust, the most valuable cargo of treasure ever carried down the Missouri River.[1] Having lost his clerk on the way up as previously related, and being himself entirely unfamiliar with bookkeeping, Captain Marsh was sorely puzzled for a time as to how he should collect and keep account of the fares of his numerous passengers and the freight charges on his cargo of gold. But he soon found in an intelligent passenger by the name of MacNeil a man eminently qualified for these delicate duties, as the results showed.

Among such a crowd there were naturally many rough characters who would use every effort to escape paying the established rates and would not hesitate to make trouble if they thought they could gain anything by so doing. All the charges were payable in gold dust, the only circulating medium, and it was a common expedient of the miners to mix black sand with their dust, which, if undetected in the weighing, saved them something of their hard-earned wealth. But the black sand never passed the vigilant eye of MacNeil. He required the passengers to pan their dust in his presence and wash out all the sand before he would accept it, a procedure which angered some of them greatly, though fortunately he was a man whose courage they respected enough to avert serious consequences.

The voyage through the Missouri's tortuous bends and narrow reaches was uneventful until the *Luella* reached the mouth of Milk River, a small stream which enters the Missouri 347 miles below Ben-

---

1. See *History of the Navigation of the Missouri River,* by Col. H. M. Chittenden, U.S.A.

ton. Here a peculiar accident occurred. As is usual at points along the Missouri where tributaries enter that stream, a sandbar existed at the mouth of Milk River difficult to cross in low water. On this bar the *Luella* ran aground. While the crew was engaged in dislodging her, the passengers, most of whom carried their gold dust in leather belts about their waists, stood along the sides of the boat, idly watching the work, and one of them, a man named McClellan, accidentally fell overboard. The water was barely two feet deep, but the current was swift. He was carried off his feet, and so great was the weight of his treasure belt that he was dragged down and drowned before help could reach him. Even his body was never recovered.

A few days later, as the boat passed below the mouth of the Yellowstone, a small camp of soldiers was discovered on the north bank of the Missouri. It proved to be occupied by Company C, 13th (later 22nd) U. S. Infantry, under Captain W. G. Rankin. The 13th Infantry had come up from St. Louis while the *Luella* was at Fort Benton, to relieve the 4th U. S. Volunteers and the 50th Wisconsin, regiments of Civil War veterans which had previously been garrisoning the river forts at Randall, Sully, Rice and Berthold. Captain Rankin had received orders to establish a new post, Fort Buford, at or near the old fur-trading post of Fort Union, and his command of seventy men was set ashore here by a steamboat and left to shift for itself. The experience of the little handful of brave spirits whose duty demanded implicit obedience to orders wherever those orders might lead them, was proving extremely hard. Their instructions were to build a post and they set about it, though their only tools were a few axes.

The second night after their arrival the Indians attacked the camp, but after a sharp fight, in which one soldier was wounded, they were repulsed. The next day the Indians unsuccessfully attempted to stampede the cattle herd, and from that time forth throughout the summer scarcely a day passed when there was not a skirmish with the hostiles. The men kept their rifles constantly beside them as they worked, ready to drop their axes in an instant and turn to defend their lives from a yelling horde of savages who swept down as swiftly as shadows from the uplands, circling close enough to fire a scattering volley and perhaps pick up a few head of stock, and then vanishing as they had come. The men cutting and rafting building logs at the mouth of the Yellowstone were so frequently attacked that a heavy guard had to remain with them constantly and, even thus protected, three wood cutters lost their lives before winter.

The Indians engaged in the depredations were Sioux, who boasted that they intended to annihilate the garrison. They seemed likely to succeed, for in January, 1867, Sitting Bull, the young and influential medicine-man of Red Cloud's army, came down the Yellowstone and joining the Indians already before Buford, laid close siege to the post. He captured the sawmill near the landing and used the big, circular saw for a war drum.[2] He established his sharpshooters on the opposite bank of the river and throughout the winter made it so dangerous for the soldiers to come to the stream after water that they were compelled to sink wells inside the stockade. Several times during the year it was reported in the East that the garrison of Fort Buford had been massacred. But the courageous band survived the winter and the next year was so largely reenforced as to make it safe against Indian attacks, though for a long time the Sioux continued to occasionally raid the herds and drive away stock.[3]

When he brought his company to this desolate spot, Captain Rankin was accompanied by his wife, a young and beautiful Cuban lady whose high-spirited courage was amply demonstrated by the manner in which she bore the hardships and dangers of that trying year. On the day that the *Luella* touched at the post, Mrs. Rankin rode down to the river bank on horseback, for the arrival of a steamboat was an exciting event at such a place. The post was but a short distance back from the bank and there were soldiers between it and the river, and also about the boat, so that apparently there was no possible danger. But a lurking party of Indians discovered her as she was riding back toward the fort, and sweeping down, endeavoured to surround her. She urged her horse forward and after a short but desperate race succeeded in reaching her husband and the soldiers who, as soon as they saw her peril, had snatched up their weapons and rushed out to save her from a fate too horrible to contemplate. Both Captain Rankin and his wife became warm friends of Captain Marsh, and while they remained at Buford he never failed to visit them in his trips up and down the river.

The difficulties experienced in establishing Fort Buford were paralleled in the founding of nearly every one of the early river posts. Even when, after vast toil and hardship, they were at last completed, so inadequate had been the tools and so wretched the materials available

---

2. *Frontier and Indian Life,* Joseph H. Taylor.
3. *The Army of the United States,* edited by Gen. Theo. P. Rodenbough and Major William L. Haskin, U. S. A.

for building purposes that they were scarcely habitable. Colonel D. B. Sackett, U. S. A., a very observant officer who ascended the Missouri in the summer of 1866 on a tour of inspection, reported[4] all of them above Fort Randall in a horrible condition. Their buildings were made entirely of cottonwood logs with dirt floors and roofs and no windows, as there were no casings for them and no glass. Being erected close to the river bank on the bottoms, they were liable to be flooded in high water, while the rains of summer soaked through the mud roofs, turning the floors to puddles, and the snows of winter drove in between the loosely-laid logs, burying everything in an icy blanket.

The cottonwood timber decayed rapidly, necessitating frequent repairs, while it also harboured swarms of bedbugs, fleas and other insects, which no efforts availed to exclude. Every post was infested with rats in such numbers that they constituted a veritable plague. It was impossible to keep either provisions or forage from them except in metal-covered cases, for they would gnaw through wood at if it were paper. At Fort Rice, Colonel Sackett estimated that the rats destroyed one thousand pounds of corn and provisions daily. All of this had been transported into the country from a long distance by steamboat and was not to be replaced except at great labour and cost.

Strange as it may seem, the destructive presence of the rats was for a number of years one of the chief considerations which deterred the military authorities from stationing a cavalry regiment in the upper country, sorely as one was needed there. It is small wonder that under such adverse conditions the soldiers of the volunteer garrisons grew disheartened and careless of personal appearance, as Colonel Sackett reported, wearing unkempt beards and ragged uniforms, or that among the regulars who followed them, desertions became unusually frequent.

The practice referred to above of sparring a boat over an obstructing shoal was a common one in the old steamboating days on the Missouri. The spars were long, heavy timbers resembling telegraph poles, and a set of them, two in number, were always carried on the sides of the boat near the bow ready for use. When she became lodged on a bar, the spars were raised and set in the river bottom, like posts, their tops inclined somewhat toward the bow. Above the line of the deck each was rigged with a tackle-block over which a manilla cable was passed, one end being fastened to the gunwale of the boat and

---

4. In report of the Secretary of War, 1866-67.

Camp of Gros Ventres Indians at Fort Buford, 1874

the other end wound around the capstan. As the capstan was turned and the paddle-wheel revolved, the boat was thus lifted and pushed forward. Then the spars were re-set farther ahead and the process repeated until the boat was at last literally lifted over the bar. From the grotesque resemblance to a grasshopper which the craft bore when her spars were set, and from the fact that she might be said to move forward in a series of hops, the practice came to be called "grasshoppering." It was only one of the many novel expedients often necessarily used in navigating those shallow waters.

CHAPTER 12

The Captain Encounters a "Bad Man"

Some days after the skirmish at the White Earth, there occurred on board the *Luella* an episode well illustrating the characters of some of the men in the floating population of the frontier. One evening at the supper table a miner named Gilmore, a swaggering fellow much given to boasting and bullying, became involved in a violent quarrel with another passenger over a trifling matter. He was the instigator of the trouble, and Captain Marsh, hurrying to quell the disturbance, reprimanded him soundly and threatened to put him ashore. The rowdy had no desire to be left alone on the prairie, where he would almost certainly be discovered and killed by the Indians, so he swallowed his resentment and became quiet for the time. But to others he breathed vengeance and openly avowed that he intended to kill the captain at the first opportunity.

A majority of the passengers were law-abiding men who had no more use for Gilmore and the few hardened spirits who consorted with *him* than the captain did, and one of them, a young man of the name of Paine, who had overheard Gilmore, came to the captain and informed him of the ruffian's threats.

"Oh, never mind that fellow," said the captain. "His actions won't reach as far as his words."

"His actions may reach pretty far if he gets a chance," answered Paine seriously, and he offered his revolver to the captain. The latter, who never made a practice of carrying small arms, had none of his own, and after some persuasion he accepted the revolver and kept it by him to be prepared for emergencies.

It was quite obvious that Gilmore was harbouring his anger until a favourable moment should arrive for seeking revenge, and this was not long in coming. In a few days the *Luella* passed beyond the Indian-haunted wilderness and came into the sparsely settled regions below Fort Randall. Here one afternoon the boat was forced to go to the bank on account of a strong head wind, and as she lay there a number of the passengers got off to amuse themselves on shore. Among them were Gilmore and his followers, who drew a mark on the ground and began a contest of broad-jumping. While thus engaged the captain passed them, going out with a party of the crew to cut some fuel in the adjacent timber, as was customary whenever the boat was tied up for any length of time. As he passed, Gilmore, whose courage had risen since the danger from Indians was over, turned to one of his friends and ostentatiously borrowing the latter's revolver, said in a loud voice:

"Watch me make that low-down dog of a captain jump the mark."

In his earnest desire to keep the peace, the captain had thus far permitted Gilmore to swagger unmolested. But this last insult was more than he would stand. Drawing Paine's revolver, he walked over to where Gilmore stood, surrounded by his companions, and looking the fellow squarely in the eyes, said:

"Gilmore, I heard what you called me just then, and the time's come for us to have a settlement. You've been looking for trouble all this trip and now you're going to get it. I'm willing you should have a fair chance, so come over here and fight," and he pointed to a clear space where there was ample room for a pistol duel.

But the bare suggestion was too much for Gilmore. His boastfulness left him instantly, his face grew pale, and he began to tremble visibly. The captain thereupon stepped up to him and slapped him full in the face.

"Now will you fight, you coward?" he demanded.

"Oh, captain, I didn't mean anything," whimpered Gilmore. "I don't want to fight."

The captain's fury was getting the better of him. He cried:

"If you won't fight, then I'll kill you right here!"

But his own friends now interfered. Paine laid a restraining hand on his shoulder, saying:

"He's nothing but a contemptible coward, Marsh. Don't kill a coward. If he was a brave man we'd insist on your killing him, but don't you dirty your hands with a sneak."

By a great effort the captain controlled himself and allowed the crestfallen *bad man* to go, since his conduct had now made him an object of ridicule to even his own associates.

Several days later the *Luella* reached Sioux City. Captain Marsh was busy for some time about the landing and then walked uptown with some friends. Most of the passengers had left the boat immediately on reaching the bank and gone out to view the village. On entering a saloon not far from the levee the captain found a number of men within and among them discovered Gilmore, seated at a table in the rear of the room. Without appearing to notice him, the captain ordered drinks for the crowd and invited everyone to step up to the bar. All complied with alacrity excepting Gilmore, who sullenly kept his seat. Captain Marsh, who felt that the fellow had suffered enough and was willing to restore good feeling, turned to him and said:

"Come on up, Gilmore, and drink with me."

"No, sir," answered the other, with a sour glance, "I won't drink with you."

His manner roused afresh the captain's ire, and picking up a heavy beer glass he stepped over and exclaimed:

"Gilmore, you come up here now and *drink* or, by the Eternal, I'll break this glass over your skull!"

Again the ruffian showed the white feather in the face of a jeering crowd and meekly went to the bar to drink at the expense of the man whom he had found to his cost that bravado could not intimidate. So completely was he cowed that a little later he came to the captain privately to beg that he be not put off the boat before she reached St. Louis, to which point he had paid his passage, as he knew of no other way to get down. His plea was granted with the express understanding that if he caused the slightest disturbance during the remainder of the trip he would be immediately set ashore. But either the difficulty he experienced in behaving himself or the open contempt of his shipmates must have finally become insupportable, for at Omaha he left the boat and never returned, much to the gratification of every one.

The remainder of the voyage was without incident, and the *Luella* arrived safely at St. Louis about October 5th, clearing on her trip $24,000, which is a fair example of the profits of Missouri River steamboating in those days.

CHAPTER 13

Blockaded by Buffalo

In the eager contest for the glittering prizes of the mountain trade it had been Captain Marsh's fortune on the trip of the *Luella* to establish the record for the richest cargo ever floated down the Big Muddy. But the following year he was destined to make another record of a nature calculated to be still more pleasing to the fortunate steamboat owner who had secured his services. This record was in the matter of net profits for the season's work, and the boat to whose credit it went was the *Ida Stockdale,* of Pittsburg, Pa. She was the property of Captain R. S. Calhoun, of that city, and surely no man had reason to feel more gratification over a business venture than he, for when he balanced his accounts at the close of the season he found that she had earned him in her five months' work $42,594 above all expenses—nearly twice her own rated value and far more than was made by any other of the thirty-nine boats which made the round trip to Benton that year.

The boat had been built under the personal direction of Captain Marsh during the previous winter, and several causes contributed to the success of this, her first trip, though the chief of these was the reputation gained by the captain in 1866 as a skilful navigator and considerate first-officer, which enabled him to fill his boat with the best class of trade both going to and returning from the mountains. Captain Calhoun accompanied him, though he made the voyage for pleasure only and had nothing to do with the management of the boat, having hired Captain Marsh at a salary of $1,200 per month to assume entire control.

The *Stockdale* made the run to Fort Benton without special incident, arriving there on June 16th, having encountered no trouble from Indians on the way up, and after loading with a valuable cargo, started on her return. One August afternoon she was bowling along at a good rate through a left-hand timber bend about 220 miles below Fort Buford, when without warning the roar of a cannon burst out, re-echoing against the bluffs, and a cloud of white smoke floated up over the left shore. Awaiting no further invitation, Captain Marsh swung the boat into the bank. A short distance back from the timber he found encamped Companies H and I, 22nd Infantry, and C, D and F, 10th Infantry,[1] while at the edge of the water stood General Alfred H. Terry, commanding the Department of Dakota, with his staff and several other prominent officers, including Major C. B. Comstock, of the Corps of Engineers, and Lieutenant-Colonel S. B. Holabird, Department Quartermaster-General. Accompanied by the troops, General Terry had come overland from St. Paul for the purpose of locating several new posts.

Colonel Holabird at once came on board and informed Captain Marsh that he wished to charter the boat to convey General Terry and staff to Fort Benton. The captain had already done an excellent business, and was anxious to get back to St. Louis as soon as possible. But after discussing the situation with Colonel Holabird and pointing out to him that such a long delay might operate to the financial loss of the boat, a contract was finally made between them for the use of the *Stockdale,* the charter to extend until she arrived at Sioux City. The colonel further agreed to furnish a detail of ten soldiers, together with two mules and a wagon, to assist the crew in getting fuel for the boat throughout the trip, this detail afterwards proving of great utility, especially in the sparsely timbered regions between Buford and Benton, where wood had to be procured several miles from the river.

Although any army officer engaged in the performance of military duties was at liberty when he needed a steamer to seize the first one which happened along and to keep it as long as required, he was also bound to arrange that she should receive fair recompense from the government for such involuntary services. The *per diem* awarded the *Ida Stockdale* was liberal, and insured her against loss, but General Terry and Colonel Holabird were glad to acknowledge before the trip was ended that the government was the gainer by their having found so excellent a craft, and so capable a navigator as Captain Marsh to handle her.

When the officers had come on board, the *Stockdale* went on down to Fort Rice after Colonel Reeve, the commander of the 13th Infan-

---

1. *The Army of the United States.*

try, and then turned about and headed for Fort Benton. On passing again the camp of General Terry's troops, the men were found cutting timber and making other preparations for the construction of a fort. Already they were beginning to undergo trials from incessant Indian attacks similar to those which had been suffered by Captain Rankin's men at Fort Buford the year before, but they were cheerfully making the best of a bad situation. The boat passed on, and continued up the river at a good speed until a point was reached about 125 miles above the mouth of the Yellowstone, where she was brought to a stop under most peculiar circumstances.

Along this section of the river the bluffs of the north bank recede several miles from the channel and the intervening space stretches away in a vast, flat meadow, covered in summer with luxuriant grasses. In the midst of the meadow and about a mile from the river stood a small, compact grove of large timber to which in the spring of the year herds of elk came from every direction to shed their horns. From this circumstance the steamboat men had named the whole bottom Elk Horn Prairie, and it was quite usual for descending boats to stop there in order that the passengers might visit the grove and gather sets of elk horns for their friends in the States. The meadow was also a favourite grazing place for the herds of buffalo which frequented this entire region. Though these animals were so numerous throughout Dakota and Montana that some of them were almost constantly visible from passing steamboats, either grazing on the open prairie or resting and wallowing near the river, it was in the country above the Yellowstone that they appeared in greatest numbers, for here they were accustomed to pass on their northern and southern migrations in the spring and autumn.

As the *Stockdale* approached Elk Horn Prairie, the buffalo increased rapidly in number on either bank. Vast herds, extending away to the horizon line of the northward bluffs, were moving slowly toward the river, grazing as they came. On arriving at the river's brink they hesitated and then, snorting and bellowing, plunged into the swift-running current and swam to the opposite shore. When the *Stockdale* reached a point nearly opposite the Elk Horn grove, excitement rose to a high pitch on board, for the buffalo became so thick in the river that the boat could not move, and the engines had to be stopped. In front the channel was blocked by their huge, shaggy bodies, and in their struggles they beat against the sides and stern, blowing and pawing. Many became entangled with the wheel, which for a time could not be revolved without breaking the buckets.

As they swept toward the precipitous bank of the north shore and plunged over into the stream, clouds of dust arose from the crumbling earth while the air trembled with their bellowing and the roar of their myriad hoofs. The south bank was turned to a liquid mass of mud by the water streaming from their sides as they scrambled out and thundered away across the prairie. To Captain Marsh and the others on the *Stockdale* it seemed almost as if they would overwhelm the boat. No one on board cared to shoot among them, for the sight of them was too awe-inspiring a demonstration of the physical might of untamed brute creation. Several hours elapsed before the *Stockdale* was able to break through the migrating herds and resume her journey, and they were still crossing when at last she passed beyond view. At Fort Benton General Terry and the other officers, with the exception of Colonel Holabird, left the boat and proceeded by the wagon-roads to the mining settlements in the interior, while the *Stockdale* immediately turned about and started on her return to Sioux City.

Chapter 14

A Game of Strategy

In due season the boat arrived at the point where she had been brought to by the cannon-shot on her previous down trip, and found the troops there making but slow progress on the buildings of the new post, which had been named Fort Stevenson. The soldiers were greatly hampered by the necessity of bringing their large building logs in wagons from the heavy timber, none of which was within several miles of the post, and the work was further impeded by the fact that a great proportion of the men had to act as escorts for the working parties.

The *Stockdale* stopped at Fort Stevenson for one day, and during the afternoon a fusillade of shots was suddenly heard out on the prairie where the live stock were grazing. The animals broke into wild commotion, scattering in every direction, and it was seen that a throng of mounted Indians was rushing down upon them from the bluffs. As Captain Marsh and his men sprang ashore from the boat they could see the mounted herders galloping about on the prairie in a desperate attempt to round the stampeding herd into the corral, at the same time returning the fire of their oncoming assailants as vigorously as their small number would permit. The soldiers about the buildings caught up their weapons and ran forward to the assistance of their hard-pressed comrades. Before their fearless advance the Indians broke and fled, but not until their crackling rifles had sent several of the infantrymen pitching headlong into the short prairie grass, while their dissolving line of ponies whirled up and swept away to the hills before them a number of the stampeded animals so sorely needed by the little garrison for the long winter months which were fast approaching.

It was now late in the autumn, and the buildings of Fort Stevenson were not nearly completed. For weeks after the *Ida Stockdale* had hurried down the river to escape the freeze-up, the soldiers of this isolated post were obliged to continue living in the tents which they had occupied since their first arrival. Winter had long since commenced, and the snow was deep upon the ground before the new quarters were at last made habitable. The troops moved in none too soon, for they had scarcely done so when a fierce blizzard, accompanied by high wind and bitter cold, swept down from the north, enveloping the post in its smothering blanket for four days. The scanty supply of fuel gave out, and as it was impossible to procure more until the storm abated, the officers had to break up their furniture and burn it to keep themselves and their men from freezing.[1] Such were some of the many hardships endured by the gallant and uncomplaining boys in blue who patiently paved the way for civilization over the length and breadth of the great West.

The *Stockdale* cast off her lines an hour or so after the skirmish, and resumed her journey. Captain Marsh was at the wheel and Colonel Holabird and Captain Calhoun were sitting on the pilot-house bench behind him when the boat swung into the head of a long, left-hand bend about twenty miles below the fort. On the right bank a high precipice, in more recent years named Plenty Coal Bluff, extended for a mile or more directly above the water. The left bank was low and timbered, and between them a large, wooded island cut the river into two narrow channels, while opposite the foot of the island the bluff swung back from the river, leaving a low, timbered shore at its base. The spot was a favourite crossing-place for the Indians, as the two narrow channels were easy to pass, either by swimming or in bull-boats.[2]

As the *Stockdale* unsuspectingly headed the bend she suddenly received a scattering volley of rifle shots from the timber bank on her left. Captain Marsh, looking down the river ahead, discovered Indians swimming horses across both channels to the south shore, and at once realized that the boat had encountered the recent assailants of Fort Stevenson making away with their plunder. The captain laid the boat over to the south bank and soon got beyond range of the enemy in the timber, but just what to do next he did not know. Therefore he signalled the engineer to stop the wheel, and held a council of war with Holabird and Calhoun. By this time a number of the Indians had

---

1. *The Army of the United States.*
2. Bowl-shaped boats of buffalo hide stretched over a willow frame and made watertight by smearing grease over the outside.

reached the south shore, and could be seen moving about there and making their way to the crest of the bluffs.

The channel invariably followed by boats was the one down past the bluff, but it would have been fool-hardiness to attempt it now with the enemy in a position to fire directly through the pilot-house roof, which was not protected like the sides by boiler-iron bulwarks. It seemed quite as dangerous, however, to attempt the left-hand channel, since this had never been run and might prove full of snags and sandbars and to be entirely unnavigable. If it did, the boat would be left helpless in the midst of the Indians, who lined both banks of this channel also and would quickly shoot down any one who exposed himself.

The situation was embarrassing, but after considerable deliberation, the captain and his advisers decided that the left channel offered the best chances for success. The *Stockdale's* head was accordingly turned toward it, and she moved cautiously forward into the unknown waters. From either bank as she entered the chute, the rifles of the Indians crackled out, their bullets crashing through her fragile woodwork. With throbbing heart but steady hand, Captain Marsh turned the wheel, his practised eyes scanning the water in front for the faintest riffle of hidden snag or shoaling bar. Behind him the cool-headed army officer and the steamer's owner stood with tense muscles, watching, helpless to aid, yet fearing each moment to feel the grinding jar which would spell destruction for them all. But their trust in their pilot was implicit, and they knew that if any man could carry the boat through to safety, he was the one who now stood at the wheel.

Down in the engine-room, the captain's brother, Monroe Marsh, was calmly handling his levers and answering the pilot's bells, while the bullets kicked splinters in his face from the stanchions along the sides and the firemen cowered in the shelter of the wood-piles. Once or twice the boat's flat bottom scraped on a bar; once or twice a jagged snag was just avoided, but at last the captain could see ahead the tapering, sandy foot of the island and the reunited waters of the river stretching away below. Slowly the *Stockdale* glided from her narrow prison, the fire of the baffled savages slackened and ceased, and the gallant little craft swept out in safety upon deeper waters, with nothing worse than a few score bullet holes through her framework by which to remember her dangerous adventure.

Colonel Holabird, whose friendship and respect for the captain were greatly enhanced by this experience, left the boat at Sioux City, after releasing her from her government charter, and she went on to St. Louis where she laid up for the winter, having been gone six months and ten days. Captain Marsh also remained in St. Louis with his family, while Captain Calhoun, pocketing his handsome profits, which had been considerably augmented by the *Stockdale's* tour of military duty, returned to his home in Pittsburg. Captain Marsh was as well satisfied as was the boat's owner with the results of his season's work. From his monthly salary of $1,200 he had paid two steersmen $125 per month each, leaving him $950 clear, which was considerably more than any other upper Missouri River pilot had ever received.

CHAPTER 15

Ice-Bound on the Nile

In the spring of 1868 the captain secured the steamer *Nile,* a St. Louis stern-wheeler of light draft, with which he made a quick trip to Fort Benton, arriving there on May 21st, the fourth boat in. The return trip was made soon thereafter, and he was back in St. Louis by midsummer, though not in time to undertake a second voyage to Benton. He therefore engaged in the lower-river trade, expecting to remain in it during the balance of the season. But late in the fall an unexpected event called him once more to the upper waters.

Early that year the Indian Commission appointed for the purpose had made the treaty with Red Cloud, chief of the Ogalalla Sioux, whereby the Montana Road was officially closed to immigration. The Fourth Article of this treaty provided for the establishment of a large agency on the Missouri River near the centre of the Indian lands, where a school should be built for the education of Indian children, warehouses erected for the housing of annuity goods, and Government officers appointed for the proper transaction of business with all Indians congregating there. Instead of a single large agency, the Government decided upon the establishment of three smaller ones; the first at the mouth of Whetstone Creek, twenty miles above Fort Randall, another opposite the mouth of the Little Cheyenne River, 270 miles further up, and the last just above the mouth of Grand River, eighty-six miles below Fort Rice.

The decision to place the agencies at the points named was not arrived at until late in the summer, and it then became necessary to send up the annuity goods destined for them in great haste if these were not to be stopped by the freezing of the river. As so often happened in later years when any task of unusual difficulty was to be performed, Captain Marsh was called upon to carry the goods to the most distant agency of the three, Grand River. The *Nile* was loaded and the start made with as little delay as possible, but in spite of all efforts she did not get away from St. Louis until October 15th. The captain was satisfied when he started that he could not deliver his cargo at its destination, but the quartermaster's department insisted on his making the effort. The government was urgently desirous of carrying out its treaty agreements in this, the first winter after they had been entered into, hoping by such an exhibition of good faith to pacify the hostile element among the Indians.

That the judgement of Captain Marsh was to be proved correct became evident almost from the moment of the *Nile's* start. As always at this season of the year, the river was very low and as the boat was riding deep in the water with her heavy cargo, her progress was proportionately slow. But notwithstanding the narrow channel and numberless shoals, she succeeded in getting 140 miles above Fort Randall without mishap. Here, however, at a point in the loop of the Great Bend of the Missouri called St. John's, or Cul-de-Sac, Island, it became impossible to go on without lightening the boat. A landing was therefore made and a considerable portion of the cargo discharged upon the island, where it was secreted in the timber and covered with tarpaulins. Thus relieved, the *Nile* pushed on 150 miles farther, to Cheyenne River Agency, where she was brought to a final standstill, as the weather had turned very cold and the ice was running heavily.

It was now obvious not only to Captain Marsh but to everyone else on board that Grand River Agency could not be reached that winter. So the remainder of the cargo was put ashore at the Cheyenne, and the *Nile* turned southward in a determined effort to escape before she should be frozen in. No boat had ever wintered on the upper Missouri and it was deemed impossible that one could do so, owing to the presence of hostile Indians who might destroy her as she lay in the ice. The *Nile laboured* down the river surrounded by ever-increasing floes, until, in a reach about four miles below the site of the present city of Chamberlain and three miles from the ruins of the old Missouri Fur Company's Fort Recovery she was forced to give up the struggle. With difficulty Captain Marsh pushed her through the closing ice until she lay against the eastern bank where she would be as far as possible removed from the hostiles who frequented the other shore, and here he and his crew prepared to make themselves as comfortable as circumstances would permit during the long winter months.

Unfortunately a large band of the Lower Brule Indians, among the most unruly of the Sioux, had gone into winter camp almost opposite the place where the boat was compelled to stop. The proximity of neighbours of such dubious temper was at best not calculated to add to the peace of mind of the boat's company, even though they were confident that they would be able to protect themselves in case of trouble. In reality there was little to be feared from the Indians, who were on good behaviour since they were depending almost entirely for their winter's sustenance upon the supplies issued to them at Fort Thompson, the Crow Creek Indian Agency, twenty-five miles above. Fort Thompson was the nearest habitation of white men to the little party on the *Nile*, and Captain Marsh and his crew came to be frequent visitors at the place, generally going for the purpose of buying provisions, but sometimes merely to relieve the monotony of their daily existence by a social call.

Major Joseph R. Hanson, chief agent for all the Sioux along the river, whose headquarters were at Fort Thompson, was a close personal friend of Captain Marsh, but he was absent that winter in Washington with a delegation of Sioux chiefs whom he had taken there on a visit to the Great Father, as the Indians called the president. However, in his absence his sub-agent at Crow Creek, Jud Lamoure, proved a most gracious host, welcoming all guests to the homely cheer of the agency with true western hospitality. Mr. Lamoure was in the habit of visiting the Brule camp, which lay near the steamboat, about once a week, to oversee the issue of rations, and on these occasions he would spend the night on the *Nile* with Captain Marsh, returning to Fort Thompson next day. They became good friends and at last on one of his visits Lamoure invited Captain Marsh and his brother, Monroe, to dine with him on a certain day at the agency, saying that he had been presented by some Indians with a saddle of excellent venison of which he wished them to partake. The larder of the *Nile* had been empty of fresh meat for some time, and the invitation was accepted with alacrity.

On the appointed day the captain and his brother appeared promptly for the feast, their appetites sharpened by their twenty-mile walk across the prairie and river. The table was bountifully spread with such good things as the storehouses could provide, the central feature being a steaming stew, whose savoury odour betokened to the hungry men venison of the finest quality. They seated themselves and partook liberally of the unwonted luxury, which they found no less palatable than it appeared. After the first keen edge of their hunger had been satisfied, however, they noticed that their host was eating only bacon, which was also on the table.

Upon being pressed to have some of the venison, he replied with an air of weariness that he had been served with it so often of late that he had grown tired of it. The two steamboat men therefore finished the dish themselves and departed feeling a sense of deep gratitude toward their thoughtful friend. Thirty-eight years afterwards, Captain Marsh read in a newspaper published in North Dakota, where Jud Lamoure still resides, (as at time of first publication), a full account by that jovial gentleman of the occasion on which he entertained his friends from the steamboat *Nile* at a *dog* feast, entirely without their knowledge. Upon completing the perusal of this chronicle, which was detailed with much relish, the captain vowed that when next he set foot upon the soil of North Dakota, he would seek out the perfidious Lamoure and challenge him to mortal combat. The threatened meeting, however, has not yet taken place.

Throughout the slow-passing months of that winter, the captain made a practice of visiting once every two weeks the *cache* of annuity goods which had been left by the *Nile* on Cul-de-Sac Island, to see that these remained safe and undisturbed. From the harbour of the *Nile* to Cul-de-Sac Island was forty-seven miles by river, though overland it was only about two-thirds of this distance.

As it was very dangerous to travel alone through the Sioux country, the captain was always accompanied either by one of the men from the boat or by some friendly agency Indian whom he would meet at Crow Creek on his way up. A muscular man, in the prime of life, he keenly enjoyed these trips over the gently rolling prairie hills and along the smooth stretches of river ice swept clean by the winter winds. He was fond of walking and had done so much of it that he had acquired an easy, swinging stride which carried him over the ground very rapidly without in the least fatiguing him. Indeed, so tireless was he that he exhausted most of his travelling companions long before they reached their destination, and his ability as a pedestrian soon began to form a topic for conversation around Crow Creek. At that time walking contests were greatly in vogue in the Eastern States, and this fact, coupled with the monotony of daily life at the agency, aroused general interest in his performances.

At length Jud Lamoure and the post traders, Major DeWitt and E. E. Hudson, put their heads together and decided to spring a surprise on the unsuspecting captain by finding a walking mate for him who would treat him as he had treated others. They canvassed the available material and settled upon an Agency Indian named Bad Moccasin, whom they induced to accompany the captain on his next trip to the island. Every one in that country, white as well as red, habitually wore *moccasins*, and the captain's competitor in this case proved to be aptly named. Either his *moccasins* or some other portions of his equipment were evidently bad, for they had not proceeded many miles when he was left far behind, astonished and panting.

Their first defeat only served to make the captain's friends at the agency more eager to find for him a rival who could beat him. Again they searched the field and unearthed a Teutonic employee at Fort Thompson known to history only as Dutch Jake. This candidate for athletic honours confidently asserted that he could out-walk any pedestrian in the West, and they decided to give him an opportunity of proving it. The path the captain always followed after leaving the agency led straight up the river bottom for a distance of eight miles along a beaten Indian *travois* track. It then crossed the river and went up the steep bluff at the narrow neck of the Great Bend, down on the other side and thence followed the middle of the frozen stream to the island.

Captain Marsh and his new comrade had no sooner left the fort, followed by the interested eyes of the assembled settlement, than the captain discovered that Jake was walking with the intention of beating him. For the first few miles the German put forth great efforts, and the captain found difficulty in keeping up. He said nothing, however, and continued his usual steady stride. As they turned to cross the river at the end of the first long stretch, Jake began to show signs of weariness. He kept on doggedly, nevertheless, until they reached the bottom of the steep bluff and began to climb. This was more than he could bear and he commenced to fall steadily behind, until, when the captain reached the island he could see Jake labouring along, a mere speck, two miles back on the shining ice.

This second discomfiture drove the conspirators to desperation. Determining upon a final, supreme effort, they sent to the hostile Brule camp for an Indian whose reputation as a pedestrian was known far and wide. Indeed, so pre-eminently was it his chief claim to distinction that it had even given him his name—Fast Walker. He was a slender, wiry fellow, whose 130 pounds of weight seemed composed entirely of springy muscles, and he kept himself in the best of condition constantly. Fast Walker was found to be quite willing to under-

FAST WALKER, BRULE SIOUX, (1909)
(The Indian walked from Crow Creek Agency to Miller, South Dakota, a distance of nearly fifty miles, to have this picture taken for "the book about his friend, Captain Marsh.")

take the trip, as he had been intending for some time to visit some of his relatives who were wintering near Fort Bennett, about 130 miles upriver, and the contest would furnish him with an interesting incentive at the beginning of the journey. He and the captain started from Crow Creek early one morning, and the Indian, who travelled at a trot, began to take the lead at once. Captain Marsh imagined that he would soon tire of the pace, but to his astonishment Fast Walker continued to gain until at the end of three hours, long before the captain had reached the island, the Indian had disappeared from view over the horizon and was seen no more. Jud Lamoure and his scheming partners had gained a victory sufficiently decisive to compensate for their two defeats.

Captain Marsh later learned that Fast Walker reached Chapelle Creek, sixty miles north of Fort Thompson, on the evening of the race. There he encamped for the night and the next night he was with his relatives at Fort Bennett, having made probably as remarkable time as any on record. The captain afterwards saw this Indian beat a thoroughbred horse from Fort Thompson to American Creek, a distance of twenty-four miles, the horse leading for the first ten miles, when his human competitor forged ahead and remained there to the end. Years later the captain wrote to his friend William F. Cody, *Buffalo Bill*, when he was touring the country with his Wild West Show, suggesting that Fast Walker be taken East to compete with some of the noted pedestrians there. Colonel Cody replied that the only difficulty would be that none of these men would make a match with him, knowing that they would have no chance of victory.

There was a pretty sequel to this race between a white man and a red, for soon after it Fast Walker came into the friendly camp where he remained, and afterwards, while Captain Marsh resided in Yankton, Dakota, as he did for a number of years, the Indian, who had become much attached to him, used often to come down with his two squaws, and camp for weeks at a time in the captain's dooryard.

With the coming of spring in 1869, the *Nile* was extricated from her uncomfortable position without damage from the breaking ice, and went on down to St. Louis, reaching there in time to participate in the annual exodus of boats for Fort Benton, Captain Marsh retaining command of her for the season.

CHAPTER 16

Wood Hawks

As has been intimated in the preceding pages, one of the chief difficulties of navigation on the upper river was the scarcity of fuel. The average boat burned about twenty-five cords of hard wood or thirty cords of cottonwood in twenty-four hours' steaming, and on the lower river, where the country was well populated, wood yards lay at frequent intervals along the banks ready to supply the demands of commerce. But above Fort Randall, where the settlements ceased, the case was different. Here the boats had to depend for their fuel chiefly upon the chance accumulations of driftwood, called *rack heaps*, piled up by the current on the sandbars in seasons of high water, or upon *deadenings* of standing timber which had been killed by fires. These sources of supply were frequently hard to reach from the river, and the collection of wood from them also often exposed the crew to the Indian attacks. Sometimes neither rack heaps nor deadenings were to be found, and then it became necessary to cut up green cottonwood trees, which were very unsatisfactory in the furnaces, burning with hardly enough vigour to keep upsteam.

In such a locality the sight of a long pile of dry cord-wood in some secluded timber bend was naturally a welcome one to the passing steamboat man, and here and there along the lonely stretches of the river nomadic wood-choppers braved the peril of the Indians for the sake of selling their wood at eight dollars per cord, which was its minimum value above Fort Randall. That their vocation was an extremely dangerous one is proved by the fact that during the summer of 1868 alone, seven wood-choppers were killed by Indians between Fort Benton and the settlements.[1] Even though profitable, it was not

---

1. Report of the Secretary of War, 1867-68.

a business to attract the timid, and the few men who engaged in it were among the most hardy and reckless that the frontier produced. In river parlance they were termed "wood hawks" a name which has been perpetuated in the great Wood Hawk Bend, about forty-five miles below Fort Rice.

Captain Marsh was acquainted with all of these adventurous fellows, and often bought from them considerable quantities of fuel. Two of the most extraordinary characters whom he ever encountered among them were a pair of partners named respectively *X* Beidler and *Liver-Eatin'* Johnson, of whom the captain relates several amusing anecdotes. They were both large and powerful men physically, ignorant in most of those matters which civilization holds as knowledge, but profoundly versed in all the strange and varied wisdom of the wilderness, which, however, they kept to themselves with the taciturnity characteristic of those whose ways lie in Nature's lonely places. Beidler had won an awe-inspiring record for courage during Montana's vigilante days when serving as a deputy under United States Marshal George M. Pinney,[2] while Johnson had earned his sanguinary title after a certain Indian raid upon the trading post at the mouth of Musselshell River. On this occasion the savages were driven off, losing several of their number in the encounter, and it was said that Johnson, in a spirit of devilish bravado, had eaten the livers of the dead warriors.

While the *Nile* was on her trip to Fort Benton in the spring of 1869, Beidler and Johnson were encountered near the mouth of the Musselshell. Their cord wood was purchased and they were, as usual, taken on board and entertained while the boat continued her journey. It so happened that on this particular day, May 11th, the crew had ice cream for dinner in honour of Captain Marsh's birthday, the ice, which was a rare luxury on the upper river, having been obtained at Fort Peck.[3] Neither of the *wood hawks* had ever seen or heard of

---

2. Contributions to the Historical Society of Montana.
3. The ice houses established at Fort Peck by the shrewd founders of that trading post had played an important part in its prosperity. The fort was built in 1865 by a party of men who had undertaken the trip to Fort Benton with a load of merchandise on the steamer *Tacony,* but were compelled by low water to abandon their enterprise a few miles above Milk River. Undismayed by this misfortune, they landed their goods at the point where the boat stopped, put up some log buildings, and began trading with the Indians. During the winter they packed ice, and the next summer dispensed free ice water to all the Indians who came into the post. The beverage met with great favour among the aborigines, and from every direction they flocked in such numbers to Fort Peck to do their bartering that the enterprising traders there were hardly able to handle the business.—J. M. H.

ice cream before, and its surprising frigidity in the heat of a summer afternoon caused them to regard it with suspicion, though Beidler was averse to admitting his ignorance. Johnson was less reticent, and straightway asked in a startled whisper of his partner:

"X, where in —— does this stuff come from?"

"Shut up, you fool," growled Beidler, bravely swallowing a spoonful of the cream. "It comes in cans."

Among the passengers of the *Nile* on this trip was a party of Eastern tourists containing several ladies who were spending the summer viewing some of the strange sections of their own country. The ladies had been interested in all the novel scenes of the frontier which the voyage had presented to them, but when the two rugged *wood hawks* appeared on board they became particularly enthusiastic. Their curiosity soon led them into conversation with Beidler and Johnson, neither of whom took very kindly to being patronized as if they were a pair of Sioux, though they maintained their stoical composure. At length one of the ladies inquired of *X*:

"Mr. Beidler, are you married?"

"Yes," grunted the *wood hawk*.

"Oh, indeed? Do you know, I hardly thought that. Is—is your wife, ah—a white woman?"

"Indian."

"How delightful! A native of these great plains. Where is she now?"

"I've sent her to Rome."

"To Rome? To be educated? Just think of such devotion!" she chirruped to her companions. "Mr. Beidler, do you mean to Rome, Italy?"

"No," responded *X* grimly. "To roam on the prairie."

At this point the conversation abruptly terminated.

In addition to the sources of fuel supply already mentioned, another developed in somewhat later years, though it was of small moment in the course of a long voyage. The Agency Indians, as they gradually began to absorb the idea of doing a little manual labour, found out that there was money to be made by cutting wood for the boats, and at a few widely separated points they commenced doing so occasionally. This was especially the case at Crow Creek, where the ravines above the Agency were full of red cedar and cottonwood timber. The cedar would burn readily even when full of sap, and the steamboat men promptly took all of it that the Indians could pile on the river bank. But when they saw only green cottonwood corded up, they would pass it by. The dusky woodsmen soon learned that cedar was what the boats wanted, and when they had only cottonwood to offer they undertook a simple deception to aid in disposing of it. Stacking the timber with the freshly-hewn ends toward the landing they would smear these ends with vermilion face-paint to make it resemble cedar, trusting that when a boat had actually stopped at the bank, she would take it away, rather than waste more time.

Another trick devised by these wily savages in the interest of trade owed its origin to the changeable nature of the Missouri's channel, which would sometimes shift across the river from the base of the bluffs where their woodpiles lay, leaving these inaccessible to boats. Not comprehending that the boatmen could have any means of knowing exactly where the channel lay, the Indians when they saw a steamer approaching would wade out through the shallow water in front of their wood-piles and there sit down. Leaving only their heads above the surface they would beckon to the pilot to come in, thinking that he would suppose them to be standing to their necks in water deep enough to carry his boat. Captain Marsh, soon becoming familiar with these subterfuges of the red men, always kept his wits on the alert when approaching Crow Creek.

CHAPTER 17

The Vegetable Trip of the "North Alabama"

The *Nile* reached Fort Benton without incident on her spring trip of 1869 and soon left there to return to St. Louis. At Fort Stevenson, whose beginnings Captain Marsh had witnessed two summers before, the boat stopped for a short time, and while lying there the captain saw an incident which impressed him deeply with the hard justice sometimes meted out for seemingly slight offences in the regular army, the only justice known at that period in a country whose sole organized communities were the military posts. Fort Stevenson, which at this time was garrisoned by two companies of the 22nd Infantry under Major Charles Dickey, stood on a bend of the river and nearly opposite a wide bottom meadow. When the *Nile* arrived, there was a party of soldiers camped on this meadow, cutting and stacking the season's supply of hay, which, when winter came, could be hauled over to the fort on the ice as it was needed. The haying party consisted of six men under a corporal, Wilson by name, who had with them six mules, a mowing machine, hay rake and wagon.

Shortly before noon on this particular day, while the hay-makers were busy with their peaceful occupation, a solitary mounted Indian rode out on a knoll at the edge of the meadow and stopping, watched them. Then he beckoned as if summoning a party of companions behind him. Corporal Wilson, mindful of the attacks often made on small parties of soldiers, hastily abandoned the mules and implements and ordered his men under the river bank. From across the river the entire garrison witnessed the movement, but could do nothing, as steam was not up on the *Nile*. The corporal's manoeuvre was an unfortunate one, for had there been any number of Indians they could have ridden over and shot the soldiers as the latter clung helplessly under the bank. The warrior, however, proved to be alone, but seeing the soldiers disappear he galloped out to the deserted mules, cut them loose from the machines, and drove them off.

As soon as the haying party could be brought across to the fort, Corporal Wilson was placed under arrest and shortly after was tried by court-martial on the charge of cowardice. He was found guilty and sentenced to ten years' imprisonment in the military penitentiary at Detroit, Michigan, and the court further ordered that while on his journey from Fort Stevenson to Detroit he should be compelled to wear a large placard on his back inscribed with the word "Coward." When the sentence was pronounced upon him, Corporal Wilson was so overcome that he piteously begged his judges to impose the death penalty rather than subject him to such degradation, but there was no appeal from their decision. Captain Marsh, who had witnessed the entire affair on the hay field, felt that the corporal's action had been merely an error of judgement not inspired by cowardice, and the punishment accorded seemed to him out of all proportion to the offence.

Upon the arrival of the *Nile* at St. Louis, the captain disposed of his interest in the boat and prepared to engage in the lower river trade. But before he could do so, his plans were changed by a call which took him in another direction. That spring a steamer named the *Tempest*, owned by Messrs. Sims, Silvers & Shields, of St. Louis, and commanded by Captain James L. Bissell, had started for Fort Benton with the mountain fleet. When she reached Cow Island, a place 130 miles below Benton, which by reason of its shallow channel bore an evil fame among pilots, the *Tempest* found herself not only unable to proceed further but equally unable to go back. Having tried in vain to extricate his boat, Captain Bissell at last sent a messenger to Helena, whence was telegraphed an appeal for help to the owners in St. Louis. Believing that Captain Marsh could save the *Tempest* if anyone could, they engaged him to undertake the task, at $400 per month. He at once set out for Salt Lake City over the newly completed Union Pacific Railroad, and there took a stage for Helena and Fort Benton. At the latter place he secured a Mackinaw boat and went down with the current to Cow Island.

Having arrived at last on board the *Tempest*, he found her in a deplorable condition. She was still confined in her watery prison, but that fact was not the worst in the situation. The captain found that the presence of a superabundance of whiskey on board had really been the cause of all the boat's mishaps. Her troubles had begun, even before Cow Island was reached, with a fight at the dinner table in which Engineer Evans killed a passenger. All the persons involved were drunk at the time, and the tragedy split the boat's company into such bitter factions that the steamer could not even be properly navigated.

When Captain Marsh arrived he found the bar running full blast, though the barkeeper was making dire threats against the besotted crew, who owed him $600. The captain instantly closed the bar, refused to let anyone have another drop of liquor, and sternly advised the barkeeper that if he ever hoped to get his money, he would do well to see that the order was observed and himself turn to and help save the boat. To his credit be it said, the barkeeper accepted his reprimand with good grace, and thereafter the captain had no more efficient assistant than he. The shutting off of their whiskey supply produced the desired effect upon the crew. Once more they became responsible men, and it was not long before the captain succeeded in working the *Tempest* out of the shoals and heading her safely down toward St. Louis.

On her way the *Tempest* touched at Sioux City, which had just become the terminus of a railroad line from the East. Here Captain Marsh was met by Captain Job Lawrence, manager of the Northwestern Transportation Company, who informed him that he might soon be needed to take a boat load of winter supplies to the upper river forts. The trip was not entirely arranged for yet, but when the *Tempest* reached St. Louis, Captain Lawrence was there waiting for her, having come down by rail. He at once engaged Captain Marsh to make the trip previously mentioned, and they set out for Sioux City without delay, for it was already very late in the season.

The captain found the boat which was to make the run loaded and waiting for him at Sioux City. She was the *North Alabama,* a well-built craft of good speed which had twice made the Fort Benton trip successfully. The morning of the 1st of October saw the *North Alabama* back away from the Sioux City levee and start on her voyage, the successful termination of which was very doubtful. To add to the captain's anxiety, her cargo was a perishable one, consisting chiefly of staple vegetables for the winter supply of the military garrisons, and a sudden cold snap, so liable to come at that season, might ruin it all. But, fortunately, for a number of days the weather continued warm.

The boat had on board a few passengers, among them Major Bannister, the department paymaster, and his clerk, Mr. Baker, who were taking up money to pay off all the troops at the posts to be visited. Two other interesting persons who occupied cabins were Mrs. Charles E. Galpin and her daughter, Miss Lou Galpin, the former being the full-blood Sioux wife of Major Galpin, the famous fur-trader who had been factor at Fort Pierre when it was bought for the government by General Harney. Mrs. Galpin was a woman of unusual mental capacity, who was well known throughout the Dakota country,[1] and her daughter had been well educated at St. Louis. They were just returning to Grand River Agency from Chicago, where they had been procuring a wedding *trousseau* for Miss Galpin, who was soon to be married to Captain Harmon, of the 17th Infantry.

The weather holding fine, Forts Randall, Hale, Sully, Rice and Stevenson were successively reached, the cargoes consigned to them discharged, and their troops paid off by Major Bannister; and Captain Marsh began to entertain hopes that he would make the whole trip without mishap, as only one more post remained to be visited, Fort Buford. But on October 17th, when the boat left Fort Stevenson, the air began to grow chill. Through the following night and day the temperature fell steadily and slush ice began forming in rapidly increasing quantities. The potatoes, turnips, onions, cabbage and apples destined for Fort Buford lay on the main deck where they were in imminent danger of freezing.

Captain Marsh therefore had them all transferred to the hold and small fires kindled there to keep the air warm. It was a dangerous experiment to try on a frail wooden steamboat, but guards were stationed in the hold to watch the fires, and no disaster resulted. Against the increasing drift ice the *North Alabama* struggled ahead, her progress becoming slower and slower, until she rounded the point at the foot of Plum Pudding Butte and came into the wide valley where Big Muddy Bend sweeps between its timbered banks. Here on the morning of October 22nd, at the mouth of Little Muddy Creek, about one mile below the site of the present town of Williston, the ice closed solid, leaving her frozen against the bank.

It seemed as if, in spite of all efforts, the garrison of Fort Buford was to be cheated of its vegetables and left to subsist on rations of salt meat, hard-tack and canned goods. The disgusting monotony of such a diet through eight long winter and spring months can easily be appreciated, and Captain Marsh, realizing it fully, did not propose

---

1. See Charles Larpenteur's *Forty Years a Fur Trader on the Upper Missouri*, edited by Dr. Eliot Coues; and *South Dakota Historical Collections*, Vol. 1.

Company "G" Sixth United States Infantry, at Fort Buford in the early '70's

that the soldiers should be subjected to such privation if he could help it. On the boat were two Arikaree Indian scouts, who had come aboard at Fort Berthold, where their tribe was located. The captain dispatched them overland with a message for the commanding officer, advising him of the steamer's predicament and asking him to come down and save the vegetables.

The appeal met with a prompt response. Though the fort was twenty-five miles distant in a direct line, the next day the men on the boat saw a train of covered wagons, escorted by a mounted detachment, come into view on the crest of the barren bluffs to northward and wind its way down across the valley toward them. When they arrived the soldiers were overjoyed to find their winter supplies still safe, and they set to work eagerly transferring them to the wagons, each one of which was equipped with a small camp stove. With their precious cargo they set out immediately for the fort, and reached there without losing anything, Major Bannister accompanying them to pay off the garrison.

Captain Marsh fully believed that winter had come to stay, and he began preparing his boat for a sojourn such as had been experienced by the *Nile*. But in a short time the temperature began to moderate, and on the tenth day after the freeze-up, to everyone's surprise and delight, the ice broke and began running out. The captain thereupon sent one of the Indian scouts post-haste to the fort with word to Major Bannister that the boat was going to leave, and that officer, only too glad to escape a winter in the comfortless quarters of Buford, hurried back to the steamer. As soon as he arrived, the *North Alabama* cast off and Started down with all speed, lest the ice again catch her. But no such misfortune befell, and she reached Sioux City on November 15th.

For the success of this trip Captain Marsh declares he received more commendation from the military authorities than for any other work he ever performed, before or since, and the officers and soldiers at Fort Buford ever after held for him a warm friendship. It was an apt confirmation of the old adage that the royal road to a man's heart is through his stomach.

CHAPTER 18

The Hare and the Tortoise

During the three years following the trip of the *North Alabama* the captain's life was uneventful, so far as adventure was concerned. The early summer of 1870 he spent on the steamer *Kate Kearney,* engaged in commerce between St. Louis and lower-river points. But the trade between St. Louis and the Northwest, which had so long flourished, was now waning, owing to the arrival of the railroad at Sioux City. That point was beginning to reap the reward of enterprise and becoming the distributing centre for Dakota and Eastern Montana, while the merchants of Chicago, who shipped to Sioux City, were wresting from their rivals in St. Louis a market which was rapidly increasing in value and which in later years the metropolis of the Mississippi Valley was to miss sorely. Later in the season of 1870, the captain assumed command of the *Ida Reese No.* 2, owned by Durfee & Peck, Indian traders, and began transporting goods for them between Sioux City and the agencies as far up as Fort Buford.

The following winter, in partnership with Durfee & Peck, he built the steamer *Nellie Peck,* at Brownsville, Pa., going there himself to superintend her construction. She was an excellent boat, costing $28,000 to build, and especially designed for the upper-river trade. The captain took her up from Brownsville in the spring and continued to command her during the seasons of 1871 and 1872. She did a good business through the summer of 1871, though nothing of interest happened to her. Late in the year, however, an incident occurred which Captain Marsh's professional friends still chuckle over, and it is worth relating because it well illustrates the dry sort of humour beloved by those old-time steamboat men.

The season's work was over, and like the southward hurrying ducks and geese which were paralleling her course in the upper air, the *Nel-*

lie Peck had turned her head downstream, bound for winter harbour at Sioux City. Late one November afternoon she had just cleared the foot of the Big Bend, above Crow Creek, when she encountered a Durfee & Peck boat called the *Silver Lake,* Captain Andy Johnson, coming up. Captain Johnson hailed and stated that the *Silver Lake* was loaded with a cargo for Messrs. Leighton & Jordan, post traders, at Fort Buford, whose freight was carried by the Durfee & Peck steamers.

Captain Johnson had been instructed by Leighton & Jordan to exchange boats with Captain Marsh when they should meet, he taking the *Nellie Peck* down to Sioux City while Captain Marsh should bring the *Silver Lake* on to Buford. Captain Marsh did not greatly relish this development, for he was anxious to get back to his family. But he knew that the post traders were relying upon him to save their boat and cargo from the freeze-up. He would not violate their confidence, so reluctantly exchanged steamers and started back.

The transfer was made not long before dusk and the *Silver Lake* had not proceeded far when night came on and the captain tied her up to the bank just below the foot of the Big Bend to wait for daylight. He had scarcely done so when to his surprise, the *Far West,* a speedy packet belonging to parties in Yankton, hove in sight upward bound, and made fast to the bank near him. The commander of the *Far West* at this time was one who is well known to all old steamboat men by the nickname of *Rodney.* He was an excellent captain and pilot, having only one failing, self-sufficiency. Above all things he disliked to admit that anyone could be better informed than himself in a given situation, and his aversion to asking advice sometimes led him into difficulties. It was now late in the year and the river very low, rendering it unusually liable to sudden changes of channel.

Rodney had not been over it for a month and he knew that Marsh had, for he had passed the *Nellie Peck* going down and learned, of course, that Marsh had just transferred from her to the *Silver Lake.* But his peculiar pride forbade him to call upon Captain Marsh during the evening, as other pilots would have done, to learn the latest news of the channel above, and he was further deterred by the presence on board his boat of several army officers going up to the forts, whom he was anxious to impress with his skill and intimate knowledge of the river. Appreciating the situation, Captain Marsh did not disturb him, and the next morning shortly after daybreak, the *Far West* shoved off and started for the bend above.

When Rodney had last come down, the channel lay as it usually does in such places, "shaping out the bend," that is, following the outer shore. But it so happened that as the river had fallen at this point, the channel had shifted, and when he was bringing the *Nellie Peck* down the day before, Captain Marsh had found it in under the point, the width of the river from its normal position. Not knowing this, Rodney now followed the channel as he knew it. As the *Far West* steamed up, the crew of the *Silver Lake* could see, through the light river mist, the army officers in their long cape overcoats gathered in a group on the forward end of the boiler deck, admiringly watching the movements of their pilot. Rodney had ordered out leadsmen with sounding poles to the bow, and while the *Far West* went rapidly up along the left bank, those on the *Silver Lake* heard the voice of the word-passer vibrating in the deathly stillness of dawn: "No-o *bottom!* No-o *bottom!*"

When he heard that cry, Captain Marsh laughed. Knowing that even at the foot of the bend there could not be more than thirty or forty inches of water, he realized at once that Rodney must have privately instructed his leadsmen for the occasion. The captain of the *Far West* himself must have known that the water would certainly be perilously low there in such a stage of the river, but he evidently expected to squeeze through and wished to add to his prestige by affecting to know so excellent a channel in so unpromising a locality. But his triumph was short-lived. He had not half rounded the bend when his vessel shivered and stopped short. Even while her leadsmen were still crying their deceptive refrain she had come head on against a bar and lay immovable.

While this was going on, Captain Marsh had cast off lines and started up also. The *Silver Lake* was emphatically not one of the river greyhounds. In fact, she might more accurately have been classed with those boats of which it was said that they "could run in the shade of a big tree all day and tie up to the foot of it at night." In a contest of speed with the *Far West,* which was one of the fastest boats on the river, she would be, to use another river definition, "like a cow racing with an antelope; the first jump would be the closest." But the *Silver Lake,* at any rate, had a pilot in her wheel-house who knew where he was going. She steamed up slowly and when she reached the point, turned in under the bluff where the channel lay. Here the captain ordered out leadsmen and, imitating Rodney, said to them:

"Boys, you'll only find about thirty inches, but whatever you find, holler, 'No bottom!'"

Then he stationed his *cub pilot,* Joe Todd, on the forward guards to pass the word, and went ahead. Todd had a voice like an angry bull, and as they steamed along the base of the bluffs in full view of the helpless *Far West,* his bellow could be heard for two miles through the pulse-less air:

"No-o-o *bottom!* No-o-o *bottom!*"

Rodney, in the other pilot-house, watched them for a time in silence, as if expecting to see them ground at any moment. But as they went on and on he began to pace back and forth nervously. At last he saw that they were really going to get through, and as he caught the derisive glances of the army officers on his own deck, he could contain himself no longer. Tearing his hat from his head he dashed it to the floor, then ran to the window and, shaking his fist at the *Silver Lake,* shouted furiously:

"You're a liar, you son of a gun! There *is* bottom!"

Amid boisterous laughter from the crews of both boats, the *Silver Lake* cleared the passage and went on her way, leaving the *Far West* to spend most of the day in sparring off.

Captain Marsh completed his trip to Fort Buford successfully, receiving as an extra token of gratitude for the safe delivery of the goods, an order from Mr. Leighton for a one hundred dollar suit of clothes, which seems to indicate that the business of post sutler was not without profit in those days. On the down trip the *Silver Lake* was fired into by Indians near the mouth of Heart River, forty miles above Fort Rice, and Pilot Joe Todd was painfully wounded, carrying the bullet the rest of his life. When the boat had almost reached Fort Thompson, the freeze-up caught her, but she was piloted into a position in which she would be safe from injury by ice when the spring break-up came, and there Captain Marsh left her, going down by wagon to Yankton. The *Far West,* which had also made a long run, escaped from the ice, but Rodney never heard the last of his discomfiture in the Big Bend of the Missouri.

CHAPTER 19

A Three Thousand Mile Race

After the close of navigation in 1871, several of the interests on the upper river combined in forming a large company, the object of which was to secure complete control of the steamboat business there. The new concern was known as the Coulson Packet Company, famous in Missouri River history, and the gentlemen composing it were Commodore Sanford B. Coulson and his brothers, Captains Martin and John Coulson, Captain James C. McVay, Captain John Todd, Captain Grant P. Marsh, and Messrs. Durfee & Peck. The boats originally owned by this powerful syndicate were the *Nellie Peck, Far West, Western, Key West, E. H. Durfee, Sioux City* and *Mary McDonald.*

With the coming of spring, 1872, there opened the most prosperous season in the history of the upper river. This was largely the result of the completion of the Northern Pacific Railroad from Fargo to Bismarck, in northern Dakota territory. As usual, a flood of settlers followed the railroad, spreading out along the eastern side of the river, and the needs of all these people greatly increased the demands for steamboat transportation. Bismarck itself, which was at first called Edwinton, was established in May. It was built on the river bank, but the following year was moved to the top of the bluff and its name changed to the one it still bears. When Captain Marsh visited it a few weeks after its first shack had been erected, it was as rough and generally disreputable a community as the Northwest ever boasted, and as such it continued to maintain its reputation for several years.

As witnessing the character of the place, an anecdote is related by a gentleman who saw it during its days of youthful exuberance. This gentleman visited a friend who was editor of a struggling but ambitious newspaper, and who possessed, besides his hand-press and case of type, a hopeful son some eight years of age. The small boy was thoroughly conversant with the class of local news which generally filled the columns of his father's paper. One day, while giving the visitor one of those searching cross-examinations to which small boys are addicted, he asked:

"You got a papa?"

"No," replied the gentleman, somewhat sadly.

"Why not?"

"Because he is dead."

"Oh!" said the questioner. He meditated this decisive fact for a moment, then inquired:

"He got shot, did he?"

"No, he didn't get shot."

"Then he drank too much whiskey?"

"No, indeed!"

"Well, then, he can't be dead," exclaimed the boy triumphantly, "'cause them's the only ways men get dead in Bismarck!"

But for all its lack of refinement, Bismarck was a lively trade centre for the steamboats, though it did not at once become the foot of navigation, the bulk of the trade continuing for some years to be through to Fort Benton from Sioux City, and, a little later, from Yankton.

Though it was a matter of indifference to the owners of the Packet Company which one of their boats might be capable of developing the greatest speed, a considerable feeling of rivalry existed between the masters of the steamers themselves. It was customary for the boats to receive their cargoes for a trip in the order of their arrival, the first one in at the Sioux City or Fort Benton levee thus being the first one out on the return trip, and it was natural that when opportunity offered, each captain should strive to secure this preference for his boat.

Moreover, the people living along the river, all more or less isolated and eager for any sort of diversion, took lively interest in the performances of the steamers and often laid wagers on their favourites and urged the masters and crews by all means of encouragement to break the records of the others. So ardent did they become in their partisanship that sometimes even bribery was resorted to if it would produce the desired results. With so many incentives to actuate them it was not surprising that the steamboat men soon began to indulge in racing, even though the practice was a dangerous one on those waters, particularly when the river was low.

It did not take long for the boats to prove themselves. The *Nellie Peck* and the *Far West* developed great superiority over the others in point of speed, and the question which of them was entitled to be regarded as the sovereign of the river came to be an absorbing one. Both boats made early trips to Fort Benton in the spring, the *Nellie Peck* arriving there on May 18th, the first boat in, and the *Far West* on May 24th, the second arrival.[1] They happened to return to Sioux City in such time that one could load immediately after the other. Captain Marsh was loading his vessel when the *Far West* appeared, her gallant captain, Mart Coulson, taking in the possibilities of the situation at a glance. The *Nellie Peck* had no sooner cast off her lines than the *Far West* took her place at the levee, rushed her cargo on board, and swung out after her rival, which had got the start. The season was the middle of June and the Big Muddy was booming bank-full through the bottom lands.

It was an ideal stage for steamboating and everything was propitious for a race to a finish. The *Nellie Peck* had the larger cargo, and both boats transacted much business at the various way landings, but Captain Marsh kept his lead for 1,370 miles. Then, at Dauphin's Rapids, only 103 miles below Fort Benton, the *Far West* overhauled and triumphantly passed him, beating him to the Benton levee by several hours on June 30th. The local admirers of the *Nellie Peck* were much cast down by this result, while the delight of the opposite party was increased by the fact that the Far West had broken all previous records for the run between Sioux City and Benton, making it in 17 days and 20 hours.[2]

But Captain Marsh was not discouraged, even though his friend Mart Coulson was now gaining the advantage of the first cargo and the start, which he had enjoyed at Sioux City. He loaded his boat as quickly as possible and started after his rival, already some hours ahead, determined to overtake her even if he collapsed a flue in doing it. There was little business to detain either of the steamers on the downward run, and officers and crews gave themselves up to the excitement of the race. Mart Coulson well knew that the *Nellie Peck* was pursuing him, and his men were using every effort to keep their lead. Neither boat stopped for storm or for night, and neither went to the bank save when compelled by the necessity of replenishing the wood piles. The *Far West* was in charge of two skilful and fearless pilots, Dan Comfort and W. H. Sims, while on the *Nellie Peck* Captain Marsh himself was standing a watch at the wheel, his partner being John LaBarge.[3] They

---

1. *Contributions to the Historical Society of Montana,* Vol. 1.
2. *Idem.*
3. Brother of Joseph LaBarge, the famous steamboat captain of the fur-trading days, whose biography has been written and published by Col. H. M. Chittenden, U. S. A.

were none of them men to hesitate for obstacles when a race was on.

A few miles west of Fort Berthold the people on the *Peck* caught sight of a feather of smoke floating off across the naked hills, for which they had long been anxiously straining their eyes, and enthusiasm rose high. It was the trail of the *Far West*. Nearer and larger it grew until, in front of the log-built stockade and clustered buildings-of the little post, the *Nellie Peck* swept past her labouring adversary, while from the crowded shore the soldiers cheered wildly and a throng of Indians gazed in wonder at the racers. With a clear river ahead, Captain Marsh did not relax his efforts. He disliked to trust the boat to another hand than his own, but at times he was forced to seek a little rest.

At length one night a short distance above the point where the Bijou Hills lie piled along the left bank, knowing that there was an easy stretch of water ahead and that everything was going smoothly on board, he surrendered the wheel to his partner at about midnight, and retired to bed. But he had scarcely fallen asleep when the watchman rushed into his cabin, crying that the boat had gone hard aground. Hurrying out, the captain found her jammed up on the bar at the head of the Bijou Hills Reach, two miles out of her proper course. He was greatly incensed, while his cub pilot, a young man named John Belt, became so furious at LaBarge that he was about to punish that offender in true Western style, when Captain Marsh took his revolver away from him and threw it in the river.

Vigorous efforts were at once begun to get the boat off, but before they were successful the *Far West* came past and continued down the river. The *Nellie Peck* was so long in regaining deep water that she could not recover her lead, and the *Far West* beat her into Sioux City by three hours, thus securing for herself the coveted supremacy of the river. She continued to hold it to the end, for a few years later Captain Marsh himself, in the most dramatic steamboat trip of the Missouri River's thrilling history, made with her a speed record which never has been and probably never will be, equalled.

In the race to Sioux City, however, Captain Marsh's partner pilot seemed to receive as many congratulations from the friends of the victor for the error in navigation which had cost the *Nellie Peck* the race, as did the crew of the *Far West* themselves. One firm, at least, in Sioux City, which had money wagered on the race, presented him with a memento of the occasion in the form of an expensive suit of clothing. But neither boat had given the owners any cause for complaint, for each cleared about $12,000 on the voyage, and each beat by several days all previous records for the round trip between Sioux City and Fort Benton.

John LaBarge a few years later met his death in a very dramatic manner, expiring literally "at the wheel." A gentleman[4] familiar with the circumstances has thus described them:

> The steamer *Benton,* Captain John C. Barr, master, backed out of the Bismarck landing on a trip up river. Captain LaBarge was at the wheel and Barr was on the roof. LaBarge stopped his engines, got her straightened up and rang his go-ahead bell. Barr on the roof noticed that she swung in and was heading for the bank and in line with the *Helena* and some other boats lying at the warehouse. He looked around and there was no one at the wheel; he called, but no answer. He then ran for the pilot-house and could not open the door, as LaBarge was lying on the floor and blocked the way. He shoved the sash, climbed in through the window, and stopped the boat just in time to save her from ramming the *Helena.* Barr dropped her back and landed, and it was found that Captain LaBarge was dead, and the verdict was heart failure.

---

4. Mr. E. P. Higbee, of the U. S. Surveyor-General's office at Bismarck, N. Dak., in a letter to Captain Marsh.

CHAPTER 20

The Railroad Comes

Along the Missouri and its tributaries through the years from 1869 to 1872, the Indians maintained a less violently hostile attitude toward the whites than they had at any time since the Minnesota outbreak. The chief reason for their good behaviour was that during those years but few encroachments were made upon the territories still remaining to them, and so little cause for friction arose. But the steadfast aim of the Government was to induce all the tribes to give up the chase as a means of livelihood and settle down to agriculture at the several agencies established for them. The efforts made in this direction were only partially successful, for of the 14,000 Indians estimated to be embraced in the Sioux Nation in 1869, over 7,000 refused to remain at the agencies and continued to roam about the Powder River and Big Horn regions of Montana and Wyoming, maintaining themselves comfortably by hunting in those great grazing grounds of the buffalo.[1] So long as they were unmolested in their chosen retreat, no trouble occurred, but it was inevitable that sooner or later they must be molested by the onward-moving forces of civilization.

As has been stated, the summer of 1872 saw the Northern Pacific Railroad completed as far as the eastern bank of the Missouri, and the country up to that natural boundary line occupied by a swarm of settlers. The ultimate destination of the railroad was the shore of the Pacific Ocean, and its next logical step in that direction would be across the Missouri and thence westward through Montana to the now well-developed mining sections at the base of the Rockies, where the inhabitants were impatiently awaiting its arrival. In making that step, the most feasible route for the line would be up the valley of the

---

1. Gen. D. S. Stanley, in *Report of Commissioner of Indian Affairs*, 1869.

Yellowstone River, through the very heart of the territory occupied by the hostile Sioux. That they would bitterly oppose any movement made toward beginning the work was a foregone conclusion.

The Indians were not without justification in fiercely resenting the idea of an invasion of this, the last province of their ancestral domain. The treaty drawn up at Fort Laramie in 1868 had distinctly acknowledged their right of possession to all the country "north of the North Platte River and east of the summits of the Big Horn Mountains," and though it did not specify what the northern boundary of the territory was to be, the Indians, and doubtless also the commissioners, who formulated the treaty, understood that it was to be the Yellowstone River. Nevertheless, regardless of their protests, the Government not only permitted the projection of the Northern Pacific up the valley of the Yellowstone, but in the terms of its charter to the railroad pledged itself to afford the enterprise every assistance of its military power.

In fulfilment of its promise, an escort of troops was furnished to a Northern Pacific surveying party which, in 1871, projected the line eastward from Bozeman to a point on the Yellowstone near the mouth of Pryor's Fork. In August of the following year, a detachment of 400 men commanded by Major E. M. Baker, 2nd Cavalry, set out with a second survey under Colonel Hayden to carry the line on from Pryor's Fork to the mouth of Powder River. It had been previously arranged that here they should be met by another party moving westward from Bismarck. But Baker and Hayden never reached the Powder. On the night of August 14th, while lying in camp opposite Pryor's Fork Bottom, they were fiercely attacked by nearly 1,000 Sioux and Cheyenne warriors under Black Moon.[2]

After a desperate fight the assailants were repulsed with loss, but the confidence of the surveyors had been so shaken that they proceeded only a short distance farther and then insisted upon abandoning the expedition.[3] Although the column from the East reached the appointed meeting place, not much was accomplished, and the close of 1872 found the preliminary line of survey still broken by a gap several hundred miles broad.

In the meanwhile, the Indians along the Missouri itself were becoming restless also. When the railroad reached Bismarck, a military post was established on the west side of the river a short distance

---

2. *History of the Sioux Indians* by Doane Robinson.
3. Lieutenant James H. Bradley's Journal, in *Contributions to the Historical Society of Montana*, Vol. 2.

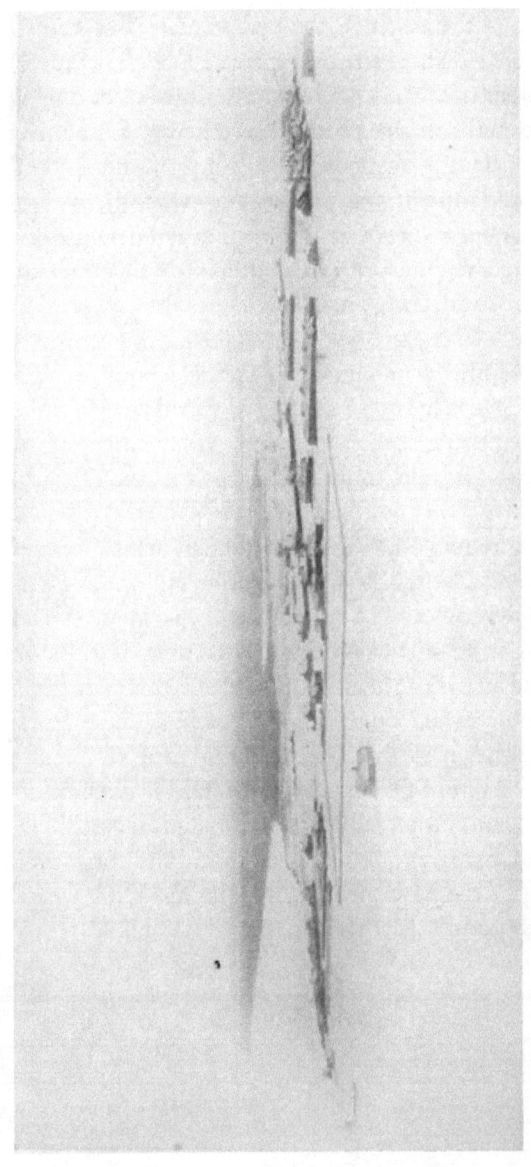

FORT ABRAHAM LINCOLN

(This photograph is of the old fort, from which the 7th Cavalry marched away on the Little Big Gorn campaign. The view is from the north, looking down the Missouri River. Assiniboine Island appears in the left distance. In 1902, all of the buildins shown in the photograph, except two, had been torn down. The post has been rebuilt on the opposite side of the river, just below Bismarck.)

below that town which was at first called Fort McKean, though the name was soon changed to Fort Abraham Lincoln. The Sioux, as usual, resented the building of the post, and those in the adjacent country, who were mainly of the Uncpapa tribe, began a series of attacks upon it of a nature similar to those which had been directed by Red Cloud upon Fort Phil Kearney. The garrison of Fort Lincoln, however, was amply large to protect itself, and suffered no serious losses during the year 1872. But the ranks of the hostiles were being constantly augmented by Indians from the agencies, who, feeling as did Red Cloud himself, that the Government was not keeping with them the faith pledged at Fort Laramie, again sought the warpath in defence of what they regarded as their rights. Under the influence and direction of such chiefs as Black Moon, Gall, Crazy Horse, and the powerful medicine man, Sitting Bull, whose sun was then in the ascendant, they were becoming so troublesome and dangerous that at length Lieutenant-General Philip H. Sheridan, commanding the Military Division of the Missouri, decided that a cavalry regiment, which could effectually pursue and punish the hostiles, must be assigned to the Department of Dakota.

In response to his request, the 7th Cavalry, Lieutenant-Colonel and Brevet Major-General George A. Custer commanding, was ordered from the Military Division of the South to the Department of Dakota. This magnificent fighting organization, recruited up to its full strength with men nearly all of whom had become veteranized in the Civil War or along the frontier, and led by the most dashing and picturesque field-officer in the service, left the South early in April, 1873, and proceeded directly to Yankton, Dakota Territory. The Dakota Southern Railroad had just been completed to this point, and here the troops were detrained and preparations were made for the long overland march up the valley of the Missouri to Forts Lincoln and Rice, where the regiment was to go into garrison.

CHAPTER 21

With Forsyth of Beecher's Island

Captain Marsh, whose life for the next few years was to be so closely connected with the gallant Seventh, was in Sioux City when the regiment passed through on its way to Yankton. Some time before, he had removed his family from St. Louis to Sioux City in order that they might be near him, as his business called him less and less frequently to the lower river. During the summer of 1873 he again moved, this time to Yankton, where he continued to make his home for the next ten years.

The Coulson Packet Company bid for the government contract for carrying troops and supplies on the river during the season of 1873, and secured it easily from all competitors. The company's proposal was made in the name of Captain Grant Marsh, and was accepted by General Sheridan in person. The captain's chief rival for the contract was Commodore Kountz, a man prominent in the Northwest at that time and possessed of considerable public influence. But the commodore's disposition was notoriously irascible, and when he learned that the contract had been awarded to Captain Marsh, he betook himself to General Sheridan in a great rage and informed that officer that before he would lose the work he would take the matter to the United States Senate. This was too much for "Little Phil," and with equal heat he replied that the commodore could take the matter to h— if he wanted to, but the contract was let to a responsible man who would undoubtedly fulfil it faithfully, and it was going to stay let to him, whether Kountz approved or not. Finding that he had met a tartar, the commodore departed, and nothing more was heard of an investigation by the Senate.

As soon as the ice went out in the spring, the steamer *Key West,* in obedience to orders from General Sheridan, started for Fort Lincoln, where instructions for her further movements awaited her. The general, who was familiar with the trips of the *Ida Stockdale* and the *North Alabama* in 1867 and 1869, directed that the boat be placed under the command of Captain Marsh. The latter, as usual, shipped as master and pilot, the other officers being Nick Buesen, pilot and clerk; Charlie Dietz, mate; and John Shacklett, first engineer.

Captain Marsh left Sioux City about April 8th and arrived at Fort Lincoln on May 2nd. Here he found General George A. Forsyth, an aide on General Sheridan's staff, who had orders to take military command of the steamer, and explore the Yellowstone River as far as the mouth of the Powder. No steamboat had ever yet ascended the tumultuous Yellowstone to this point, and the object of the trip was to learn whether it was navigable thus far. If it proved so, the intention was that one or more boats should later on carry up supplies for the military expedition which had been planned to ascend the Yellowstone Valley during the summer as an escort to the Northern Pacific surveyors.

General Forsyth, the officer selected to conduct this preliminary exploration, was a man admirably fitted for the work. He was called "Sandy" Forsyth out on the plains of Kansas and Nebraska, where he had gained wide fame for bravery and resourcefulness as an Indian fighter, especially in 1868, when, with a handful of scouts, he made his splendid defence of Beecher's Island, on the Arikaree Fork of the Republican River, Colorado, against an overwhelming Cheyenne force under Roman Nose. A brigadier-general of volunteers in the Civil War, he had been given a major's commission in the permanent establishment at its close, and for his work at Beecher's Island was brevetted brigadier-general of regulars. A close personal friend of General Sheridan, he had accompanied that dashing commander on his famous ride down the hard-pressed Union battle-line at Winchester in '64, and "Little Phil" had kept him close to his side ever since. At the time Captain Marsh first met him at Fort Lincoln, he was a young man hardly past thirty, keen-eyed, square-jawed, and quick of speech; an energetic, observant cavalryman of the best type, thoroughly trained in the rough school of active service.

The *Key West* was setting forth to penetrate the centre of the hostile country, and she could not safely attempt it without strong military protection. But no escort could be obtained at Fort Lincoln, for the post was garrisoned that spring by only two companies of the 6th Infantry, under Lieutenant-Colonel W. P. Carlin, who had enough to attend to in guarding their immediate territory without sending detachments elsewhere. The escort was therefore to come on board at Fort Buford, the headquarters of the 6th Infantry, where the commanding officer, Colonel W. B. Hazen, had five companies of his regiment.

At Lincoln, however, General Forsyth secured the services of two French and Indian half-breeds as guides for the trip. They were really nothing more than loafers about the post, or "coffee-coolers," as such men were termed along the river, but tempted by the high wages paid to scouts, they undertook the part, professing an intimate knowledge of the country to be visited. The general at first relied upon their claims, until the test of actual service proved their ignorance, for the little knowledge they did possess they had picked up by listening to the talk of the Indians in their camps. No sooner had the boat progressed a short distance along the Missouri than they became hopelessly confused, and when questions were put to them concerning the topography of the country, they resorted to a pretence of being unable to understand English.

The general began to fear that he would have to enter the Yellowstone without suitable guides, and in this dilemma came to Captain Marsh for assistance. As has been said before, the captain was well acquainted with nearly all of the few hardy men who then frequented the wild banks of the Missouri, and he at once recollected one among them who, he felt sure, would meet General Forsyth's most exacting requirements. The man in question was an individual remarkable even in that country of strong personalities and one who later became familiar in the annals of the Northwest as a trusted scout of Generals Terry, Custer and Miles in some of their most important campaigns. His name was Luther S. Kelly, though he was better known as "Yellowstone" Kelly, and his career had been of a nature to compare favourably with those of the most desperate heroes of *Wild West* novels. An outline of it is well worth recording:

In 1864, Kelly was living in New York State, a boy of fifteen, the son of a prosperous family and with a good preparatory education so far as he had gone. Being of a restless and adventurous turn of mind he contrived to enlist in the regular army, although under age, and he saw service in the South during the last year of the Civil War, participating in the Grand Parade of the Union armies in Washington, in May, 1865. After that event the battalion to which he belonged was ordered to Minnesota and, in 1886, relieved the garrison of Minnesota volunteers at Fort Wadsworth, Dakota, and later built Fort Ransom. Two years later he was honourably discharged from the service and, securing a pony, rode down Red River to Fort Garry, Manitoba, and later started across country for the Missouri River. On the way he fell in with a party of half-breeds on a buffalo hunt and remained with them for a time, during which he first saw Sitting Bull, accompanied by a war party of Sioux.

Eventually leaving the half-breeds, he resumed his journey to the Missouri and encountered some Mandan and Arikaree Indians, whom he accompanied to Fort Berthold, on the river, going thence to Fort Buford. The men about the post, recognizing his youth and knowing nothing of his already wide experience as a frontiersman, tried to make life a burden to him by all manner of fun and petty persecution. But Kelly maintained his composure and good-naturedly bore their treatment until an opportunity should arise for showing his mettle. After a while it came.

The country about Fort Buford, as usual, was infested with hostile Sioux, who made war not only upon the whites but also upon their hereditary Indian enemies, the Mandan, Arikaree, and Grosventre Indians, whose agency was at Fort Berthold. So dangerous was the road that when a mail passed between Fort Buford and Fort Stevenson, an escort of mounted troops usually accompanied it. Shortly after Kelly's arrival, the regular mail carriers became long overdue and were given up as killed. There was some important mail to go to Stevenson, but most of the garrison was out on scout so that no troops were available to escort it to its destination. Kelly learned of the situation and, seeking the commanding officer, coolly offered to take the mail through alone. The astonished soldier at first refused to treat the proposal seriously, for it seemed nothing short of madness. But finally Kelly was given a mustang and at dusk of a winter evening he started, the little package of mail secured under his belt.

When he set out, his late associates crowded around him with cheering predictions that before he had gone a mile from the post he would be killed, but he merely laughed and went on. Crossing the Missouri on the ice he arrived at the winter camp of the Mandans about midnight. Two days later he walked into Durfee and Peck's trading-store at Fort Berthold, two hundred miles from Buford. His appearance created a sensation, especially among the Indians, who, decimated by long and disastrous warfare, were crowded together there in a great stockade, practically besieged by the Sioux. These unfortunate

"Yellowstone" Kelly in 1870
(Mr Kelly is seated at the right; John George Brown at the left; and Ed Lambert a Canadian character of the upper Missouri, in the centre.)

people thronged about the mail carrier in wonder, for it seemed to them little less than miraculous that a white man could come alive through a country haunted, by their stealthy foes.

But Kelly pressed on to Stevenson, where he delivered his letters to Col. De Trobriand, —the Count Philip Regis De Trobriand of Civil War fame,—and then started on his return. Fifty miles above Berthold he camped over night with Bloody Knife and some Arikaree hunters. Leaving them in the morning, he proceeded on his way. Suddenly, on turning a point, he came face to face with two mounted Sioux warriors who sprang to the ground and fired point-blank at him, wounding his horse with slugs and inflicting an arrow wound in Kelly's knee. But Kelly was nearly as quick as they in reaching the ground and, felling one of them at the first shot, turned his attention to the other, who had taken refuge behind a cottonwood tree.

Then ensued a duel between rifle and bow-and-arrow, in which the cunning of the Sioux manifested itself in thrusting his robe to one side of the tree to draw the fire of his opponent. When the latter had fired the Indian would spring out and discharge an arrow, then leap behind his cover again. His tree was barked on both sides by Kelly's bullets without result, but finally he played his trick once too often and fell dead. Kelly's horse had stampeded with the others and, not knowing how many hostiles were in the neighbourhood, he returned to Bloody Knife's camp. That doughty warrior and his followers, on hearing of the fight, immediately rushed out and secured the scalps of the dead Sioux, with which they rode post-haste to Berthold, where the entire camp danced for three days and nights over the scalps.[1] Kelly went on to Buford without further adventure and delivered his letters, after which he took the mail regularly for a time between that post and Stevenson. The admiration of the Fort Berthold Indians for him became unbounded and they dubbed him "The-Little-Man-with-a-Strong-Heart."

---

1. Despite this act of cowardly bravado, Bloody Knife was a courageous warrior, of whose daredevil exploits many stories once existed. Some of these have been preserved in Joseph H. Taylor's invaluable personal recollections of the North-western frontier, embraced in his *Kaleidoscopic Lives* and *Frontier and Indian Life*, published by the author at Washburn, North Dakota. Years later, Bloody Knife was one of Custer's most trusted scouts in the Little Big Horn campaign, and was one of the first to fall with Reno's command on the fatal 25th of June, 1876. He was at the side of Major Reno when killed and it was said that that officer first lost his self-control when the brains of Bloody Knife were spattered in his face by the bullet which crushed the Arikaree's skull.—J. M. H.

But he soon tired of so prosaic an occupation as carrying mail, though it would seem that under the circumstances it ought to have furnished him with enough excitement. His restless spirit longed for regions never trodden by the feet of white men, and the next summer, quite alone, he set out up the valley of the mysterious Yellowstone. All that season he remained there, hunting, trapping and exploring the hidden fastnesses of a country rich in rugged beauties. Love of the land and its solitude kept him there, but in the autumn he returned to Buford and quietly took up his winter abode in one of the timbered bends of the Missouri. In the meantime, however, the tale of his hardihood had passed from mouth to mouth along the borderland, and far and wide he was known by the sobriquet which has outlived all his previous ones, "Yellowstone" Kelly.

With this hermit of the water courses Captain Marsh was intimately acquainted. In 1871 and 1872 his boat had been the first one up in the spring, and in both years he had found Kelly at his winter camp and conveyed him to the nearest fort to sell his pelts and furs, the fruits of his winter's trapping. When General Forsyth asked him to recommend a guide for the Yellowstone, Captain Marsh therefore gave him an account of Kelly and his history. The general was delighted, for in the description he recognized a man after his own ideals, but he expressed a fear that, much as they wanted him, Kelly might not be found. The captain replied that he need feel no uneasiness on that score, as the frontiersman would certainly be met with somewhere between Stevenson and Buford.

CHAPTER 22

"Yellowstone" Kelly guides the "Key West"

The next afternoon the *Key West* was steaming leisurely through one of the sweeping bends near the spot where the *North Alabama* had become icebound four years earlier. As the boat headed the bend, Captain Marsh from the pilot-house discovered, on the next timber point, a rude log cabin partly hidden in the forest. It was just such a place as an experienced frontiersman would select for a camp of some duration, for the heavy woods on every side concealed it entirely from the prairie bluffs where Indian scouts might prowl, and protected it against the storms of winter. Near by and close to the cut-bank lay a long, even pile of freshly hewn cord-wood, and before the cabin door stood a solitary human figure, leaning motionless on a rifle and watching the approaching boat. The captain, recognizing the figure instantly, put the wheel over and brought the boat to land, and Kelly, a little more mature, but otherwise unchanged since their last meeting, stepped to the deck.

An extremely taciturn man, his greeting was brief and a bargain was soon struck for the welcome pile of cord-wood which he had cut during the winter to sell to the first boat up. Then, while the crew were busy carrying it aboard, the captain led him to the boiler deck and introduced him to Forsyth. As he looked up, the General could not conceal his surprise and admiration. Before him stood a man reticent of speech and modest of demeanour, yet highly picturesque in appearance and bearing himself with an air of self-reliance and hardihood which could not be mistaken. He was dressed entirely in a suit of fringed buckskin, and his feet were encased in beaded *moccasins*. His face, darkly tanned by sun and weather, was smooth-shaven except for a slender moustache, and his features were lean with the hard, muscular gauntness of a hunting animal that carries not an ounce of superfluous flesh.

A mass of thick hair, straight and black as an Indian's, was swept back from his forehead and hung below his shoulders. Across his arm he carried a long, breech-loading Springfield rifle, army model, on the butt of which was carved the name he had bestowed upon this trusty companion and guardian of his lonely life, "Old Sweetness." The rifle's barrel from muzzle to stock was covered with the skin of a great bull-snake, shrunk on so tightly that it resembled varnishing.

It was small wonder that the man's appearance impressed General Forsyth, who questioned him briefly as to his knowledge of the Yellowstone, and then informed him that the boat was going up for the purpose of exploring that stream and that his services as guide would be very welcome if he would consent to act. The young man answered the general's questions in the fewest possible words, but it was plainly to be seen that his interest was aroused and that he was anxious to accompany the expedition.

Turning to Captain Marsh, he said that he would be glad to go if the captain would take his peltries on board and stop at Fort Buford long enough for him to dispose of them. To this the captain readily consented, the fur packs were brought on deck, and leaving his little winter's home to crumble away on its lonely timber point, Kelly steamed off up the river as a government scout.

At Fort Buford, two companies of the 6th Infantry, under Captains M. Bryant and D. H. Murdock, were taken on board and the *Key West* entered the Yellowstone on May 6th, where she remained for nine days. The water was found to be very low, for the winter's snows had not yet commenced to melt in the mountains where the Yellowstone and its tributaries take their rise. But the deposits of driftwood along the banks indicated unmistakably that during the summer season the volume of water would be much greater. The boat had gone but a few miles when she came to a spot where the stream spread out into a great shallow full of sandbars and intersected by numerous small chutes. It seemed that she had already reached her journey's end, but by sounding carefully with the yawl a channel was at length found through which she could be worked by using the spars. She was taken through safely, and though several more such places were encountered, she surmounted them all.

The channel of the Yellowstone, except near the mouth, differs radically from that of the Missouri. From Stanley's Shoals, forty-two miles above Fort Buford, it has a gravel bottom, interspersed with many dangerous rock-reefs, in passing which the most skilful navigation is necessary. But Marsh and Buesen proved equal to the task. Much time was consumed in cutting fuel, the soldiers assisting in the work, always as guards and sometimes as choppers and sawyers. The fuel problem, on this as on subsequent voyages up the Yellowstone, proved one of the most serious the captain had to contend with. In recent years, however, he has noticed a curious change in the flora of the country, due, so he believes, to the removal of the Indians. During the early '70s, the absence of large timber in the valley was very noticeable. The cotton-woods, the largest tree indigenous to the section, were small and scattering, and it was difficult to find even green wood to cut, for though willow brush extended all along the banks, the individual trees were mere saplings.

The Indians then were in the habit of making their winter camps along the valley, of course bringing with them their great herds of ponies, of which the Montana tribes, both Sioux and Crows, possessed an unusual number. These tribes were constantly engaged in war with one another, and it behooved every camp to guard its herd carefully against raiding parties of the enemy. The timber furnished the safest hiding place, and here the ponies roamed during the winter. Forage being naturally poor in such localities, the animals gnawed the bark of the cottonwoods, the most palatable food they could find, and thus in the course of a few months the pony herd of a single camp would girdle and kill the cottonwoods for miles around.

After his last trip up the Yellowstone during the Sioux wars, Captain Marsh did not again ascend the river for more than twenty-five years, and in the meantime the Indians had long been removed to their reservations elsewhere. When he next breasted the current of the stream, he found its banks lined with magnificent forests of cottonwood, which had found opportunity to grow and flourish after the calico ponies, with their gnawing proclivities, had vanished.

As the *Key West* penetrated farther up the valley, game was encountered in more than mere abundance; the country fairly teemed with it. Vast herds of buffalo were migrating over the prairies, and in the river bottom and among the broken stretches of rough bad-lands back from the stream, antelope and elk wandered in droves, like cattle. The elk, indeed, were so numerous in this region that the Indian name for the Yellowstone had always been Elk River. In the long spring evenings, after the boat's headlines had been made fast to the bank for the night, Yellowstone Kelly would set out with *Old Sweetness* across his arm and a blanket over his shoulders and stride away alone into the darkness. Sometime the next moaning the boat, steaming around a bend, would find him waiting on the bank with the choicest parts of several antelope, elk, buffalo or perhaps other game, in sufficient quantity to keep the boat's company on royal fare for two or three days. Since the steamer had to follow all the meanderings of the channel while Kelly could move across the necks of the bends, he had ample time for hunting before she could overtake him.

Nor were the spoils of his rifle the only results of these excursions. He would return to the *Key West* with a fund of information concerning the country through which he had passed; the woods and prairies and bottom-lands, where the creeks headed and how they took their course, and what signs of Indians he had met with. Much of this information proved not only of immediate benefit but was valuable to the expeditions of subsequent years. Kelly, indeed, made himself the most useful member of the exploring party, excepting only Captain Marsh, and gained by his services not alone the confidence but the friendship of General Forsyth.[1]

At the mouth of Glendive Creek, about 125 miles above Fort Buford, General Forsyth had reason to believe that the Northern Pacific would cross the Yellowstone, and here an excellent location for a supply depot was found and reconnoitred. No Indians were encountered, and though the boat's people were constantly on the alert for them in case they should appear, the trip was a pleasant one for all concerned. Over the valley and the vast, ridge-ribbed prairies beyond, the promise of spring was beginning to break the long spell of winter. The grass and the brilliant early flowers of that northern latitude had not yet started up on the level plains which invariably border the Yellowstone on one side or the other, but the vivid green of the bottom-land

---

1. The Yellowstone Kelly of the Sioux wars was later Major Luther S. Kelly of the United States Indian Service, agent for the Apaches and Mohaves at San Carlos, Arizona. His life, ever since the close of the North-western border disturbances, was an active and adventurous one, and spent chiefly in the service of his country, as is shown in the succeeding extract from a letter received from him by the author: "I was a scout until 1883, then went into the War Department, and in 1898 went to Alaska, exploring, later coming back to take my commission as Captain in the Volunteers. I then went to the Philippines, where, after my service in the army, I was appointed Treasurer of one of the large provinces. I was appointed U. S. Indian Agent at San Carlos, Arizona, after spending four years in the Islands."

willow thickets, as yet untarnished by the scorching breath of summer, formed an aisle of verdure along the swift-running river for the progress of the boat.

In the years after the traditions of the pioneers have died out, it is often a mystery how and why the natural features of a region originally received the names by which they are known. No such mystery exists regarding the Yellowstone Valley, for nearly all of its natural features were given their names by Captain Marsh, and for a very simple reason. Like any pilot who feels a pride in professional knowledge, the captain always kept a detailed log of his trips, especially on waters which he had not previously navigated. Therein he recorded the course of the channel, the locations of the islands and chutes, the nature of the banks and any other data which might prove useful in future voyages.

If names were given to these topographical formations, their later identification would be much simplified, and so, during this first exploration of the valley by steamboat, Captain Marsh, assisted by Clerk Buesen, bestowed names right and left upon islands, bluffs and rapids. These were later recorded by a representative of the War Department and applied in official maps and documents to the points designated, thus becoming permanently embodied in the nomenclature of the region. The appellations given to some of the more important of these points may be mentioned, as well as the reasons for their use.

Forsyth Butte, the first prominent bluff on the east bank of the Yellowstone above its junction with the Missouri, was so called in honour of the military commander of the expedition. Cut Nose Butte, Chimney Rock and Diamond Island were named because of their fancied resemblance to these objects. A group of seven small islands a few miles above Diamond Island were called by Captain Marsh the Seven Sisters Islands, in remembrance of his seven sisters.

Crittenden Island was so designated for General T. L. Crittenden, commanding the 17th Infantry, which at that time was garrisoning various posts along the Missouri. Mary Island became a perpetual monument to the chambermaid of the *Key West,* wife of the steward, "Dutch Jake." Reno Island was named for Major M. A. Reno, of the 7th Cavalry; Schindel Island, for a captain of the 6th Infantry; Bryant's Buttes, for Major M. Bryant, commanding the escort of the *Key West;* Edgerly Island, for Lieutenant W. S. Edgerly of the 7th Cavalry; Monroe Island, for the captain's brother, Monroe Marsh; DeRussy Rapids, for Isaac D. DeRussy, later Lieutenant-Colonel of the 14th Infantry;

McCune Rapids[2] for one of the captain's old friends in St. Louis; and Barr's Bluff, for another old friend.

Almost at the Powder River, Stanley's Point was named for the colonel of the 22nd Infantry, while immediately across the Yellowstone from the mouth of that stream, a gigantic bluff, rising abruptly above the valley and dominating the country for miles around, was fittingly christened Sheridan's Buttes, in honour of the indefatigable lieutenant-general under whose direction the land was being slowly won from the sway of the red man.

Besides the points mentioned by reason of their association with the gallant men of the military frontier, the captain gave titles to many other buttes, islands and rapids for more trivial reasons. In fact, nearly every natural object along the Yellowstone from its mouth to the Powder, received its name, if it has one, from him, excepting only the creeks, most of which had been named by Captain William Clark when he descended the river in 1806. On the seventh day after her departure from Fort Buford, the *Key West* arrived within two miles of the mouth of the Powder, and here her progress ended. An insurmountable reef of rocks prevented her going further, though it was evident that later in the season this would offer no serious obstacle. Moreover, the indications were that the river would then prove navigable far above that point, and Kelly's previous observations also tended to confirm this. The object of the trip, however, had been attained, and the boat turned about on her homeward run.

To the commander of the *Key West* probably more than to any other, the expedition had owed its complete success. The skill with which he navigated his vessel through the intricate channel of a river never before ascended thus far by a steamboat, elicited the praise of all the army officers on board. In this connection, the comments of General Forsyth, together with his graphic description of Captain Marsh as he remembers him at that time, are of interest.[3]

> During the years 1866 to 1871, (says General Forsyth), I had occasion to go up and down the Mississippi River from New Orleans to St. Louis several times, and made the acquaintance of a number of well-known steamboat captains of those days.

---

2. Incorrectly spelled *McKeon* on Government maps.—J. M. H.
3. These are contained in a letter written to the author by General Forsyth, whose own published works, which include, *The Story of the Soldier*, and *Thrilling Days in Army Life*, (the latter also published by Leonaur), contain no account of the trip of the *Key West*,—J. M. H.

They were all good men and competent, too, but none of them impressed me as did Captain Marsh in our first interview at Fort Lincoln. General Sheridan had told me that I would meet in him one of the best specimens of the river man whom he had ever known, and one who was absolutely reliable in all respects and safe to be depended upon in any emergency. I was, therefore, already impressed in his favour, and my first interview with the quiet, cool, self-contained and straightforward river captain, satisfied me that he was the ideal man of his profession. Years of considerable experience since those days among steamboat men of his rank, have only confirmed me in the accuracy of the opinion I then formed.

At that time, to the best of my recollection, Captain Marsh was a man about thirty-five or possibly thirty-eight years of age, straight as an arrow and, while not spare in person, not overweighted with flesh. He was pleasant-spoken and gentle-mannered, with clean-cut features lighted up by a pair of wonderfully clear eyes that caught my immediate attention; quick of movement but reserved in manner and quite deliberate in speech.

In our trip up the Yellowstone, which we ascended at a very low stage of water, he was constantly on deck and always alert, whether his boat was in the stream during the day or tied up against the river bank at night. His judgement as to what he could do with the *Key West* in threading the unknown shoals and working through the rapids among dangerous and partially submerged rocks, was good to see, and his skill in handling his boat and in using his spars and hawsers to force her over and through sandy shallows and gravelly riffles showed a most capable knowledge of his vocation.

Our guide, known as 'Yellowstone' Kelly, was another capable character, who gave us much information of the country on each side of the river through which we were passing, and he has since won a lasting reputation on the old Western frontier as an able scout and a reliable guide. The report of Captain Marsh upon the river conditions found on that trip was the nucleus upon which in later years was built up the knowledge of all Yellowstone River pilots.

At the time this voyage was made, the whole upper country was in the possession of the hostile Sioux, and the fact that such conditions prevailed was the reason I was detailed to go with the expedition, as it was thought not at all unlikely that the boat would be attacked by the Indians. But, if my memory serves me aright, we did not see an Indian either going up or coming down the river. Our pilot, Nick Buesen, was another unusually capable man and well worthy of mention.

On the day that the *Key West* re-entered the Missouri, before the escort disembarked at Fort Buford, all the army officers on board signed an engrossed letter of commendation which they presented to Captain Marsh, and which he has treasured ever since. The text of this letter is as follows:

Steamer *Key West*
May 15th, 1873.

The thanks of the undersigned officers of the army are due, and are hereby tendered, to Captain Grant Marsh and the officers under his command, for the ability and energy which have characterized them during the trip of the Steamer *Key West* from Fort Buford, D. T., to Powder River, Montana.

 (Signed)   R. T. Jacob, Jr.,
       2nd Lieut., 6th Infantry.
       Geo. B. Walker,
       2nd Lieut., 6th Infantry.
       D. H. Murdock,
       Captain, 6th Infantry.
       Josiah Chance,
       2nd Lieut., 17th Infantry.
       Thos. G. Townsend,
       2nd Lieut., 6th Infantry.
       Geo. A. Forsyth,
       Major & Bvt. Brig. Gen., U. S. A.
       M. Bryant,
       Capt., 6th Infy., Bvt. Maj., U. S. A.
       E. R. Ames,
       Captain, 6th Infantry.
       Fred W. Thibaut,
       1st Lieut., 6th Infantry.

After quitting the Yellowstone and disembarking her escort, the *Key West* proceeded at once to Yankton. At Buford and the other posts along the river she was received with enthusiasm, for the feat she had accomplished was regarded as a remarkable one. From Yankton, General Forsyth made a full report of the expedition to General Sheridan, in Chicago. The latter was much gratified at its success and requested General Forsyth to convey his thanks to the officers and crew of the *Key West*.

CHAPTER 23

Campaigning With the Seventh Cavalry

When the *Key West,* downward-bound, passed Bismarck the surveyors of the Northern Pacific were already assembled there, waiting to start westward, while across the river, at Forts Lincoln and Rice, General Alfred H. Terry, commanding the Department of Dakota, was making ready the military column which was to accompany them to the Yellowstone. The hostiles were known to be in large force somewhere in the wilds of the Big Horn or Yellowstone valleys, and it was General Sheridan's desire that the escort to be sent with the surveyors should be strong enough to deal the Indians a crushing blow if they could be brought to battle. He therefore instructed Terry to mobilize at Rice and Lincoln as much of the infantry of his Department as could be spared, and to General Custer, in cantonment at Yankton, he sent orders to hasten the march of the 7th Cavalry up the Missouri and report to General Terry at the earliest possible moment. Captain Marsh was instructed by Sheridan to place his vessel at the disposal of General Custer.

The *Key West* had arrived at the territorial capital while the town was passing through the turmoil incident to the departure of the cavalry. General Custer ordered Captain Marsh to take on board the women and children of the regiment and the personal baggage of the officers, such room as remained after these had been accommodated being used for some of the supplies destined for use during the coming campaign. The greater part of the latter, however, were conveyed north on the steamers *Far West,* Captain Mart Coulson, and *Peninah,* Captain Abner Shaw, which were chartered by the Government for the purpose.

The voyage from Yankton to the forts, which occupied several weeks, was without incident; so much so, indeed, that it proved extremely monotonous to the women on board, among whom were included most of the feminine element of the regiment, the wives of officers and enlisted men and laundresses. Mrs. Custer and Mrs. Calhoun, General Custer's sister, had gone with the column, travelling in an ambulance. The regiment, in order to have as good a road as might be, marched along the upland prairies, avoiding the river bottom, and though now and then the river wound close enough to the bluffs to permit of the troops bivouacking near the boat, this happened but seldom and the women were generally obliged to pass several days at a time without seeing or hearing from their husbands. Captain Marsh did all he could for the entertainment and comfort of his passengers, but his resources were limited, and about the only advantage the people on the boat enjoyed over those with the column was in the fact that they were protected from the violent storms of early summer.

After the arrival of the Seventh at Fort Rice, only a few days were spent there, then the farewells were said to the families left behind, and on the 20th of June the column moved out on its long march into the uninhabited wilderness. The force consisted of the entire 7th Cavalry with the exception of two troops, headquarters and five companies of the 22nd Infantry, six companies of the 9th Infantry, four of the 8th Infantry, two of the 6th Infantry, three of the 17th Infantry, and a detachment of Arikaree Indian scouts.[1] General David S. Stanley, Colo-

---

1. *The Army of the United States.* In his article on *The Yellowstone Expedition of 1873*, published in the *Journal* of the U. S. Cavalry Association, October, 1905, Lieutenant Charles Braden, U. S. A., retired, is made to add to the above enumerated list of companies, "several of the 7th Infantry." In writing to the author on the subject, however, Lieutenant Braden says of his article in the *Journal* of the U. S. Cavalry Association:

"My article, as written, did not mention any part of the Seventh Infantry as forming a portion of the command. The error is the printer's. The article as published was, much to my displeasure, printed without any proofreading. The proof sheets were sent to me. I marked a number of errors and revised some of the text. The Secretary of the Association did not wait for the return to him of the proofs, but printed the article with all of its errors. I wish you would add the above to your notes, so as to place me in a proper light."

The 7th Infantry, at the time of the Stanley Expedition, was garrisoning some of the posts of western Montana. The facts concerning the events of the expedition which appear in the text, aside from those in which the steamboats were concerned, are mainly gathered from Lieutenant Braden's published articles and letters to the author, and from the regimental sketches embraced in *The Army of the United States.*—J. M. H.

Group of officers and ladies of the Seventh United States Cavalry at Fort Lincoln about 1875.

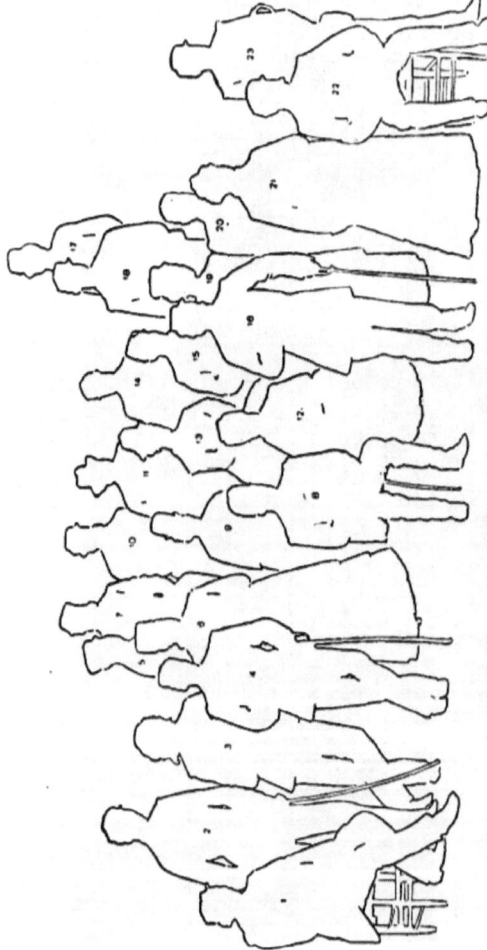

KEY TO THE FOREGOING PHOTOGRAPH

1. Second Lieutenant Bronson, 6th Infantry; 2, 2d Lieut. G. D. Wallace, 7th Cavalry; *3, Gen. G. A. Custer, 7th Cavalry; *4, 2d Lieut. B. H. Hodgson, 7th Cavalry; 5, Mrs. T. M. McDougall, 7th Cavalry; 6, Mrs. G. A. Custer; 7, Capt. T. M. McDougall, 7th Cavalry; *8, Capt. G. W. Yates, 7th Cavalry; 9, Mrs. G. W. Yates; 10, First Lieutenant Badger, 6th Infantry; 11, Mr. Charles Thompson (son of Captain Thompson); 12, Miss Annie Bates; 13, Mrs. James Calhoun; 14, Col. J. S. Poland, 6th Infantry; 15, 1st Lieut. Charles A. Varnum, 7th Cavalry; 16, Lieut.-Col. W. P. Carlin, 17th Infantry (B. G. Everett); 17, Capt. Wm. Thompson, 7th Cavalry; *18, Capt. T. W. Custer, 7th Cavalry; 19, Mrs. M. Moylan; *20, 1st Lieut. James Calhoun; 21, Mrs. Donald McIntosh; 22, Capt. Myles Moylan, 7th Cavalry; *23, 1st Lieut. Donald McIntosh, 7th Cavalry. (Note: Of the officers shown in the photograph, six were afterward killed at the battle of the Little Big Horn. Their names are marked with an asterisk.)

nel of the 22nd Infantry, was placed by General Terry in command of the column, which aggregated eighty officers and 1,451 enlisted men.[2] A large wagon-train accompanied the troops for carrying the supplies necessary for the overland march.

As soon as the expedition left Fort Rice, the three steamboats started for the Yellowstone and the mouth of Glendive Creek, where General Forsyth had recommended that the supply depot be established. As had been expected, the water was high and the obstacles which had been encountered in May gave no trouble, so that the boats reached their objective point some time before the column made its appearance. At Glendive the *Peninah* and *Far West* unloaded their cargoes, were discharged by the quartermaster and returned to the lower river. The *Key West*, with Captain Marsh in charge, was retained to act as a transport or patrol boat as occasion might require. At Fort Buford on the way up, a company of the 6th Infantry under Captain Hawkins had been taken on as escort, and these men remained with the boat throughout the campaign. While waiting for Stanley to arrive, they commenced the erection of a stockade at the landing place.

The main column, in the meantime, had been seriously delayed by heavy rains, which softened the ground and hindered the long wagon-train. In 1872 a similar but smaller expedition under General Stanley had marched from Fort Rice to the mouth of the Powder in twenty-four days; in 1873 forty-one days were consumed in reaching Glendive Creek, though the distance was less. Before the journey was half completed many of the wagons were emptied and sent back to Fort Lincoln for additional supplies. The troops traversed practically the same route as that followed by General Sully in 1864, but under much more favourable circumstances. No Indians were encountered to harass them and while the spring rains delayed the train, they assured, on the other hand, an abundance of forage for the animals. The march, indeed, partook much of the character of a holiday excursion. General Custer, who possessed a reputation as a royal entertainer, seldom set out on an expedition unaccompanied by several guests, and the present occasion was no exception to the rule. He had with him R. Graham Frost, of St. Louis, the son of the distinguished Confederate General, D. M. Frost, and also Lord Clifford and another British nobleman.

The engineer in charge of the railroad surveyors was likewise an intimate friend of General Custer. This was General T. L. Rosser, who

---

2. Report of the Secretary of War, 1873-1874.

had been Custer's classmate and room-mate at West Point. When the Civil War broke out, Rosser resigned from the Academy and accepted a commission in the Confederate service. He rose rapidly to prominence as a brilliant cavalry leader, displaying in the field many of the same fearless and dashing qualities which distinguished Custer. Several times the fortunes of war caused the two friends to be pitted against each other in battle, but even the passion of conflict never chilled the warm personal regard which they held for each other. They had not met since the close of the Rebellion, but when thrown together on the far North-western frontier their delight was sincere, and throughout the campaign they spent as much time as possible in one another's company.

General Custer, who was an indefatigable sportsman, had with him, as usual, a fine pack of hounds; the 22nd Infantry had a regimental pack and the English noblemen also had a pack. There was no dearth of pedigreed dogs in camp, and ample opportunity for using them was found during the march to the Yellowstone, for the country teemed with antelope, deer, wolves, and other game. After the column reached Glendive, Lord Clifford told Captain Marsh an amusing story concerning the dogs. In the 22nd Infantry was a young lieutenant named W. W. Daugherty, who, in the previous year, had been presented with a deer-hound pup of exceedingly hazy and uncertain lineage. But the lieutenant was much attached to his lowly four-footed friend and avowed great confidence in his hunting qualities. As the dog had been *given* to him, Daugherty whimsically named him *Given*. Shortly after the expedition left Fort Rice, the officers, eager to try their animals on the first available game, started two hapless jack-rabbits from their coverts on the open prairie. Instantly the hounds were released, and put out in a frantic mob after the bounding fugitives.

Amid the commiserating smiles of his brother officers, Lieutenant Daugherty unleashed the plebian Given and sent him to join the chase, though no one but himself imagined that the dog could even remain within barking distance of his blooded competitors. But Given took the trail with an earnestness and speed astonishing to all beholders. After being started, the jack-rabbits had parted in their flight. Given went through the pack like a torpedo-boat through a fleet at anchor, caught and killed one of the rabbits which was loping away in front, and then, turning, overtook and disposed of the other before the rest of the hounds could reach him. After this performance of his pet, no one smiled commiseratively at Daugherty. Given's speed and endurance became the wonder of the camp.

One difficulty met with in running the dogs arose from the quantities of prickly pears which grew all over the country. The small, keen thorns of these plants penetrated the feet of the hounds and soon lamed them. Then some ingenious sportsman thought of the expedient of having the dogs shod with leather. It worked admirably, and after finding that their feet were safe, the animals paid no more attention to the thorns, but ran as well as they would have done on bare ground. After the column had reached a region where antelope were plentiful, some of the best hounds were picked out to run these nimble-footed animals, though the officers had no hope that any could be caught unless previously wounded. But one day in a fair, straight-away chase on the open prairie Given overtook and brought down an unwounded antelope, a feat which Lord Clifford, who was well versed in the annals of sportsmanship, declared to Captain Marsh was unprecedented. The remarkable nature of the exploit was emphasized a few days later, when the pack came suddenly upon four antelope at graze in a swale of the prairie. The dogs were among them before they could start to run, yet every one escaped, leaping over their pursuers and scurrying quickly beyond reach.

The *Key West* had been lying twelve days at Glendive, when early one afternoon, General Custer suddenly appeared, riding down the valley of the creek, accompanied by a single troop of his regiment. After cordial greetings, he informed Captain Marsh that the scouts had located a more convenient camping-place twenty miles upriver and that the main column was heading for that point. He therefore instructed the boat to proceed there also, and came on board with his men for the short trip. The *Key West* reached her destination about dusk. The main column had not yet arrived, but late that night the 7th Cavalry band came into the valley ahead of the troops and going aboard the boat, serenaded the crew. Never before had the air of the lonely Yellowstone Valley echoed to any music save the rude beat of Indian *tom-toms*, and the sweet strains of this splendid military band, on such a silent, moonlit night and in such surroundings, made a weirdly solemn impression on the listeners which time could never efface. Early the next morning, July 31st, the remainder of the expedition came up.

The troops now went into camp for several days to rest and replenish the train. In the meanwhile the *Key West* was busy bringing up supplies from Glendive for the column to take on the next and most difficult stage of its advance. At the new camping place the soldiers constructed a fortification which was named Stanley's Stockade, for protecting the stores which were to be left behind. After he had brought up all the goods from Glendive, Captain Marsh was instructed to take a party of surveyors about fifty miles further up the river, where they surveyed a section of the valley. On returning from this duty, he found the troops and General Rosser's men ready and waiting to be ferried across the Yellowstone, the former to engage in their active Indian campaign and the latter to prosecute their railroad work. Though the Northern Pacific was eventually built along the south bank of the Yellowstone, these early preliminary surveys, so costly in life and labour and money, were run along the north bank and proved futile after all.

Just before the troops moved a stir was caused among them by the arrival of a Catholic priest, Father Stephen, who had come alone all the way from Fort Rice over the route previously followed by the column. Driving a single horse attached to an old buggy, over the top of which he had erected a large cross, this devoted man, utterly unarmed and defenceless, had ventured upon a journey which the most hardy frontiersmen would have hesitated to undertake. Eager to reach the army in Montana, to whose spiritual needs he felt called to minister, he had travelled across the desolate Bad-lands, regardless of the dangers of swollen streams, prowling wild animals and skulking Indians with which his pathway was beset. With the sublime courage which has characterized the missionaries of the Roman Catholic Church throughout the history of the North American Continent, he had not hesitated to jeopardize his life for the sake of the object he wished to attain. His faith was not misplaced, for he came through safely and his courage made him an object of such respect to the soldiers that the work he was able to do among them must have been gratifying to him. He accompanied them on their westward march and was present to give Christian burial to those who fell in action.

The passage of the Yellowstone was accomplished quickly with the aid of the boat, and the expedition at once departed, leaving only one company of the 17th Infantry and two troops of the 7th Cavalry, to guard the stockade. Shortly after it had gone, a mail came into the stockade from Fort Rice containing letters and papers for all the command. Captain Marsh took it on board the *Key West* and hastened up the river, hoping to overtake them. He did so opposite the mouth of Powder River, much to the satisfaction of the soldiers, who were thus enabled to hear again from the friends and dear ones left behind, which they could not otherwise have done for a number of weeks. The *Key West* did not go above the Powder, but after delivering the mail returned to Stanley's Stockade.

As General Stanley moved forward, signs of Indians were not at first noticeable. But it was felt that somewhere ahead in the fastnesses of the mysterious hills, stealthy tribesmen must be watching and gathering. The march was conducted with every precaution. A strong advance guard of cavalry scouted in front, the infantry marched ahead and in the rear of the wagon-train, while on both flanks of it was the remainder of the cavalry, except such as was daily detailed for immediate escort to the surveyors. The latter were running their line along the river bank, while the wagons followed the top of the bluffs where travelling was easier.

On the afternoon of the 4th of August, a day when the thermometer was standing at 110° in the shade, Doctor Honzinger, the veterinary surgeon of the 7th Cavalry, and Mr. Baliran, the regimental sutler, together with two troopers, straggled from the column in search of water. They found a spring, and were resting beside it when, without warning, a party of Indians rose up before them and fired point-blank into their faces. Three of them fell dead, but the surviving trooper escaped to the train, and several troops of cavalry at once made chase up the valley after the fleeing hostiles, who were led, as was afterwards learned, by Rain-in-the-Face, a young Ogalalla chief. To the surprise of the pursuers after they had ridden a few miles, they came upon General Custer and the advance guard, surrounded by several hundred Indians in a strip of timber near the river. Their timely arrival raised the siege and the enemy retreated.

This day's attack was the first intimation the expedition had of the proximity of the Indians, but thereafter the evidences of their presence became plentiful. The sites of large camps recently abandoned by them were passed daily, while their scouts constantly observed the progress of the column from distant hilltops. Sometimes the retreating *travois* trains bearing their families and camp equipage could be seen on the horizon, and on August 8th General Stanley instructed Custer to take all the mounted troops, including the Arikaree scouts, and by a forced march endeavour to overtake and destroy the villages.

Custer started with his command in light marching order, but after pursuing the enemy all the next day, he arrived at a point on the Yellowstone near the mouth of the Big Horn River, where he was disappointed to find that they had crossed all their belongings in bull-boats and escaped to the south bank. He spent the following day seeking a ford, but without success. That night, war parties of the Indians recrossed the Yellowstone above and below his position, and at sunrise furiously attacked the cavalry as it lay in bivouac on the river bank. The first attack came from a strip of timber across the river, but directly west of the bivouac was a high bluff, which, if gained by the Indians, would make the position untenable. Lieutenant Charles Braden, with half of his troop, L, hurried forward to occupy the crest of the bluff. He and the Indians reached it at the same moment, and a struggle almost hand-to-hand ensued for its possession. The Indians were at last driven back, but with most unusual tenacity made several charges, all of which were repulsed, though Lieutenant Braden received a terrible wound which crippled him for life. Shortly afterwards, a general advance was ordered by Custer, and the enemy was scattered in every direction. The Indians had suffered heavily in the engagement, while the cavalry lost four men killed and one officer and three men wounded. Although routed on the field, the enemy continued to hold the strip of timber across the river from which they fired during the day, and were only driven out at last by shells from the two field-pieces under Lieutenant Webster, 22nd Infantry, which came up toward evening with General Stanley and the main column.

Their severe handling in this affair demoralized the savages and they gave the troops no more trouble, save for a slight skirmish a few days later near Pompey's Pillar. This point marked the end of the westward march, for here the line of the surveyors connected with that run eastward from Bozeman in the two previous years. The column turned north and crossed the high plateau into the valley of the Musselshell. This it followed for a distance, then went along Great Porcupine Creek to the Yellowstone, and marched down the bank of the latter stream until the starting-point, opposite Stanley's Stockade, was again reached on September 10th.

During the absence of the troops, the *Key West* had spent most of her time in the vicinity of the stockade, occasionally making short trips up and down river for the purpose of examining the channels and chutes more carefully than had hitherto been possible. About the middle of August, while on one of these brief voyages down toward Glendive Creek, she encountered the steamer *Josephine*, Captain John Todd, coming up. This boat had long been expected by Captain Marsh, who at once transferred to her from the *Key West,* the latter being taken down to the Missouri by Captain Todd, while the *Josephine* proceeded to the stockade.

The new boat, which was an addition to the fleet of the Coulson Packet Company, had been built under instructions from Captain Marsh and for his own use. She had come from the marine ways at Freedom, Pa., whither Captain Todd had gone to hasten her completion and to bring her up to the Yellowstone, where she was seriously needed, as the river was falling.[3] She was of very light draught, having been designed for use on those waters, and was better adapted to such work than the *Key West*. Captain Marsh had named her after Josephine, the little daughter of General Stanley, whose home was then at Fort Sully, the headquarters of the 22nd Infantry.

When, three weeks after the arrival of the new boat, the returning expedition at last made its appearance on the opposite bank of the Yellowstone, the troops were worn down by hard campaigning, for their march had been an arduous one. With them they brought Lieutenant Braden who, contrary to the expectations of his comrades, had survived his desperate wound. Since the fight near the Big Horn, it had been a difficult matter to bring him through all that long and torturing journey of 400 miles across the hill country. His injury had been caused by a rifle ball which passed through his left leg, shattering the bone from hip to knee. The command was provided with few surgical appliances and, lacking splints or plaster bandages, the officer's injured limb was placed in a wooden trough, made by a blacksmith and a carpenter.

The next problem was to carry him. The jolting of the ambulance nearly killed him, while hand and mule litters proved nearly as bad. At last the ingenious wagon-master rigged up a litter slung on poles thirty feet long, the ends of which were fastened to the running-gear of an ambulance. The contrivance was hauled by men, and an officer, three non-commissioned officers, and thirty troopers were detailed to handle it. In it the heroic Braden travelled for thirty days, and as soon as the column reached the river bank, he was taken on board the *Josephine* and tenderly placed in one of her comfortable cabins, as were the several wounded soldiers who had suffered with him.

---

3. The contributions to the Historical Society of Montana place the *Josephine* in the list of steamboat arrivals at the Fort Benton levee during the season of 1873. This is an error. Under orders from Captain Marsh she went direct from Freedom, Pa., to the Yellowstone for Government contract service with the army in the field.— J.M.H.

After this work of humanity had been done, the boat ferried the cavalry and some of the infantry to the east bank, whence they marched for Fort Rice, arriving there September 22nd. The battalions of the 8th and 9th Infantry were taken on board and conveyed to Sioux City, *en route* to distant stations. At Fort Buford, Captain Marsh found a young man by the name of William H. Seward, anxiously awaiting his arrival. Seward was clerk to the Department Paymaster, Major William Smith, and, in the absence of his superior, was paying off the troops at the river posts. Shortly before the arrival of the *Josephine,* he had received word from the East that his wife had given birth to a daughter and he was naturally very desirous of reaching home. But he still had to pay off the troops at one more post, Fort Stevenson.

On the way down from Buford he confided the situation to Captain Marsh. The *Josephine* was under Government charter and the captain was supposed to take her through to her journey's end without any unnecessary delays, yet if Seward were set ashore at Stevenson and left there by the boat he would have no means of reaching Bismarck and the railroad for a long time, and might even be compelled to remain at the fort all winter, since no more boats were expected there that year.

Captain Marsh did not wish the young paymaster's clerk to suffer such a misfortune, which would seem all the harder from the fact that Seward's actual business at Fort Stevenson would only occupy him for about half a day. So just before the *Josephine* reached the fort, the captain went down to the main deck and inquired of First Engineer Charlie Echols:

"Charlie, don't you think the engine valves ought to be ground?"

Echols intently scrutinized the face of his chief. "Well, I don't know but they had, captain," he replied, with a grin.

"Take you about half a day, won't it, Charlie?"

Again the engineer looked at him closely.

"Yes," he answered, "I reckon it will; about half a day."

"All right," said Captain Marsh, "we'll do it at Fort Stevenson."

Echols put in the time industriously, though just what results he accomplished are not matters of record. But at almost the moment when Seward finally appeared on the bank, hurrying down to the landing, the work on the valves came to an abrupt termination, the stage was hauled in and the vessel resumed her journey. Seward left the boat at Bismarck and caught the first train for the East. Nearly eight years passed before the captain saw him again. Then he came to Bismarck, accompanied by his wife and eight-year-old daughter, for no purpose save to pay the captain a visit. They had been in Minneapolis and Mrs. Seward had insisted on making the journey in order that she might meet and personally thank the man who had once saved her a six months' separation from her husband at a time when she sorely needed him at her side.

Lieutenant Braden was carried off the *Josephine* at Fort Lincoln, where he lay in the post hospital for some weeks, and was then taken by rail to St. Paul. He remained in that city through the winter, and in the spring returned to his home in Michigan, hoping to recover fully. But it was impossible for him to do so, and eventually he was promoted to the rank of first lieutenant and then retired, on account of "wounds in the line of duty." Captain Marsh greatly admired the young officer's cheerful courage while he was lying on the *Josephine,* making no complaint over his wound and submitting without a murmur to the diet of pork and beans, which was all the larder of the boat could furnish him. When he was taken ashore at Fort Lincoln, his campaign hat was left hanging on a nail in the cabin he had occupied. Captain Marsh would not allow it to be removed, and as long as he continued to command the boat Braden's hat remained where he had placed it, a memento of the fortitude of one American soldier.

CHAPTER 24

Pioneer Paths

Regarded superficially, the objects of General Stanley's expedition had all been attained. The railway survey had been carried to completion, and the Indians had been driven before the military advance and defeated in several engagements. But in a deeper sense, the results were far less satisfactory. As soon as the troops retired, the country was reoccupied by the hostiles, whose bitterness against the Government had been increased ten-fold by the invasion. Those of their number who ventured into the river agencies after supplies recited their grievances with redoubled vehemence to the reservation Indians, and many of these, whose friendship for the whites was at best but lukewarm, were converted to the hostile cause.

How many thus became converted was not known or even suspected by the military authorities until the battles of the Rosebud and the Little Big Horn three years later opened their eyes to the terrible earnestness with which the great Sioux Nation clung to its last wild hunting ground. The climax of the mighty drama of warfare for possession of the North-western territories, was rapidly drawing near, and the Yellowstone Expedition of 1873 contributed not a little to its consummation.

So far as fighting was concerned, comparative quiet I reigned throughout the Sioux country during the year 1874. The management of the Northern Pacific was not yet ready either to prosecute its construction work or to elaborate its surveys, and the Indians in the disputed region were not irritated by any military movements there. On their part the red men remained quietly within their proper boundaries, undertaking no offensive movements, but during the year two events transpired which were well calculated to arouse their anger.

The first and least important of these was an expedition of civilians undertaken from Bozeman in February, March and April. Its object was a double one; to prospect for gold and to reconnoitre a wagon road from Bozeman to the head of navigation on the Yellowstone and there establish a town as a base of communication with the terminus of the Northern Pacific at Bismarck. Judging from the observations of the *Key West* in the previous summer, this Bozeman party concluded that the head of navigation was near the mouth of the Tongue River, and toward this point their expedition proceeded, following as usual the north bank of the river.

But the provisions running short, the eastward march was given up long before the mouth of the Tongue was reached, and, crossing the Yellowstone, the column moved up the valley of the Big Horn River, exploring for gold. Here it was severely and constantly harassed by the hostiles, though no heavy engagements occurred, and after swinging in a wide circle along the base of the Big Horn Mountains, it returned to Bozeman by the old Montana Road, having accomplished practically nothing, except to incense the Indians.

But the event of 1874 which most deeply stirred the Sioux was the military expedition under General Custer which visited the Black Hills in the summer of that year. This beautiful region of pine-covered hills and park-like valleys, watered by innumerable crystal streams, possessing many thousands of acres of fertile agricultural land and great stores of mineral wealth, was regarded by the Indians as the chief jewel of their empire. Relying upon their treaty rights, they had felt little apprehension of being disturbed in its peaceful possession.

But early in 1874, General Sheridan, actuated entirely by considerations of military policy, recommended to the Government that an army post be established in the Black Hills, which, lying near the centre of the Sioux country, would greatly simplify the problem of keeping that restless people in subjection. In pursuance of this plan and quite regardless of the nice points of treaties, Sheridan ordered Custer with his regiment to march from Fort Abraham Lincoln into the Hills and thoroughly explore the region, for the double purpose of ascertaining its natural resources and of locating a favourable site for a post.

General Custer carried out his instructions promptly and thoroughly. The Indians were not aware of his movements until he was in the centre of the Black Hills. Here, scattered about in summer camps, he encountered a few of them, who fled at his approach, dismayed by the appearance of an army in the midst of their quiet valleys. The general, whose official reports were usually made in forceful and picturesque language, on the completion of his expedition, sent to his superiors a description of the country so glowing and enthusiastic that, when made public, it precipitated into the Black Hills a rush of home-seekers and prospectors similar to that which had invaded western Montana several years before. The aggressors were promptly ejected by troops, but the mischief had been done.

All over the country a popular clamour arose for the Government to open the Hills to settlement by purchase from the Indians, if possible, but, if not, then by forcible seizure. The Sioux, on the other hand, furious over the invasion, and feeling that no promise of the government, however solemnly pledged, was worth the paper on which it was written, became ready to cast aside all caution and sacrifice their lives in a last despairing contest for their oft-violated rights. How deeply, how vitally, this proud and freedom-loving people cherished the crumbling ideals of their old, wild life, the Government could not seem to realize until, in the final cataclysm, their devotion stood revealed, and half a thousand white men were blotted out by dying savagery at bay before the cupidity of civilization.

CHAPTER 25

Bound for the Mountains

The season of 1874 Captain Marsh spent quietly, operating the *Josephine* in regular commerce between Yankton, Bismarck, and Fort Benton, and finding plenty of business though little excitement in transporting Government stores and post trader's goods. On one of his first trips up river in the spring he had as a passenger for Fort Lincoln, a banker from Beulah, a hamlet in eastern Iowa. The nature of the business which was calling this gentleman so far from home did not at once become apparent. But one day he, together with several other passengers, was in the pilot-house while Captain Marsh was on duty and in the course of conversation he related the circumstances which had caused him to make the journey.

It seemed that during the previous summer, while the 7th Cavalry was out on the Yellowstone, a young man had gone from Iowa to Fort Lincoln and there entered into a contract to furnish hay for the cavalry horses during the coming winter. He purchased a number of mules and some machinery, the money thus expended having been furnished to him by the Beulah banker, who took a chattel mortgage on the property to insure his investment. The contractor set to work on the prairie meadows near the fort, but being unfamiliar with the ways of the wily red man, he permitted his mules to wander at large during the night, and presently a marauding band of Sioux swept down and ran off the entire herd. The contractor possessed no money of his own, and the banker, who had been obliged to stand the loss, was now going up to learn whether he could recover anything on his unfortunate venture.

When he had concluded, Captain Marsh asked him whether he had ever taken the matter up with the military authorities.

"Oh, yes," he answered, in an injured tone. "I have written to General Custer asking him if he did not think that the Indians would give those mules up to me if they knew I held a chattel mortgage on them, since I am not connected with the army. But he has never replied to my letter."

The story of the Iowa banker's artlessness went the rounds of the frontier posts, and an echo of it was heard several years later. One day when General Miles was going up the river on Captain Marsh's boat, on coming around a bend, a fine looking horse was observed quietly grazing out on the prairie and not far from a heavy strip of timber. The captain called General Miles' attention to it, and gravely asked whether he should land so that it might be captured, though he well knew that the animal was a decoy put out to draw them from the boat. But the general was not to be trapped. He regarded the horse and the strip of timber for a moment, then turning a quizzical smile on the captain, remarked:

"Yes, that certainly seems to be a good horse. But I'm afraid there may, be some Indians around here who hold a chattel mortgage on him, and they might not want to give him up!"

The autumn of 1874 found the captain again in the place he most enjoyed, at home in Yankton with his family around him, and here he remained through the winter. But the season following was to prove a more eventful one for him. Shortly after New Year's Day, 1875, General Sheridan requested Commodore S. B. Coulson, the manager of the Coulson Packet Company, to come to headquarters in Chicago for a consultation. Upon the Commodore's arrival, Sheridan informed him that he wished a suitable boat under Captain Marsh to be sent to Bismarck as early as practicable in the spring for the purpose of conveying an exploring expedition up the Yellowstone to the head of navigation. It was finally agreed that the *Josephine* should be used, and upon the opening of navigation, General Sheridan issued the following order to Lieut.-Col. James W. Forsyth, Military Secretary on his staff:

      Headquarters Military Division of the Missouri,
         Chicago, Ill., May 19, 1875.

Colonel:—

Pursuant to an agreement with Mr. S. B. Coulson, the contractor for freight on the Upper Missouri, the steamer *Josephine* will be placed at your disposal at Bismarck, Dakota Territory, for an examination of the Yellowstone River from its mouth to the

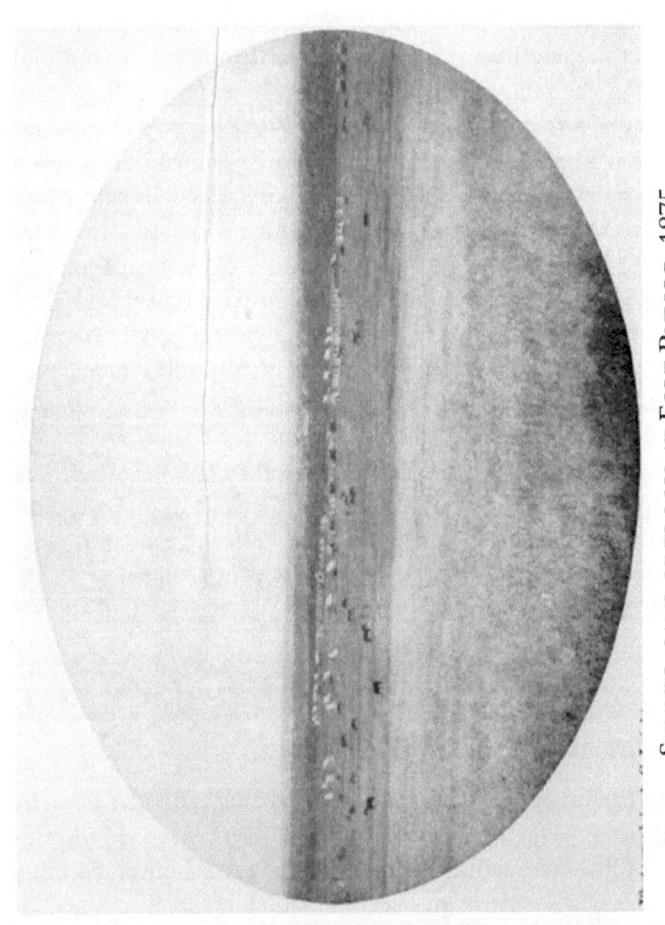

Summer camp of troops at Fort Buford, 1875

mouth of the Big Horn, or still further up, if practicable.

You will therefore proceed to Bismarck without delay, accompanied by Lieut.-Col. F. D. Grant, of my staff, where the steamer *Josephine* will be in readiness for you; and after landing such freight as she may carry for Forts Stevenson and Buford at these respective points, you will take on board from the garrison at Fort Buford a sufficient escort for the accomplishment of the object in view. I want a careful examination made of the south bank of the Yellowstone and the mouths and immediate valleys of the rivers coming in from the Black Hills, and especially those of Tongue River, Rosebud, and Big Horn, and if you go higher up the Yellowstone, the Big Rosebud, giving an account of the timber, soil, and geological formation, also the depth of the water in a general way, and the character of any rapids passed over above the mouth of Powder River. Make your examination as complete as possible, without any unnecessary detention of the boat, and return from any point when, in your best judgement, there is not sufficient water, or any other obstacles to impede your progress.

It may be necessary, at some time in the immediate future, to occupy by a military force the country in and about the mouths of Tongue River and the Big Horn. You will, therefore, make especial examination of these points with this view.

    Yours truly,
        P. H. Sheridan,
            Lieutenant-General.

Lieut.-Col. J. W. Forsyth,
    Military Secretary."

Like the other officer of the same surname who had ascended the Yellowstone two years earlier, James W. Forsyth was the possessor of a brilliant Civil War record. He had received several brevet commissions for "gallant and meritorious services," first at Chickamauga, then at Cedar Creek, then at Opequan, Fisher's Hill, and Middletown, and last at Five Forks, while the grade of brigadier-general, with which he had been retired from the volunteer army, was conferred upon him specifically "for gallant and meritorious services" during the war, an honour accorded to but few officers.[1] He was a gentleman of noble character and unfailing courtesy, with whom it was a constant pleasure

---

1. *Official Army Register.*

to associate, and a soldier of high professional attainments, beloved by his subordinates and respected and trusted by his superiors. The command of such an expedition as he was to undertake could not have been placed in more competent hands.

The *Josephine* left Yankton early in May with Grant Marsh as master and pilot; Joe Todd, pilot and clerk; Andrew Larson, mate; Monroe Marsh and George Britton, engineers; Lew Miller, steward, and thirty-seven men. Going straight through to Fort Lincoln, she stopped there to pick up Charlie Reynolds, the scout and hunter, then crossed to Bismarck, where General Forsyth and Lieutenant-Colonel Grant came on board, accompanied by several professors of the Smithsonian Institution bent upon scientific research.

Having no freight to deliver, the *Josephine* proceeded without delay to Fort Buford, where she arrived on the 25th of May, and took on the escort, consisting of Companies E, G, and H, of the 6th Infantry, commanded respectively by Captain Thomas Britton, 1st Lieut. W. H. H. Crowell, and 2nd Lieut. R. E. Thompson, a total force of seven officers and one hundred enlisted men. There were, in addition, four mounted scouts, of whom Charlie Reynolds was the chief. One one-inch Gatling gun, with 10,000 rounds of ammunition, was carried, and the troops were provided with 350 rounds of rifle ammunition and with one month's subsistence per man. Thus loaded, the *Josephine,* which registered 300 tons burden, drew only twenty inches of water.[2]

All was now ready for the start into the wilderness. The prospect before the voyagers was enough to arouse the enthusiasm of any man having within him the love of primeval nature and feeling the fascination of mysteries unsolved which lead the feet onward along a pathway of discovery. Comfortable quarters had been prepared for each of the 160 men on the boat and they were plentifully supplied with all necessary provisions, while the spice of danger added to their enterprise by the possibility of encountering hostile Indians was just sufficient to be exhilarating without causing serious apprehension. It is rarely that an exploring expedition can set out into a savage region provided with so many of the comforts of civilization.

Captain Marsh was anxious to be well within the mouth of the Yellowstone before darkness fell, in order that good progress might be made the following day, so at six o'clock on the evening of the 26th,

---

2. Report of an expedition up the Yellowstone River, made in 1875 by James W. Forsyth, Lieutenant-Colonel and Military Secretary, and F. D. Grant, Lieutenant-Colonel and *Aide-de-Camp.*

as soon as the escort was on board, he backed off. Before sundown the *Josephine* had passed out of the Missouri and was breasting the impetuous current of the Yellowstone, which leaping from its steep channel into the larger stream with the full force of the spring freshets behind it, seemed determined to entirely usurp the place of the latter. Before the last streaks of the long twilight had faded from the west, the boat had plowed her way twelve miles up the headstrong river and come to rest for the night at the foot of Forsyth's Butte, towering high above the bottoms of the right bank. She had no sooner been made fast than General Forsyth ordered a strong cordon of guards to be posted out on the prairie, extending in a semi-circle to the bank above and below the boat, as a protection against Indian surprise. This practice was adhered to throughout the voyage, both at night and when, during daylight, a landing was made to procure fuel.

The next morning at four o'clock the *Josephine* was off again, and by the afternoon of May 29th had reached Wolf Rapids, just below the mouth of the Powder, the most formidable obstruction to navigation yet encountered. The river had been found at a good stage, about two feet below high water mark, and the current over the normal channel averaged four miles per hour. On Wolf Rapids it attained the high velocity of six miles, but the boat was easily able to steam about over them, taking soundings and finding a minimum depth of eight feet along the channel.

On the right bank of these rapids a perpendicular cliff rises sheer from the water to a height of fifty feet, its face seamed with veins of bituminous coal, the largest as much as five feet in thickness. Bituminous coal along the upper Missouri and the Yellowstone is common, vast fields of it underlying portions of North Dakota and Montana. In recent years some of these have been developed in a very limited way, and as the country becomes populated they will doubtless be worked more extensively. But during all his early years in the north-west, neither Captain Marsh nor any other of the steamboat men were able to make any use of the native coal deposits. The difficulty of procuring firewood induced them to make every effort to utilize the coal, which might have been shovelled from the river banks in hundreds of places where it had broken off and fallen in heaps from outcropping veins. Had it been of any value, it would have solved the fuel problem completely. But it could not be made to burn by any means.

On his boats at different times Captain Marsh tested it in the laundry stoves and tried to keep up steam in the boilers with it over night.

Then he had some of it thoroughly dried and, piling seasoned wood around and under it in the furnaces, subjected it to the greatest heat that could be produced. But without avail. Like iron, it would redden around the edges, but it would not burn, and after each experiment it had to be pulled from the furnaces and thrown in the river. When he returned to North Dakota in 1903, after an absence of twenty years, the captain found to his surprise that all steamboats were using the native coal to the exclusion of wood. It seems hardly conceivable that the coal can have undergone a change in quality in so short a time, but it is nevertheless true that now an excellent quality of fuel is gathered from the same deposits which two decades ago were as useless for the purpose as so much rubble-stone.

CHAPTER 26

Breasting Unknown Waters

On the same afternoon that Wolf Rapids were explored, the *Josephine* reconnoitered the mouth of Powder River and then, passing on beneath the shadow of Sheridan's Buttes, the last familiar landmark, came to rest for the night ten miles above. From the time that the Powder was left behind timber was found to be very scarce, even on the islands, and the boat was obliged to make frequent stops while the woodcutters and their guards went out for fuel. This condition prevailed until the mouth of Tongue River was attained, thirty-eight miles above the Powder. But from its valley on westward the timber became magnificent, many of the cottonwoods having a diameter of five feet and some of six feet. General Forsyth, in his official report of the expedition, declared that some of the large, wooded islands "are so handsome that they almost make the voyager believe that they are the well-kept grounds pertaining to some English country-house. I never saw so fine a growth of cottonwood in my life as on the Yellowstone twenty-five miles above Tongue River."

No Indians were seen until the Tongue was reached, on the evening of May 30th, though the mounted scouts had been off scouring the northward hills for *signs* all that day. But as the boat, in the light of the setting sun, approached the finely timbered valley of this tributary, a considerable Indian camp was discovered, nestled among the trees. The red men sighted the boat at the same moment, and were evidently terror-stricken thereby, for they fled precipitately, abandoning some of their camp equipage and leaving their *tepee* fires burning. So hasty was their departure that no movement could have been made against them even if any had been contemplated. From the time that this encampment was encountered, the men on the boat could now and then see signal smokes rising back among the hills or on the buttes along the river. Warned by these mute evidences that the enemy was observing their progress, the guards were cautioned to renewed vigilance at night.

The method employed by these Indians, and by all the Sioux, in manipulating their signal fires, was interesting. The dusky scout who had news to convey to other scouts or to distant camps would first select as the location for his fire the crest of some conspicuous elevation. Here with his knife he would dig a small hole in the ground, fill it with damp prairie grass and light it, making a smudge, the smoke from which would rise high in a straight column through the still summer air. After he had permitted it to smoulder for a minute or two, he would throw his blanket over the hole, cutting off the smoke for a time, and then withdraw it and send up another column. In this way many signals, previously arranged, could be transmitted to distant points by various combinations of smoke columns and intervals, as telegraphic messages are transmitted by dots and dashes.

General Forsyth had been instructed to make an examination of the mouth of Rosebud River, which point was reached on the 1st of June. But, strangely enough, after a careful survey the General came to the conclusion that it was not the mouth of the Rosebud and that, in fact, this stream did not empty into the Yellowstone at all, but into the Tongue. Though the Rosebud is one of the chief affluents of the Yellowstone, for some reason its bed happened to be dry at the time of the *Josephine's* visit, so that General Forsyth's conjecture was not unnatural.

Until the Big Horn had been passed, on the afternoon of June 2nd, the soldiers of the escort enjoyed an easy existence. Their quarters were comfortable and they passed many hours daily in lounging about their bunks, talking, playing cards and writing letters to be mailed on their return. It was part of the business of the contractor for steamboat transportation to build temporary bunks along the sides of the main deck, back of the boilers, for the accommodation of the enlisted men, on boats which were to carry escorts. The officers were always quartered in the cabins on the deck above, which in steamboat nomenclature is known as the "boiler deck"; for what reason no steamboat man seems able to explain, since the boilers really stand on the main deck, below. The soldiers did not even have to go out in hunting squads, as was often the case on such trips, because the indefatigable Charlie Reynolds, alone, supplied them with more fresh meat than they could use.

On the islands and in the valleys of the Yellowstone grew quantities of wild plums and cherries, buffalo-berries, gooseberries, currants and strawberries, and the troops sometimes found opportunity for gathering such of these fruits as were then ripe to add to their bill of fare. The nightly guard duty had, of course, to be performed, but at other times, save when wood was being cut, all the men were at leisure except three, who were constantly occupied while the boat was in motion, in measuring distances.

This last was an important duty and the method pursued, which had been employed also on the *Key West* in 1873, was a novel one. It was out of the question on such a trip to have men walk along the bank and accurately determine the distances from point to point; time would not allow it. So the work was done on the boat. The men having it in charge were stationed on the top, or "hurricane" deck, the length of which from bow to stern was exactly 150 feet. One of them took his place at the stern to keep the record and the other two at the bow.

As soon as the boat got under way, one of the men at the bow selected an object on shore and keeping abreast of it, walked toward the stern. When he reached the latter, still abreast of his marking point, he had walked 150 feet and the boat, obviously, had advanced a like distance. Upon his gaining the stern, the second man started from the bow, similarly covering an object on shore, while the first returned to the bow to repeat the process, and so on. While not to be compared in accuracy with a survey, this method established the distances along the river with approximate certainty, and from that day to the present the measurements taken by the *Key West* and the *Josephine* have been regarded as the standard ones for the Yellowstone, no regular survey of the river having ever been made.

Taking up the work where he had left it in 1873, Captain Marsh began naming the prominent points along the river as soon as the Powder was passed. Among the eminences thus named were Devil's Back Bone Buttes, Cap Butte, Tower, Bad Land, Marsh's, Lookout, Sundown, Rosebud, and Bessie Buttes, The Palisades, Gray's and Huntley's Bluffs, Cape Horn, just above Big Horn River, The Turrets, two fantastic, castle-like rocks standing side by side on the north shore thirty-five miles beyond Cape Horn, and Belle Butte, the later marking the highest point attained by the *Josephine*. Some of the rapids receiving titles were Baker's, Dixon's, and Bear Rapids, The Narrows, and Hell Roaring Rapids, the last, of sulphurous suggestion, lying at the foot of Belle Butte. The chief islands which were given their designations by the Josephine's master were Reynold's, Eagle, Poncie and Bear Islands, and The Thousand Isles.

When he personally was navigating the boat, Captain Marsh always kept beside him in the pilot-house a notebook, in which he recorded for his own future use the characteristics of the channel and the adjacent shores. This detailed log, which has been previously mentioned in connection with the exploring trip of the *Key West,* the captain grew so accustomed to maintaining that invariably after completing a crossing and getting the boat straightened up on her new course, he would pick up his notebook and enter his observations on the section of river just passed. The entries would read somewhat as follows:

> Run left-hand shore up past a big bluff. Plenty of dead timber in this bend. Then cross from the dead wood in the left-hand bluff over to a short, right-hand bend. Small timber in the head of this bend. Run to the head of this short, right-hand bend, then circle out between two islands (first island named Crittenden Island for General T. L. Crittenden, 17th Infantry; second named Elk Island) and come back to a right-hand prairie bend. Run this bend to the head of it, then cross from the dead timber in the head of the right-hand bend over to a deep, left-hand bluff bend (bluff named Calf Head Butte).[1]

It did not occur to Captain Marsh that the entries in his notebook could be of interest to any one except himself. But one day General Forsyth was sitting on the pilot's bench behind him, and observing him writing, inquired:

"Captain, what is it that you are always putting down in that book?"

"Notes about the channel," replied Captain Marsh.

The general was interested, and after the nature of the entries had been explained to him, he exclaimed:

"Well, by George, I want that information; it is exactly what I am after and have never been able to get."

---

1. Extract from log of steamer *Mandan,* Captain W. H. Gould, of trip up the Yellowstone River in July, 1905, with additions applicable to the trip of the steamer *Key West,* in 1873. The log of the *Mandan* was kept by Captain Marsh, who was employed by the government to make an examination of the Yellowstone with her, and the vessel was chartered for his use.

"Why, I thought you were after information about the country, general," said the captain. "You have engineer officers and professors from the Smithsonian along with you, and I didn't suppose my little notes could be of any value to you compared with the ones they are getting."

"You didn't?" cried the general. "Why, what do you suppose I care about the geological formation of this country or the traces of Mesozoic formations? I want military information for the use of campaigning troops; I want to know about this river for the transportation of supplies, and all the engineers and professors on earth can't give me what you have in that book. I want it to take back to headquarters with me."

At the end of the voyage the captain accordingly turned over his notebook to General Forsyth, exacting a promise, however, that it should be used only for military purposes and should not be copied for the use of other pilots who might later want to ascend the Yellowstone. The captain maintained that the book was of pecuniary value to him, and that he could sell copies of it to other pilots for considerable sums. He regarded it as his personal property, but General Sheridan took a different view of the matter. A year or so later, when many boats had occasion to ascend the Yellowstone on government business, Sheridan had copies made of the log of Captain Marsh and gave them to all pilots who applied. General Forsyth protested, saying he had promised the captain that his book should not be made public. Sheridan disposed of the objections summarily by exclaiming to Forsyth:

"You tell Marsh to go to a warmer climate! Ask him if he thinks we've been paying him four times as much as any other steamboat man all these years just to have him keep his knowledge bottled up for private use? His work on a government boat belongs to the government; he's paid to know about the river and to tell us about it, and I'll use his logbook for any purpose I think proper."

When he heard of this outburst on the part of his good friend Sheridan, Captain Marsh laughed and mentally bade farewell to his log, for he knew that the general was right.

CHAPTER 27

Lonesome Charlie

Reynold's Island, which was mentioned a little way back, was given its name in honour of the gallant scout and hunter of the expedition, who was best known through the north-west as "Lonesome Charlie" Reynolds. This man had attained a fame along the frontier as wide as that of *Yellowstone* Kelly, and his character and exploits were similar in many respects to those of "the-little-man-with-a-strong-heart." Like him, Reynolds had come of a good family in the East, where he had lived until 1860. Then, at the age of sixteen, his restless nature impelled him to seek the West. He joined an emigrant party bound for California, which was driven back by the Indians. But his short experience with the ill-starred enterprise had given the boy a taste of the wild life which he craved, and he remained in the border country, hunting and trapping, exploring and scouting, from the plains of old Mexico to the forks of the Republican River, serving for three years during the Civil War in a Kansas regiment along the frontier, and some years afterwards drifting to the Northwest.

Here his marvellous gifts as a hunter, more remarkable even than those of Kelly, quickly earned him a wide reputation, and for some time he was employed by contract to supply the garrisons of Fort Rice and Fort Stevenson with fresh meat. The phrase, "Reynold's luck," became a familiar one, and other hunters, envious of his success, resorted to all manner of plausible explanations for their failure to emulate his performances. Among the Gros Ventres, Mandan and Arikaree Indians at Fort Berthold, with whom he frequently came in contact, his prowess was attributed to magic, or *medicine*, and their superstitious jealousy sometimes placed him in danger of his life.

On one occasion, in the dead of winter, when the Indians at the agency were actually suffering for want of the meat which their hunters could not procure, Reynolds started out from Fort Berthold for a hunt, accompanied by a young half-breed Arikaree named Peter Beauchamp. They took with them a wagon and made their way southward to the valley of the Little Missouri, where they almost immediately came upon a herd of eight elk. With his customary skill, Reynolds got to leeward of them, crept within long rifle range and succeeded in picking them all off. Beauchamp and he then dressed them, loaded the wagon with as much meat as it would carry and, caching the rest, returned to the agency.

Seeing Reynolds come in loaded down with game from a place where they had hunted in vain, the Indians, especially the Gros Ventres, became very angry, and Beauchamp aroused them to frenzy by telling them, purely for his own amusement, a story about the *medicine* which Reynolds had used on the hunt. He declared that when "the-white-hunter-who-never-goes-out-for-nothing," as Reynolds was called by the Indians, first came upon the trail of the elk, he examined it to see that it was fresh, then took from a hidden pocket a black bottle and poured a few drops of its liquid contents upon the trail. Then he sat down on a log and waited for an hour, when all the elk returned upon their tracks and he had nothing to do but shoot and dress them.

The story aroused the Gros Ventres to such a pitch of superstitious fury that to the number of two hundred they rushed to Malnorie's trading-store, where Reynolds, all unsuspicious of coming trouble, was quietly resting after his long journey. They surrounded the building and demanded from him the black bottle, threatening that if he did not give it up they would kill him. The employees of the trading establishment, when they saw the angry mob approaching, fled to the stockade, leaving Reynolds and his friend Malnorie to face the sudden peril alone.

Reynolds, of course, had no bottle to give and told the Gros Ventres so, whereupon they drew their knives and made a dash upon his team of horses, which still stood hitched before the store, intending to cut the animals' throats. But the hunter threw his dreaded rifle to his shoulder and warned them that the first man who touched a horse would die. They knew him to be as good as his word, and at last sullenly withdrew, vowing vengeance, which, however, they never dared attempt. To the Arikaree tribesmen, who had taken no part in the attack, Reynolds gave two of the dead elk, but to the Gros Ventres he gave nothing, a procedure not calculated to restore the good humour of the latter.

In 1875, when he accompanied the *Josephine,* Reynolds was about thirty-one years of age, a slender, sinewy man five feet eight inches in height, slightly stoop-shouldered, with restless gray eyes and a voice as gentle as a woman's. Like Kelly, he was very chary of speech, seeming even surly on short acquaintance, though such was not the case, for his disposition was cheerful and his generosity such that he would hesitate at no sacrifice for a friend. As a scout his services were of great value to the expedition and the slaughter he wrought among the wild animals of the country caused continual astonishment to the soldiers, whom his rifle kept constantly supplied with such a variety of choice game. as would have tickled the palate of an epicure.

The friendship existing between Captain Marsh and Lonesome Charlie was close and warm, and it continued up to the day when the brave scout, after passing through countless dangers, laid down his life in the service of his country and in the midst of the wild land which had so long been his home.[1]

---

[1] An extended account of the life and adventures of Charles Reynolds is contained in Joseph H. Taylor's *Frontier and Indian Life.*

CHAPTER 28

By Line and Spar to the Head of Navigation

Early on the morning of June 2nd, the mouth of Big Horn River came into view, and the explorers were surprised at the size and volume of the stream. It was fully 150 yards wide, with a powerful current hurling its waters forward into the Yellowstone. The *Josephine's* prow was turned into the mysterious torrent, whose name for years had been a synonym for the stamping-ground of the dreaded hostiles, and she forced her way for twelve miles above its outlet. But at length the channel became so broken by chutes and so obstructed by mud-banks that further progress was impossible. General Forsyth concluded that they had reached the Big Horn's head of navigation, but the next year Captain Marsh succeeded in ascending it very much further with the steamer *Far West*.

Although this tributary seemed to contribute so much to the volume of the Yellowstone, the latter did not appear to diminish above the Big Horn's mouth. It continued to vary in width from 300 to 1,000 yards, though the *Josephine* found as she went on that the current was gradually increasing in velocity. From the time she had entered the Yellowstone until the Big Horn was passed, she had not required the assistance of either spars or lines. But about the middle of the forenoon on June 3rd, when twenty-seven miles above the Big Horn, the pilot noticed that the rugged bluffs bordering the valley were closing in ahead of them. As the boat moved forward, the bed of the stream became more and more contracted, while momentarily the current increased in depth and rapidity, until she found herself in a place where the bluffs stood only eighty-five yards apart, towering straight above her.

Between them, the torrent swirled like a mill-race, running no less than nine miles per hour. Every pound of steam was crowded on the *Josephine's* boilers, and her paddle-wheel beat the water into foam, but the utmost speed she could make was one-sixth of a mile an hour, and most of the time she seemed to be standing still. The captain ordered the spars set, and after an exhausting struggle of several hours the boat was finally forced through *The Narrows*, as the place was appropriately termed, into the wider channel beyond.

For some miles now the steaming became easy, and in the latter part of the afternoon the *Josephine* drew in sight of an isolated butte rearing its head high above the southern bank and, from the point where it was first seen, apparently standing in the river itself. The appearance of it aroused the greatest enthusiasm on board, for it was at once recognized as Pompey's Pillar, the famous landmark discovered by Captain William Clark, of the Lewis and Clark Expedition, in 1806, when conducting their exploration of the country between the Mississippi River and the Pacific Ocean. Everyone in the Northwest had heard of it, but no one on the *Josephine* had dared hope that she could reach it. But at its base the boat's lines were made fast, and the remainder of the day was spent by the crew and escort in examining the historic rock.

Pompey's Pillar[1] is composed of yellow sandstone, and stands quite alone on the edge of the river, in the midst of a level valley. On July 18, 1860, Lieut. Henry E. Maynardier, commanding a detachment of Captain William F. Raynolds' Yellowstone exploring expedition, conducted observations of a solar eclipse from the top of the Pillar. In his report[2] he stated the Indian tradition to be that at some remote time the massive rock had fallen from the bluffs on the opposite side of the river and rolled across to its present resting place. But the logical explanation of its formation is, that the ridge once connecting it with the bluffs had been worn through by the erosion of the river. Its soft sandstone was easy to cut, and high up on its face the *Josephine's* men found inscribed the words, "Wm. Clark, July 25, 1806," the letters still as clearly defined as when chiselled there by the illustrious explorer, sixty-nine years before.

Many of the steamboat men and soldiers followed Captain Clark's example by cutting their names on the rock, and in a prominent place

---

1. In his *Journal*, Captain Clark writes the name, "Pompey's Tower."
2. Embraced in the *Report on the Exploration of the Yellowstone River*, by Bvt. Brigadier-General W. F. Raynolds, published in 1868.

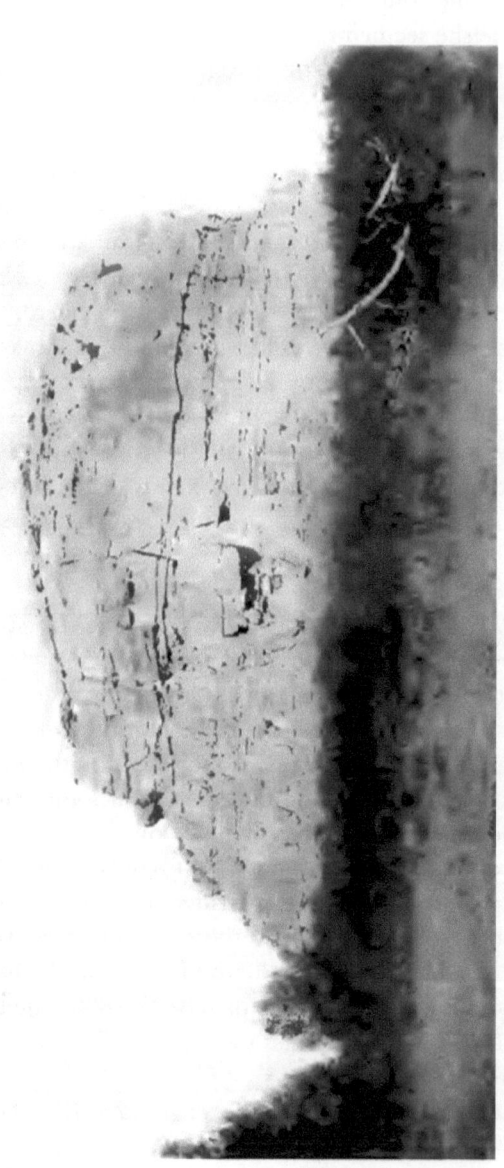

Pompey's Pillar on the Yellowstone River, Montana, reached by the steamer Josephine on June 3, 1875

Captain Marsh inscribed: "*Josephine,* June 3, 1875." After completing this record of the achievement of his vessel, the captain stood looking up at the crest of the Pillar, rearing itself majestically overhead and bathed in the sunlight of late afternoon, and the thought came to him that in such a place it would be eminently fitting to raise the Stars and Stripes, where the winds of Montana's prairies had never caressed them before. The *Josephine* was the possessor of two handsome flags, for, in accordance with custom, one had been given her by the builders at the time of her launching, while the second she had received some time later from General Stanley, as a token of his appreciation that she had been made the namesake of his daughter. Captain Marsh now went down to the boat, and, securing the first flag, carried it to the top of the Pillar, where he nailed it fast to a stout staff and left it, an emblem of Columbia's supremacy over the lonely land, to wave in solitary beauty until storm and wind should wear its fabric away.

Some of the men spent the late afternoon in fishing, and with great success, for the river was full of mountain trout, catfish, shiners and jack salmon. Then after a refreshing sleep in the deliciously cool air of the Montana summer night, the voyagers resumed their onward course at 3:45 o'clock next morning. But their journey now became fraught with many and increasing difficulties. The great river, though apparently undiminished in volume, grew more and more swift, constantly breaking into rapids through which it was necessary to warp and spar the boat, while numberless small islands split the channel into chutes, no one of which was large enough for easy navigation. At times it seemed that a smooth stretch of water had been reached, where it would be possible to coil the ropes, ship the spars and stop the "nigger" engine, but invariably just beyond, another rapid would be encountered, again forcing these clumsy implements into use. At length, after two days of incessant struggle, Pryor's Fork was reached, opposite the mouth of which, three years before, Major Baker's detachment had been attacked by Black Moon and his Sioux and Cheyenne warriors.

Here, on the north bank of the Yellowstone and almost at Baker's battleground, was encountered a large camp of Indians, principally Mountain Crows, on their way down to the Big Porcupine to hunt buffalo. The *Josephine* had met the buffalo on her upward journey. They were crossing the Yellowstone in countless numbers between the Tongue and the Big Horn, migrating north from their wintering places among the foothills of the mountains, and, as the Indians well knew, the Big Porcupine lay right in the centre of their usual line of advance. The Crows, always friendly to white men, were delighted to meet the expedition, and General Forsyth and some of his officers paid them a visit in their village, leaving the steamer after nightfall, in the yawl. They found the village to consist of 351 lodges, 270 being those of Mountain Crows under Iron Bull, Black Foot, Crazy Head, Long Horse, and Bear Wolf; fifty Nez Perces lodges under Looking Glass; twenty lodges of River Crows under Black Bull and Forked Tail; ten lodges of Gros Ventres of the Prairie under Brass Bracelet, and one Bannock lodge.

The Mountain Crows at this time were reputed to be the wealthiest Indians on the continent, their riches consisting of rare and elaborately decorated robes and skin lodges, and, more largely still, of vast herds of ponies. The herds of this hunting party were great enough to substantiate the statement, for they seemed to be grazing everywhere about the village. All the warriors in the encampment were well armed with Sharp's carbines and they had a reserve ammunition supply of over 15,000 rounds, furnished them by the Indian Bureau. They boldly announced that, equipped as they were, they would wipe out Sitting Bull and his Sioux followers if only the latter could be brought to battle. They claimed the Big Horn country as Crow territory and declared that if necessary they would kill the whole Sioux Nation in order to possess it. These people were intelligent and thrifty above the average of their race, and quite as brave as the Sioux, with whom they had long been at enmity. Had occasion offered, they would very probably have tried to make good their threats.[3]

The meeting with this friendly camp of aborigines was a pleasant diversion, and the next day the *Josephine* pushed on along her difficult pathway. Before nightfall a tremendous rapid was encountered and though, after a hard struggle, it was successfully passed, so forbidding was its aspect and so savage the resistance it offered, that it was appreciatively named "Hell Roaring Rapids." At the head of it the boat lay up for the night, with a line stretched to the bank ahead to help her forward in the morning. But when dawn came, General Forsyth seeing the nature of the river in front, ordered out a reconnoitring party who marched up the bank for several miles, examining the channel.

---

3. See *Report of an Expedition up the Yellowstone River, made in 1875*, by Lieutenant-Colonel James W. Forsyth and Lieutenant-Colonel P. D. Grant, which has been referred to for dates and other data in preparing the account of the *Josephine's* trip.—J.M.H.

On their return they reported the whole river ahead so broken up by islands and with so powerful a current that it could not be navigated without constant resort to warping and sparring.

General Forsyth and Captain Marsh held a consultation and decided that no adequate reward for the labour involved was to be gained by going further. So, at two o'clock p. m. on June 7th, the boat was turned about and started on her return. She had reached a point estimated to be forty-six miles from Pompey's Pillar, 250 miles from Powder River and 483 miles above the mouth of the Yellowstone, and her stopping place, measured in a straight line, lies less than sixty miles from the north-eastern corner of the present Yellowstone National Park. Before leaving this highest point attained, Captain Marsh blazed the trunk of a gigantic cottonwood to which the *Josephine* was tied, and carved thereon the name of the boat and the date. It is exceedingly improbable that a steam vessel will ever again come within sight of that spot or be entitled to place her name beneath the *Josephine's* on that ancient tree trunk, almost under the shadow of the Rocky Mountains.

Borne downward by the swift current, the return trip was quickly made, and in four days the voyagers were back at Fort Buford. The escort was here disembarked and the boat went on to Bismarck, where the army officers and scientific men left her and departed for the East by rail.[4]

General Forsyth reported to General Sheridan that the voyage of the *Josephine* had proved the Yellowstone to be navigable for commercial purposes as far as the mouth of Big Horn River; Colonel Grant stated that it was so to Pompey's Pillar, and both expressed the opinion that, owing to its gravel bed, its stable banks and islands and its freedom from snags, it offered a much better highway for commerce from Fort Buford to the settlements of western Montana than did the shifting and dangerous Missouri from the same point to Fort Benton. Their judgement was doubtless correct, though the opportunity never came for demonstrating it, because the advent of railroads soon after put an end to all through river traffic. But their report aroused much interest in Montana, and in the autumn an expedition was organized

---

4. General J. W. Forsyth on this trip of the *Josephine* was as much impressed with the skill and dexterity of Captain Marsh as General G. A. Forsyth had been two years before. In a recent letter to the author, he takes occasion to say of Captain Marsh: "I considered him the finest Captain that navigated the upper Missouri. He was exceedingly popular with all the army officers stationed in that country."—J. M. H.

at Bozeman which set out to establish a town at "the *Josephine's* head of navigation."

The point selected was nearly opposite the mouth of the Big Horn, and here a small stockade was erected and a town site laid out, the promoters of the enterprise expecting to create a metropolis which should eclipse Fort Benton in its palmiest days. They called their settlement Fort Pease, in honour of F. D. Pease, the chief of the expedition, and their idea was to open a road between it and Bozeman, tranship freight from the boats to wagons and haul it over to the settlements, as was done at Fort Benton. But unfortunately their location was in the centre of the region occupied by the hostiles, and they had scarcely arrived before the Sioux appeared and placed them in a state of close investment.

From that time forth throughout the winter, the colonists were engaged in a constant battle for existence. They could not venture from the stockade without being fired upon, for some of the enemy were always sure to be on the alert, and even when within the defences they could not feel altogether safe from stray bullets. Occasionally some Mountain Crows would visit the post, though usually they found it perilous to do so. But one winter's afternoon, so a survivor of the venture afterwards related to Captain Marsh, a strong war party of these friendly Indians came in just as the garrison was being treated to a long-range bombardment by some Sioux stationed on the bluffs across the river.

The Crows were braving the inclement weather for the sole purpose of securing a few choice scalps from their hereditary enemies, and inasmuch as the Sioux were evidently in small number, they were delighted at the situation of affairs. Informing the settlers that they would soon be rid of their persecutors, the Crows drew their robes about them and solemnly marching off in single file, disappeared in the brush. They walked directly away from the river in order to lull the enemy's suspicions, but, once out of sight, they made a wide detour, crossed the river at a concealed point above and swinging around behind the bluffs, suddenly rushed upon the Sioux, who were too much absorbed in dropping bullets into the stockade to keep watch of their line of retreat. The hostiles, who were only three in number, were taken completely by surprise and fell easy victims to the attack. Two were killed outright while the third, badly wounded, escaped into a thicket.

There was with the Crow party a youth who had still his warrior's spurs to win. For a long time he had been expressing his ardent desire to prove his metal by slaying a Sioux. The warriors now crowded around him, telling him that if he was as brave as he boasted, he should go into the thicket and kill the wounded man with his knife. Nothing daunted, the boy rushed in. For a few moments his eagerly waiting companions listened to the sounds of a terrific struggle deep among the bushes. Then ensued a significant silence and presently the young Crow emerged, triumphantly holding aloft in the cold air the steaming scalp of his victim. He had entered the thicket a stripling; he came out a full-fledged warrior, to be honoured by his nation.

After mutilating the dead bodies according to time-honoured custom, the Crows marched back to Fort Pease as solemnly as they had gone forth. They said no word of their success upon entering the stockade, but three of the warriors advanced, thrusting their hands from their blankets. As the white men who met them grasped the proffered hands, these fell from the blankets and were left dangling in their startled grip, while the Crows gave themselves up to uproarious laughter. They had cut the forearms from the dead Sioux and used these gruesome trophies for announcing their victory.

Such successes, however, were rare in the short but eventful history of Fort Pease. Though many a Sioux fell before the rifles of the besieged, six of their own number were killed and nine severely wounded before the winter was half over. The garrison thus became reduced to twenty-five, while the Sioux seemed steadily to increase in number. As day after day passed with no sign of relaxation in the vigor of the attack, there gradually crept over the little party of pioneers, exhausted by ceaseless vigil, the dreadful fear of total annihilation. For a time no one would confess it, but at length it became impossible longer to conceal that which was in all their minds. Then one of their number volunteered to attempt the delivery of an appeal for relief to the commanding officer at Fort Ellis, 175 miles away. He bade farewell to his comrades, crept from the stockade and did not return. More weary days passed while the garrison, ignorant of his fate, waited for either the help which they knew would come if he had escaped or the death which it seemed equally certain would be theirs if he had not.

Finally, one day in March, 1876, their eyes were gladdened by the sight of a column of horsemen marching into the valley, four troops of the sturdy old 2nd Cavalry, under Major Brisbin. Thankfully the garrison abandoned the town site which they had laid out with such high hopes a few months before and returned to Bozeman. They left the flag fluttering defiantly over the stout walls which had stopped so many a singing bullet and the fort itself to become one of the heroic traditions of the frontier.[5] Major Brisbin's relief expedition was the first military movement against the hostile Indians of the memorable battle year of 1876, and it was a bloodless victory for the whites. Yet, exciting as had been the meteoric career of the post which he rescued and which had been established in consequence of the *Josephine's* exploring trip, far more momentous events were soon to follow on which the results of that trip were destined to exercise a potent influence,[6]

---

5. Lieutenant J. H. Bradley's *Journal*, in the contributions to the *Historical Society of Montana,* Vol. 2, contains an interesting account of the defence of Fort Pease.—J.M.H.

6. The manuscript of the foregoing chapters relating to the *Josephine's* exploration of the Yellowstone in 1875 was in the possession of the late Major General James W. Forsyth for revision or correction at the time of his death, October 24th, 1906. The author owed a debt of gratitude to General Forsyth for assistance previously rendered in the preparation of these chapters and it will always be a matter of regret to him that the general could not have read them in their completed form. Few American soldiers have served their country with more distinction and honour than did General Forsyth, yet little concerning his brilliant career has ever been written, either by himself or by others. After General Forsyth's death, Major W. H. H. Crowell, U. S. A., who commanded a company of the *Josephine's* escort in 1875, kindly gave the above chapters a critical reading.—J.M.H.

CHAPTER 29

First Blood For Crazy Horse

Thirteen long years had now passed since that summer of the Minnesota massacres, when the skirmish line of the Republic was first checked in its onward sweep by the outposts of the Sioux. Through those years the red enemy had been driven backward and ever backward from one stronghold to another. But the paths of conquest were marked by the bleaching bones of hundreds of white men to attest the vigour of barbarian resistance, while in the fastnesses of the Big Horn country still roamed defiantly those powerful factions of the Northwestern tribes whose spirits were yet too proud to bend to the yoke of civilization. They were fighting hard for their old, wild life, the only life they and their race had known from time immemorial.

Ever since the days when Sully forced his toilsome way through the Bad-Lands of the Little Missouri, the Department of the Interior, having in charge the conduct of Indian matters, had been endeavouring by every peaceful means to induce the hostiles to come into the agencies and settle down. These efforts had apparently been quite fruitless, and as time went on the Government officials lost patience. Having seen during the summer of 1875 that the nomadic element among the Indians was no more inclined than formerly to obey his orders, the Commissioner of Indian Affairs at last, early in December, 1875, instructed his agents to notify them that if they did not come in by the 31st of January, 1876, they would be regarded as enemies of the United States, and the army would be empowered to force their submission. Up to this time they had never, in theory, at least, been consigned absolutely to the mercy of the army, the latter having been employed only in a defensive capacity, to protect emigration and commerce from their attacks.

However justifiable this order may have been, the time given for its execution was certainly very short. It was issued on December 6th, and did not reach the Cheyenne River Agency until December 20th, or the Standing Rock Agency until December 22nd. From these points messengers had then to be despatched to the absent Indians. January, 1876, came in with bitter weather. Even the upper Missouri Valley, accustomed to severe winters, had not known such cold in years. The runners carrying the message of the Indian commissioner were delayed in reaching the camps in the buffalo country, and when they finally arrived they found the hunting parties waiting for the inclement weather to relax so that they might begin killing game. Whether any of the absentees had been willing to comply with the order or not, it was past the first of February before any of them would have been able to return to the agencies from their distant wintering places; meantime, the commissioner, true to his threat, had given into the hands of the army the task of forcibly bringing them in.[1]

General Sheridan, following a carefully matured plan, thereupon prepared to institute a vigorous campaign against them. At three different points on the borders of the Sioux country he ordered the concentration of strong mobile columns, with the intention of undertaking a winter campaign. The three bases of operation were Fort Abraham Lincoln, Dakota; Fort Fetterman, on the Platte River, Wyoming, and Fort Ellis, Montana. From these points it was designed to drive converging columns wedge-like into the enemy's country, catching and crushing between them any force which might oppose. At Fort Lincoln, Gen. Alfred H. Terry was in charge of local operations, at Fort Fetterman, Gen. George Crook, and at Fort Ellis, Gen. John Gibbon.

Through the first two months of the year the severe weather forbade any attempt at carrying the plans into execution. The country lay buried under heavy snows while blizzards of frightful intensity swept down from the north at frequent intervals. But finally, on the first day of March, Crook got away from Fetterman with five troops of the 3rd Cavalry and five of the 2nd, under Col. J. J. Reynolds, and four companies of the 4th Infantry. Pushing forward vigorously, on the morning of March 17th he succeeded in surprising and capturing the village of Crazy Horse, the leading war chief of the Ogalalla Sioux, on the headwaters of the Powder River.

Though the soldiers destroyed the village of 105 lodges together with a large quantity of supplies, and captured the Indian pony herd,

---

1. History of the Sioux Indians, by Doane Robinson.

General Gibbon's wagon-train parked on the Yellowstone, opposite the mouth of the Tongue River, 1876

Cavalry camp on the Yellowstone, 1876

Crazy Horse rallied his followers so promptly and made such a vigorous fight, that the troops were forced to retire under fire. Encumbered with wounded and suffering agonies from the cold, their return march was a bitter ordeal. The pony herd was recaptured by the Indians, and when the command finally re-entered the post, in addition to the wounded of the engagement, sixty-six men were badly frostbitten. Though they had lost their village, the moral effect of the entire movement had been rather to embolden than to intimidate the warriors of Crazy Horse.

With the opening of spring, however, affairs assumed a more active and promising appearance in the theatre of war. At Fort Ellis, General Gibbon had concentrated about 450 men, consisting of six companies of his own regiment, the 7th Infantry, a strong detachment of Crow scouts, and the four troops of the 2nd Cavalry embraced in that faithful squadron which, from its fifteen years of continuous service in the territory, came to be known as *the Montana Battalion*. Accompanied by a large wagon train, Gibbon's force left Fort Ellis on March 30th and proceeded by easy stages down the Yellowstone. They encountered very few Indians during the first two months they were out, and through this time the expedition partook of many of the enjoyable features of a pleasure excursion.

The function of the column was chiefly to guard the north bank of the river and prevent the Indians from crossing in case they should thus seek to escape from Crook and Terry, and its work was performed with complete success. According to the prearranged plan, Gibbon was to meet Terry at Stanley's Stockade, near the mouth of Glendive Creek, after which the two were to co-operate in further movements. As will be presently seen, the arrangement was practically carried out on June 8th, when the two forces came into communication at the mouth of Powder River.

Having reorganized and increased his expeditionary force, General Crook again left Fort Fetterman on May 29th. He now had ten troops of the 3rd, and five of the 2nd Cavalry, three companies of the 9th, and two of the 4th Infantry, 200 Crow scouts and considerable wagon and pack trains; in all, nearly 1,500 men. He pushed north by the old Bozeman Road, and upon reaching the site of Fort Phil Kearney, turned east and struck the Tongue River on June 9th. Crazy Horse had sent Crook a warning that if he attempted to cross Tongue River, he would be attacked. No sooner had the troops appeared on the forbidden stream than the doughty Ogalalla, true to his promise, massed his warriors on the opposite bluffs and opened fire. They were soon dislodged by a gallant assault of Mills' squadron of the 3rd Cavalry, but they fell back fighting.

Leaving his trains parked under guard of the infantry, Crook now pushed across the Tongue, his men carrying four days' rations and one hundred rounds of ammunition each, and made a forced march for the upper Rosebud River, where he had reason to believe the village of Crazy Horse lay. Early on the morning of the 17th, his command was roused from its bivouac on the banks of the Rosebud by a furious attack of the entire Indian force, so formidable a body of warriors that it deserves the name of army. The troops in the valley with difficulty drove back their assailants to the surrounding bluffs, but could press them no further. Through all that long day a conflict, perhaps the most stubbornly contested in the history of Indian warfare, raged over the hills and ravines of the Rosebud.

General Crook's column was the largest ever sent against the hostile Sioux, excepting only that of General Sully in 1864. What were the numbers of the Indians opposed to him can never be known with accuracy, but that they largely outnumbered him is certain. And they made good use of their superiority, for they fought Crook to a standstill, held him back from even a glimpse of their lodge villages and finally forced him into a retreat on his wagon trains at the crossing of the Tongue, carrying twenty-seven wounded with him and leaving ten dead on the field.

Crook[2] and his officers were dumbfounded at the resistance which they had met. The battle of the Rosebud opened their eyes to the fact which neither they nor any other white men had apparently understood before, that the bulk of the Sioux Nation had taken up arms against the Government. For years the prevailing estimates of army officers and others in a position to be well informed had placed the number of Sioux hostiles at less than one thousand. Crook's battle proved conclusively that there were several times this number in his front alone, while there could be no means of knowing how many more might be in other camps not far distant. In addition to their own numbers, the Sioux were assisted throughout the campaign by a heavy contingent of northern Cheyenne warriors from Nebraska, who were thus repaying the debt they owed for help rendered them by the Sioux when, in 1868, under Roman Nose, they were opposing the building of the Union Pacific.

2. *On the Border With Crook* by John G. Bourke also published by Leonaur.

Crazy Horse was well aware that other troops were moving against his people from Fort Lincoln and Fort Ellis. With strategical skill of a quite uncommon quality, he availed himself of his interior lines to fight his opponents in detail. After defeating Crook's column and rendering it, at least for the time, incapable of further offensive movement, he quickly put his army in motion for the other hostile camps on the Little Big Horn, and united with them in time to be in at the death when Custer was crushed eight days later.

CHAPTER 30

Custer to the Front

Having outlined the movements of the co-operating forces up to the time of the appearance on the field of General Terry's column, we may now turn to the latter, as it was with this body that Captain Marsh was chiefly identified. By reason of the terrible disaster which overwhelmed it at the climax of the campaign, Terry's column has received far more attention from historians and been the subject of more popular interest, than any other of the strategical units in the operations of 1876. Though the record of its movements stands out so prominently as to quite overshadow those of the others, this force was smaller in point of numbers than that of Crook. The greater part of it assembled at Fort Lincoln, early in May and consisted of the entire twelve troops of the 7th Cavalry, under Lieut.-Col. George A. Custer, two companies of the 17th and one of the 6th Infantry, forty Ree scouts and a battery of three Gatling guns, manned by soldiers of the 20th Infantry and commanded by Lieutenant Low of that regiment.

One battalion of the 6th Infantry, comprising Companies B, C, D, and I, under Maj. Orlando H. Moore, was to join them on the Yellowstone, the entire expedition being under Brigadier-General Terry, commanding the Department of Dakota. Most of the 7th Cavalry had been in garrison at Forts Lincoln and Rice during the preceding winter, while the infantry companies had been occupying other of the river posts. General Sheridan was loath to withdraw so many men from these garrisons, as it left several of the forts almost defenceless, but the need was so urgent for dealing the hostiles a decisive blow that he felt it imperative to put every available man into the field. The force, without Moore, was 950 strong.

A strange feeling of foreboding seemed to hover over the frontier that spring. Though no one knew positively that the Indians in the field were any more numerous than they had been for years past, mysterious excitement prevailed among those about the agencies, and a few observant persons noticed as the spring wore on that the able-bodied young warriors grew daily less numerous in these peaceful camps, while the old men and the women and children remained as before. But the soldiers who were to march to the Yellowstone laughed at such disquieting rumours, for, as always, they felt themselves amply able to deal with any hostile force in existence.

A short time before the expedition was to start, General Custer and his wife returned to Fort Lincoln from the East, where they had been spending the winter, and he resumed command of his regiment. The 7th was in splendid fighting trim when, with the battery, it marched out from Fort Lincoln on the morning of May 17th, bound for the Yellowstone at the mouth of the Powder. Yet so great was the grief and anxiety of the wives whom officers and soldiers were leaving behind, that, in order to reassure them, Custer paraded the regiment at the post before starting. While the band played *Gary Owen*, the valorous old regimental pibroch, the troops marched around the parade ground. Yet even the sight of that magnificent body of 600 warriors but partially allayed the fears of the women, for with the unerring intuition of their sex, they felt impending evil in the air. It was with aching hearts and streaming eyes that they saw their dear ones finally ride away across the prairie, until the dust from the feet of the horses blurred them from view and the stirring strains of *The Girl I Left Behind Me*, died away into silence.

For several months before the expedition left, the troops had not received their pay. A paymaster who had come up by steamer when the river opened, accompanied the column on its first day's march and paid off the men at the evening bivouac, returning to Fort Lincoln next day. This was done in order that the soldiers might have an opportunity of saving their money, instead of spending it recklessly to their own loss and the detriment of discipline, as many of them would have done had they received it a few days earlier. Most of this money was still in their possession when the battle took place five weeks later, and a great portion of it went to swell the war fund of the Sioux, along with the other booty of the Little Big Horn's bloody field.

Perhaps it would have been better, after all, if the poor fellows who had earned it had been given a chance to spend it in a last good time, even though it passed through their fingers lightly and to little purpose. The column carried with it only provisions enough to last to the Powder, where a supply steamer had been ordered to meet it. The provisions were transported in wagons drawn by mules, and 250 pack saddles were taken along to be used on these same animals for carrying a few days' rations at a time when active campaigning should commence.

When the troops reached the Powder on June 7th, they found awaiting them the steamer *Far West,* under Captain Grant Marsh, which had proceeded there from Stanley's Stockade in obedience to orders sent ahead by General Terry. How Captain Marsh with the *Far West,* instead of his own steamer *Josephine,* came to be at the Powder, and the events preceding his arrival there, form a separate chapter in the chronicles of that memorable summer.

CHAPTER 31

The Heroine of the Upper River

Thus far in its eventful history, every steamboat which had braved the perils of the upper Yellowstone had been commanded by Captain Marsh. He had consequently acquired an intimate acquaintance with the changeful stream not possessed by other navigators, and it was but natural that General Sheridan should look to him to command the supply boat when plans were being formulated for the campaign of 1876. Early in the spring the General notified Captain Marsh, through Commodore Coulson, that his services would be required and requested him to select a steamer adapted to the work ahead.

After thoroughly considering the situation, the captain decided that of the several boats of the Coulson Packet Company at his disposal, the *Far West* would be the most suitable. She was not so comfortable nor commodious a craft as the *Josephine,* but she possessed ample freight carrying capacity together with light draught, and the fact that she could accommodate but few passengers was one of his chief reasons for selecting her. He knew that he was setting out upon a summer of arduous work, during which the boat would be obliged to remain in close touch with the troops in the field and he did not wish to be burdened with many passengers for whose safety and comfort he would have to be responsible.

From previous experience he knew that more or less wounded men would probably have to be accommodated from time to time, whose presence would inconvenience any idle pleasure seekers on board. The absence of a large cabin furthermore rendered the *Far West* a very manageable boat in the high winds which often prevailed in northern Dakota and Montana during the summer months, for it had no *Texas* and its short upper works offered little resistance to the wind.

The *Far West* had been built for the Coulsons at Pittsburg in 1870. She was 190 feet long, 33 feet beam and her draught, when loaded to her full capacity of 400 tons,[1] was 4 feet, 6 inches, while unloaded she drew 20 inches. Thirty passengers were all her cabin could accommodate. Her motive power consisted of two fifteen-inch diameter engines of five-foot piston stroke, built by the Herbertson Engine Works of Brownsville, Pa., and she carried three boilers. She was also provided with two steam capstans, one on each side of the bow, being the first boat ever built with more than one, though afterwards all Missouri River steamers were similarly equipped. Light, strong and speedy, she was eminently a vessel for hard and continuous service. During her long tour of duty that summer the Government paid $360.00 per day for her use.

At Yankton, where the *Far West* had spent the winter, she began loading with Government stores for Fort Lincoln and the troops in the field as soon as she could be brought to the levee after the ice went out, and with a full cargo she left Yankton about the middle of May. Her officers, who remained with her throughout the summer, were as follows: Grant Marsh, captain and pilot; Dave Campbell, pilot; Ben Thompson, mate; George Foulk and John Hardy, engineers; and Walter Burleigh, clerk. The trip to Fort Lincoln was quick and uneventful, and she reached the post on May 27th, to find that the expedition had started for the Yellowstone ten days before.

The few persons remaining at the fort, including the families of the absent troops, hailed the appearance of the boat with rejoicing. It was the first break in the monotony of their existence since the departure of the column, and the day of her arrival was treated by them as a holiday. The wives of the officers in Custer's regiment all came down to the river and made themselves at home on the boat while she was unloading, as was customary at the isolated frontier posts. Captain Marsh was busy throughout the morning superintending the discharge of cargo, but he instructed the steward to prepare as dainty a luncheon as the larder of the boat would afford, and spread it in the small cabin for the ladies.

When informed of this pleasant attention, they were much pleased and accepted it gratefully. Before they took their seats, Mrs. Custer sent to Captain Marsh an invitation to preside at the table, which he, being very busy, had not intended doing. But he heeded her urgent

---

1. The Quartermaster General's report for 1876-77 gives her exact tonnage as 397.81 tons.

Steamer *Far West*. The heroine of the upper river.

(The spars so frequently called into use in navigating the upper Missouri and the Yellowstone are seen, suspended, upright, near the bow. When Reno's wounded were carried down to Fort Lincoln, they were disposed on the main deck beneath the cabin, at the point where the after wood-pile appears in the photograph.)

request and, hastily making himself as presentable as possible, joined them at the board. Mrs. Custer and Mrs. Algernon E. Smith, wife of a lieutenant in the 7th, with whom Captain Marsh was unacquainted, seated themselves beside him and were at particular pains to treat him cordially. When the agreeable meal was concluded and the captain was about to withdraw, Mrs. Custer and Mrs. Smith took him aside and asked him if they might accompany the boat to the Yellowstone, Mrs. Custer[2] stating that her husband had authorized her to go if Captain Marsh was willing.

The captain was much taken aback at this request, as under the circumstances he believed that such a trip would be both dangerous and uncomfortable for them. He pointed this out, showing them how limited were the accommodations of the *Far West* and what inconveniences they would have to put up with. As they still remained undiscouraged, he at last fell back upon a feeble subterfuge and mendaciously expressed regret that he had not brought his own comfortable boat, the *Josephine,* declaring that if he had, he would gladly take them along. Finally seeing that it would be impossible to gain his consent, the ladies reluctantly gave up their plan, though with evident disappointment. It was well that the captain stood firm, for had he yielded to their wishes through a mistaken sense of courtesy and allowed them to go, all the heart-breaking suspense and horror of those days so soon to follow, might well have bereft them of reason.

During the afternoon the supplies waiting at the fort for the cavalry were taken on board, consisting of forage such as oats and bran, commissary goods, medical supplies, tents, tarpaulins and other quartermaster's stores, and small arms ammunition. The total weight of the new cargo was about 200 tons, as much as it was safe to carry into the Yellowstone, since it brought the boat to a draught of thirty inches or more. The next morning the *Far West* started up the river. At Fort Buford the escort came on board, consisting of Company B of the 6th infantry; Captain Stephen Baker, commanding, and John A. Carlin, 1st Lieutenant. The company numbered about sixty men, and they made their quarters as usual on the main deck, the officers taking cabins above. The other three companies of the battalion, under Major Moore, had already marched up the east bank of the Yellowstone for Stanley's Stockade. The *Far West* at once followed, and in a few days reached the rendezvous to find Major Moore and his command al-

---

2. *Tenting on the Plains, Following the Guidon* and *Boots and Saddles* by Elizabeth Custer all published by Leonaur.

ready encamped there.

The major had received despatches from General Gibbon, who was coming down the left bank of the river, and on the arrival of the Far West he forwarded them, as well as one from himself, to General Terry. His courier travelled eastward along the old Stanley trail and encountered Terry just west of the Little Missouri, still several days' march from the Yellowstone. Learning from the despatches the location of Gibbon and also that the supply steamer had arrived, Terry diverted the march of his troops up the valley of Beaver Creek toward the mouth of the Powder, where the junction with Gibbon could be sooner accomplished, and sent back instructions to Major Moore to have the *Far West* meet him there. Captain Marsh proceeded thither, and tied to the bank on the 7th of June.

Toward evening of that day, several skiffs were seen floating down the river. Upon sighting the steamer they pulled in and were found to contain Major Brisbin, Captain Clifford and others of Gibbon's command—Captain Clifford carrying despatches for General Terry. They had floated thirty or forty miles, meeting no Indians on their journey. The next morning while the crew were engaged in cutting wood, a body of horsemen was discerned rapidly approaching through the valley of the Powder. When they drew up on the bank they proved to be General Terry and his staff escorted by two troops of cavalry, who had ridden down in advance of the main column, leaving the latter in camp about twenty miles up the Powder. The General immediately came on board to make his headquarters, and he gave Captain Marsh a cordial welcome, congratulating him on his prompt arrival. After reading Captain Clifford's despatches, Terry sent couriers to Gibbon with orders to leave his command and himself come down to meet the boat, which would steam up until he was encountered.

The following morning the *Far West* got under way and went up until she reached a point about fifteen miles below the mouth of Tongue River where a trooper hailed her from the shore. She came in and General Gibbon was found, accompanied by cavalry and the company of twenty-five mounted Crow Indians, who, under Lieut. J. H. Bradley, had served him efficiently as scouts during his march from Fort Ellis. The two generals who had so long been planning for the junction now successfully accomplished, greeted each other at the bow of the *Far West* and then repaired to the cabin to discuss future movements. Finding that Gibbon's main body was resting but a short distance above, General Terry instructed Captain Marsh to steam up to their camping place.

This was reached about noon and Terry invited all the officers on board, where a reunion affording opportunity for pleasant exchange of experiences occurred between them and the members of Terry's staff. After lying at the camp for some two hours, Gibbon and his officers took their leave and the boat returned to the Powder, where Terry also left for Custer's camp, after instructing Captain Marsh to return to Stanley's Stockade and bring all the supplies there up to the Powder, where a new depot was to be established. He also sent orders to Major Moore to bring his troops to the same point. By the 15th of June, Captain Marsh had accomplished these transfers and held his boat at the Powder, ready for further work.

It would be hard to estimate from a military standpoint the value of the services already rendered to the troops in the field by the *Far West,* slight as they had been compared with those which she was to render later in the campaign. In the many accounts which have been written of that summer of battle, the share of the *Far West* in the work has been little dwelt upon unless we except that spectacular portion of it immediately following the disaster on the Little Big Horn. Yet throughout the season she was constantly employed in duties of the utmost importance. She maintained a communication between the scattered bodies of troops operating on opposite sides of an unfordable river which otherwise could hardly have been maintained at all; on several occasions she transferred a base of supply from one point to another, miles distant, in a fraction of the time which a wagon-train would have required, and frequently she was called upon to ferry from shore to shore, or to transport up and down stream, troops which, without her, could not have been brought to the positions where they were needed.

Difficult as was campaigning in that sterile country, it would have been infinitely more difficult if a steamer had not been at hand, ready for any kind of work at a moment's notice. The *Far West* was used in a half-dozen different capacities by the army during its months in the field; as ferry-boat, despatch-boat, patrol-boat, gun-boat, transport, or hospital-ship, each as occasion demanded, and in herself she demonstrated perfectly how valuable even a single unit of floating transportation, under an intelligent and obedient commander, may be made to an expeditionary force.

CHAPTER 32

Strong Men and True

On the morning of June 11th, from the camp of the 7th Cavalry in Powder River Valley, Maj. Marcus A. Reno with six troops, and ten days' rations on pack mules, set out to reconnoitre the country south of the Yellowstone from the Powder to the Tongue, in search of Indian trails. North of the Yellowstone, Gibbon's men were toiling back over the road they had come, delayed by heavy rains, but still bent upon their purpose of holding back the enemy from crossing if he should become alarmed by the movements of the other troops. When the *Far West* reached the depot at the Powder after her last trip from Stanley's Stockade, she found that Terry and Custer, with the remaining six troops of the 7th, had come down during her absence.

Along the river bank, where a few days before unbroken silence had reigned, now resounded the voices of hundreds of men, the trampling of horses and all the busy hum of a great military encampment. General Terry resumed his headquarters on the boat and for the next few days it became the centre of activity of the whole campaign. Back and forth across its decks hurried officers and soldiers, Indian scouts and white frontiersmen, whose names stand in history and story for courage, strength and loyalty.

Among them all, the dominating figure was that of General Terry himself. Quiet and undemonstrative, he sat hour after hour at his desk in the cabin, poring over maps and papers, consulting with the officers who came and went, working with an energy which seemed tireless upon the innumerable problems of the campaign he was conducting. The calm eyes which looked forth from his strong, bearded face inspired in the observer a sense of confidence and security. His brain seemed one capable of grasping so firmly every phase of the situation, of guarding so carefully against every danger, that his plans could not miscarry. The military impulses of his nature were tempered and strengthened by the legal acumen derived from his years of practice at the bar, for Terry had not been a soldier from his youth.

At the outbreak of the Civil War he had resided in Connecticut, where he was a practising attorney, and he had entered the Union army as a volunteer in one of the first regiments organized by that State. There was little about him to suggest such a spirit of reckless heroism as he had displayed on that January afternoon in 1865 when he led his division forward through the shattered palisade and across the yawning ditch of Fort Fisher, fighting hand-to-hand over the traverses and through the casemates, until he had planted the flag of the Union above the greatest earthwork fortress that the modern world had ever known. He was a man whose words were not many, but, once spoken, they were remembered. When he praised, the praise was merited; when he censured, it was for grave cause. Though he was not one whose characteristics suggested the ideal Indian fighter, he wove a plan of campaign against the savage foe in his front which was almost faultless in conception, and when it was jeopardized by an appalling disaster in execution, he skilfully gathered together again its broken threads and brought it ultimately to success.

Far different in appearance and temperament from the commanding general was that other noted leader who was a frequent visitor on board the *Far West* during those days. Indeed, so strongly did the brilliant record and romantic personality of Custer appeal to the imaginations of the bold spirits gathered in the warrior camp, that his presence nearly overshadowed that of his chief. Custer's tent was pitched on the river bank but a few feet away from the *Far West* and he was on the boat almost hourly, dressed in his picturesque modification of the regulation uniform, with flowing red tie, wide-collared campaign shirt and broad felt hat; a costume the graceful abandon of which made him seem half soldier and half the border scout. He was a figure to attract attention anywhere. His form was straight and slender, his speech quick, his movements restless. He had been disappointed when he first heard of the arrival of the *Far West* to find that his wife was not on board, but he did not permit this to affect his pleasant relations with Captain Marsh, whose reasons for not bringing her he well understood.

It was noticeable at this time that Custer's usually buoyant spirits were somewhat depressed, for he was suffering under the displeasure of several persons high in National authority. When, during the previous year, the campaign had first been planned, it was intended that Custer should have chief command of the eastern column. But during the winter, while visiting in Washington, he had become involved in a difficulty with President Grant and Secretary of War Belknap. In consequence of it the President, in the spring of 1876, was on the point of withholding him from any participation in the campaign. But at the earnest solicitations of General Sheridan and General Terry, who felt his services to be indispensable, he was permitted to command his own regiment, though not the entire column. The wound thus inflicted upon his proudly sensitive spirit caused him to be more eager even than usual to win fresh laurels on the battlefield and, it has often been urged, contributed in no small degree to the impetuosity with which he flung himself upon the enemy at the first opportunity.

To the *Far West* often came also General Custer's brother, Captain Tom Custer, as well as Captains Keogh and Yates, Lieutenant Calhoun, and others of those gallant troop officers who, a few days later, were destined to fall with smoking revolvers clutched in their dying hands, on the barren ridges above the Little Big Horn. Maj. James S. Brisbin, Gibbon's commander of cavalry, was another visitor to the boat at different times throughout the summer. He was an elderly officer, whose deep interest in the agricultural possibilities of eastern Montana, constantly manifested in conversation, earned for him from the soldiers the good-natured sobriquet of "Grasshopper Jim."

In addition to the professional soldiers there were a number of others as brave, though they did not wear the uniform of the regular service. There was Frank Girard, the noted scout; there was "Lonesome Charlie" Reynolds, the remarkable guide and hunter who had done such good work on the *Josephine* during the previous summer. The latter was Custer's favourite scout and the general relied upon his judgement implicitly. There was Mark Kellogg, the correspondent representing the Bismarck *Tribune,* and, through that paper, also the New York *Herald,* a faithful worker and graphic writer, whose detailed descriptions of events up to the time of the battle in which he fell close beside Custer, are now among the most reliable data in existence on the history of that campaign. Kellogg boarded the *Far West* at Bismarck and was the guest of Captain Marsh on the up trip, making his quarters on the boat until the columns separated on June 22nd. Charlie Reynolds also occupied a cabin until that day, for he was suffering great pain from a felon on his left hand, and was under the care of Doctor Porter, one of the surgeons of the 7th Cavalry.

As always, General Custer had brought guests with him from the East who were anxious to see and enjoy the wild West under his skilful guidance. This time they were his nephew, Autie Reed, and his younger brother, Boston. The latter, a light-hearted, companionable young fellow whom everyone affectionately called "Boss," became a great friend of Captain Marsh after they met at Powder River, and the captain offered him a cabin and asked him to remain on the boat as long as he wished. "Boss" gladly accepted the invitation, for it was cold comfort sleeping under a dog-tent on the prairie through the chill Montana nights.

Of Captain Marsh himself, who so often welcomed to the decks of his vessel the members of this famous company, a few appreciative words from General Edward S. Godfrey, U. S. A.,[1] lately commandant of the School of Application for Cavalry and Field Artillery, Fort Riley, Kansas, but at that time one of Custer's troop commanders, may be fittingly inserted here as indicating the place which the captain held among his associates during those busy weeks of preparation.

> He was, indeed, a familiar figure, (says General Godfrey), and his presence was always welcomed in any gathering of the officers at their bivouacs and on board his boat. When he was at leisure he was sure to be surrounded by a crowd, to each of whom he was a friend and companion. He was bluff, frank, *original,* honest and generous. He was intense, or, in modern parlance, strenuous. In all that pertained to his boat and crew he looked to their best interest; there was no trifling. When he was in the employ of the government, and he generally was on these expeditions, he never hesitated in any emergency to take all chances to serve it, and his rare good judgement carried him and his charges through many a tight place. Of course, he knew the government was behind him.

---

1. Contained in a recent letter to the author.

CHAPTER 33

The Last Council of War

On the morning of the 15th, General Custer, with his six troops and one Gatling gun, marched for the Tongue, leaving Major Moore at the Powder with the infantry and all the wagons. Custer took with him a train of pack mules loaded with provisions, while the *Far West,* carrying an ample reserve supply, followed up the river, with General Terry and staff on board. The cavalry reached the Tongue on the 16th, where the boat rejoined, and all remained until the 19th, impatiently waiting for news from Reno. While they were lying there through the 17th, Crook was fighting his stubborn battle on the Rosebud, though, of course, no one in Custer's camp knew of it or could dream that one hundred miles away events were transpiring which would so deeply affect their own fate.

The news from Reno came about sunset of the 19th, in the form of a despatch in which he stated that he had scouted to the Rosebud and beyond and had found a heavy Indian trail. After following it until he was satisfied that it led to the Big Horn, he had left it and swung off to the Rosebud again, descending that stream to its mouth, from which point he was now returning to the Tongue. General Terry at once sent an order to him to halt and await the arrival of Custer with the remainder of the regiment. The latter resumed its march westward that night and after reuniting with Reno, the whole command bivouacked at the mouth of the Rosebud on the morning of the 21st. Across the Yellowstone, General Gibbon's troops were lying in the camp which they had been occupying for over a week, sending out patrols along the left shore and scouts along the right, and waiting for the *Far West* to arrive and place them in communication with General Terry.

The information now at hand, gathered by Reno and by Gibbon's

WHERE RENO CROSSED.

scouts, seemed to indicate that not more than eight hundred or a thousand warriors were in the hostile camps. Lieutenant Bradley with his untiring Crows, scouting through the hills along the Rosebud on May 27th, had discovered a Sioux village of several hundred lodges whose occupants were engaged in hunting, as was amply evident from the number of buffalo carcasses scattered over the country from which the hides had been stripped for lodge skins. Major Reno, three weeks later, had come upon the same camping place, finding it abandoned. But he had counted nearly 400 extinct lodge fires, indicating that the village had contained about 800 warriors upon the usual calculation of two men to each lodge. From the deserted camp led the trail which he had followed toward the Big Horn.

Since neither Reno nor Bradley had discovered other camps, General Terry, as well as his subordinates, concluded that this body of hostiles was the only one in the country and he made his dispositions accordingly. The event proved his conclusion to be very far from correct, but he had no means of knowing it. It was at about this time that General Sheridan forwarded him advices that nearly 1,800 lodges had departed for the Big Horn country from the Missouri River agencies,[1] but Terry did not receive them until some days after the Little Big Horn battle, nor did he hear until that time of Crook's defeat on the headwaters of the Rosebud. Hence he could not imagine that another Sioux army had joined the one already in his front, and much less that the enemy was now led by a general capable of grasping fully the advantages of interior lines for defeating his opponents in detail; the same advantages which were seized by Napoleon before Paris and by "Stonewall" Jackson in the Valley of Virginia.

The main position of the Sioux, however, was now approximately located, the expeditionary columns were united, and everything was ready for the striking of that swift and decisive blow which was the object of the campaign. The activity on board the *Far West* was redoubled. Captain Marsh had started from the Tongue with General Terry when the cavalry left there and he outstripped them, reaching the Rosebud on the morning of the 21st, early. The boat landed at Gibbon's camp and took that officer on board for a conference to be

---

1. In his *Century* article, General Godfrey said: "Information was despatched from General Sheridan that from one agency alone about eighteen hundred lodges had set out to join the hostile camp." General Godfrey has advised the author, however, that this was "a camp rumour. Sheridan's despatch, I believe, was that about eighteen hundred lodges had been reported absent from the agencies."—J. M. H.

held between himself, Terry and Custer as soon as the latter should be up, while Gibbon's troops were immediately put in motion toward the mouth of the Big Horn, their commander intending to join them later. About noon the long line of the 7th Cavalry appeared, marching across the tableland and into the valley, where it halted. The boat crossed to their camp and toward evening General Custer came on board.

Then ensued in the cabin of the *Far West* that memorable council of war between the three veteran generals at which were determined the details of the offensive movement against the hostiles. Gibbon's command was to continue the march already begun up the north bank of the Yellowstone until it should reach a point opposite the mouth of the Big Horn, where it would halt and wait for the boat. The latter was then to ferry it across after which it would move up the Big Horn to co-operate with Custer in attacking the Indian villages. On his part, Custer was to march up the Rosebud until he found the trail discovered by Reno. This he was to follow westward, scouting carefully to his right and left for signs of Indians, and to so time his movements that he would reach the immediate vicinity of the enemy on the Big Horn about the 26th, at which time it was expected that Gibbon would have arrived in the same neighbourhood from the north. The written orders given to General Custer by General Terry after the conference on the *Far West,* though they have been so often quoted before as to be familiar to every student of that campaign, may be referred to again as most clearly indicating what he was expected to accomplish. They were as follows:

> Camp at Mouth of Rosebud River, Montana Territory,
> June 22nd, 1876.

Lieutenant-Colonel Custer, 7th Cavalry.

Colonel:—

The Brigadier-General commanding directs that, as soon as your regiment can be made ready for the march, you will proceed up the Rosebud in pursuit of the Indians whose trail was discovered by Major Reno a few days since. It is, of course, impossible to give you any definite instructions in regard to this movement, and were it not impossible to do so the Department Commander places too much confidence in your zeal, energy, and ability to wish to impose upon you precise orders which might hamper your action when nearly in contact with the enemy. He will, however, indicate to you his own views of what your action should be, and he desires that you should conform to them unless you shall see sufficient reason for departing from them.

He thinks that you should proceed up the Rosebud until you ascertain definitely the direction in which the trail above spoken of leads. Should it be found (as it appears almost certain that it will be found) to turn towards the Little Horn, he thinks that you should still proceed southward, perhaps as far as the headwaters of the Tongue, and then turn towards the Little Horn, feeling constantly, however, to your left, so as to preclude the possibility of the escape of the Indians to the south or southeast by passing around your left flank. The column of Colonel Gibbon is now in motion for the mouth of the Big Horn. As soon as it reaches that point it will cross the Yellowstone and move up at least as far as the forks of the Big and Little Horns. Of course, its future movements must be controlled by circumstances as they arise, but it is hoped that the Indians, if upon the Little Horn, may be so nearly enclosed by the two columns that their escape will be impossible.

The Department Commander desires that on your way up the Rosebud you should thoroughly examine the upper part of Tulloch's Creek, and that you should endeavour to send a scout through to Colonel Gibbon's column, with information of the result of your examination. The lower part of this creek will be examined by a detachment from Colonel Gibbon's command. The supply steamer will be pushed up the Big Horn as far as the forks if the river is found to be navigable for that distance, and the Department Commander, who will accompany the column of Colonel Gibbon, desires you to report to him there not later than the expiration of the time for which your troops are rationed, unless in the meantime you receive further orders.

Very respectfully, your obedient servant,
E W. Smith,
Captain 18th Infantry
Acting Assistant Adjutant-General.

It is not desired here to enter into any discussion of the unfortunate controversy which has been waged by various authorities ever since the battle of the Little Big Horn, as to whether General Custer did or did not obey these orders. But the opinion of Captain Marsh on the subject is worthy of record because he was entirely familiar with conditions at the time of Custer's departure and, though he was not present at the conference in the cabin, he was, of course, on the boat and immediately afterwards gathered from officers the general purport of the plans laid.

General Terry, in a subsequent official report, said that during the conference he verbally informed Custer that Gibbon's column would probably reach the mouth of the Little Big Horn on June 26th. Captain Marsh is firmly of the opinion that Terry did not desire nor intend Custer to give battle to the Indians before that date. Indeed, after the disastrous culmination of the movement, General Terry personally told the captain that such was the case, and both he and General Gibbon have so stated in their official reports of the campaign.

Lieut. James H. Bradley[2] has voiced in his journal the sentiment then current in the camps of both Gibbon and Custer, relative to the intentions of the latter officer. Writing in this journal, or diary, on Wednesday, June 21st, he says:

> ...though it is General Terry's expectation that we will arrive in the neighbourhood of the Sioux village about the same time and assist each other in the attack, it is understood that if Custer arrives first he is at liberty to attack at once if he deems prudent. We have little hope of being in at the death, as Custer will undoubtedly exert himself to the utmost to get there first and win all the laurels for himself and his regiment. He is provided with Indian scouts, but from the superior knowledge possessed by the Crows of the country he is to traverse it was decided to furnish him with a part of ours, and I was directed to make a detail for that purpose. I selected my six best men, and they joined him at the mouth of the Rosebud. Our guide, Mitch

---

2. Lieutenant Bradley's Journal has been constantly referred to in the preparation of the account of the Little Big Horn campaign. The *Journal*, which has been published in Vol. 2 of the *Contributions to the Historical Society of Montana*, contains a detailed record of the movements of General Gibbon's column from the time it left Fort Ellis until it arrived on Custer's battlefield. It teems with interesting notes upon the early history of Montana and of the Indian tribes residing therein. lieutenant Bradley, who was killed in the battle of the Big Hole, Montana, in 1877, was a gallant soldier, a keen observer and a graphic writer, and his literary works, though left in a very incomplete state by his untimely death, are yet among Montana's most valuable historical documents.—J. M. H.

Bouyer,[3] accompanies him also. This leaves us wholly without a guide, while Custer has one of the very best that the country affords. Surely he is being afforded every facility to make a successful pursuit. . . .

At the conference, Gibbon's four troops of the 2nd Cavalry, under Major Brisbin, were offered to Custer. He refused them, stating that any Indian force which would be too big for the 7th Cavalry would be too big for the 7th Cavalry and these four troops. He was urged to take the three Gatling guns under Lieutenant Low, which, though already across the river and moving up to join Gibbon, could have been easily recalled had Custer so elected. He declined them, declaring that they would only impede his movements. The conference lasted until late in the evening and at its conclusion Terry and Gibbon walked out with Custer to his tent, which was pitched near by, where they remained only a few minutes, returning to sleep in their cabins.

As soon as they had departed, Custer caused officer's call to be sounded, and when his staff and line were assembled he gave them their instructions. These were to have the pack mules carry fifteen days' rations and fifty rounds of reserve carbine ammunition for each man. Every trooper was to carry one hundred rounds of carbine and twenty-four rounds of pistol ammunition in his saddlebags and twelve pounds of oats for his horse. The general seemed in an irritable frame of mind that night, and Lieutenant Godfrey, commanding K Troop, has the following to say concerning his further instructions: [4]

> The pack-mules sent out with Reno's command were badly used up, and promised seriously to embarrass the expedition. General Custer recommended that some extra forage be carried on the pack-mules. In endeavouring to carry out this recommendation some troop commanders foresaw the difficulties, and told the general that some of the mules would certainly break down, especially if the extra forage was packed. He re-

---

3. Bouyer was one of the noted characters of Montana's early mining days, he was a man perfectly reckless of danger, as was made plain one day during Gibbon's march down the Yellowstone. A party of about a dozen Sioux warriors appeared on the opposite bank of the river, without, however, discovering Gibbon's men. Bouyer stripped himself naked and, unarmed, swam the river to attempt the capture of some of the Indians' horses. He had almost succeeded when they detected him creeping up, but he made his escape as he had come, unharmed.—J. M. H.

4. *Custer's Last Battle,* by General Edward S. Godfrey, U. S. A., *Century Magazine,* Vol. 43, No. 3.

plied in an excited manner, quite unusual with him:

'Well, gentlemen, you may carry what supplies you please; you will be held responsible for your companies. The extra forage was only a suggestion, but this fact bear in mind, we will follow the trail for fifteen days unless we catch them before that time expires, no matter how far it may take us from our base of supplies; we may not see the supply steamer again,' and, turning as he was about to enter his tent, he added, 'You had better carry along an extra supply of salt; we may have to live on horse meat before we get through.'

He was taken at his word, and an extra supply of salt was carried.[5]

---

5. General Godfrey, in reading the manuscript of the above chapter, noted that himself and Captain Myles Moylan, Troop A, were the troop commanders who held with General Custer the conversation regarding the extra forage and salt.—J. M. H.

CHAPTER 34

The Seventh Marches Into the Shadow

The supplies for the 7th Cavalry were drawn from the hold of the *Far West* early on the morning of Thursday, June 22nd. It was a beautiful morning, that one of Custer's start; such a morning as only the high plateaus of the Northwest, with their sweeping winds and invigorating air, can yield. Over the valley and the rugged hills beyond, the sparse vegetation of bunch grass and prickly pear took on the appearance of velvet verdure until the rough buttes in the distance resembled well-kept terraces. Here and there on the bottom groups of buffalo grazed quietly, while the swift-running Yellowstone sparkled and flashed over its gravelly bed and between its wooded islands, like a mountain torrent. The cavalry camp on the river bank seemed a puny thing and its activities insignificant in the vast tranquillity of nature.

Hours before sunrise Captain Marsh was about directing the discharge of cargo and keeping his thirty deckhands rushing, and when, at the first streaks of dawn, the bugles' echoing reveille roused the sleeping soldiers, the fifteen days' supplies were ready for issue on the bank. After the bustle of breakfast was over the camp quieted for a few hours, while the men arranged their belongings for the hard march ahead. A number, including the officers, seized the opportunity for writing letters to dear ones at home. For many of them, alas, these were to be the last messages of love they would ever send on earth.

Though the morning was glorious, and though the soldiers were veterans, accustomed to hail the approach of action with enthusiasm, strangely enough a sense of depression seemed to pervade the camp and not a few of the letters voiced this feeling. It was as if a premonition of coming catastrophe was in the men's hearts which they could not shake off. General Custer himself was affected by it and so were many of his officers. It is only fair to say, however, that the dejected spirits of several of the gallant cavalrymen may have resulted from a more substantial cause than premonition of coming ill. This is mere conjecture, but the fact remains that through the small hours of the previous night, more than one of them had remained awake to attend a meeting of absorbing interest in the cabin of the *Far West*. Captain Marsh was there, also Captain Tom Custer, Lieutenant Calhoun, Captain Crowell, of the 6th Infantry, and others, and the matter which kept them from their blankets on the eve of a hard campaign was one which rarely fails in its attraction to an American—poker.

It had been a battle royal between the different arms of the service, with fortune varying from one side of the table to the other. Now the cavalry leaped ahead, as if emulating the rush of squadrons on the battlefield; now the navy, as represented by Captain Marsh, swept all before it. But in the end the steady, plodding infantry was left in sole possession of the field, as so often happens in actual warfare, and Captain Crowell arose from the board a winner by several thousand dollars. Perhaps the thought of the perils they were about to face tended to make the participants reckless, but, be that as it may, Captain Marsh remembers that poker game on the eve of the Little Big Horn campaign as one of the stiffest ever played on the rivers, and he has witnessed some wherein fortunes were won and lost.

Once during the morning, while busy about his manifold duties, the captain came face to face with Charlie Reynolds. The features of the scout were haggard with pain and the captain asked him solicitously how the felon was on his hand.

"No better," answered Reynolds. "Doctor Porter can't seem to cure it and my hand is no use."

"See here, Charlie," exclaimed the captain, "I wish you would give up going with General Custer and stay on the boat. It will be a hard march for you in your condition, and you can't do any fighting, anyway, with that hand."

The gallant fellow flushed and straightened. "Captain," he said, earnestly, "I've been waiting and getting ready for this expedition for two years and I would sooner be dead than miss it."

It was useless to argue with such a spirit and when the column left, Captain Marsh regretfully saw Reynolds start with it, never to return.

Another friend whom he wished to save from the rigours of the march was Boss Custer. Passing the boy's cabin during the morning the captain saw him writing a letter to his mother, and stepped in. He talked for a few moments, pointing out to Boss what an exhausting journey was ahead of the 7th Cavalry, and telling him how welcome he would be if he would remain on the boat, as General Terry and General Gibbon were going to do for the present.

The captain also reminded him that he owed it to his mother to take care of himself, and that the march his brother was about to undertake would not be without many dangers. The result of these persuasions was that Boss decided to remain on the boat. He hastened to finish his letter home, as a skiff was to go down the river with the mail at noon. He then stepped ashore, telling Captain Marsh that he was going to say goodbye to his brother, get some tobacco at the commissary tent and would then be back. A few moments later, the captain passed General Custer's tent. The general was writing, and called out:

"Captain, "Boss" tells me he is going with you."

"Yes," answered the captain, "he has decided to."

"I am glad of that," returned the general. "But I am afraid he will eat you out of house and home."

Nevertheless, despite the fact that his brother wished him to remain on the *Far West,* the prospect for excitement was evidently too much for the boy. He did not return to the boat but went with the ill-fated column, and Captain Marsh never saw his young friend again.

At noon, every preparation having been made, the 7th Cavalry was formed and marched out of camp, passing in review before Generals Terry and Gibbon as it went. When the last sturdy troop had swept by, fit from fetlock to campaign hat for any work ahead, Custer turned with a flash in his eyes of the old, imperious pride which he always felt in his regiment, gripped the hands of Gibbon and Terry in a last, strong farewell, then touched his horse and galloped after the column, never to be seen again by the world whose applause he had so often nobly earned. General Gibbon has recorded that he said to Custer as the latter left them:

"Now, Custer, don't be greedy, but wait for us."

And the brave cavalryman called back: "No, I will not"; an ambiguous answer which might have been intended to apply to either part of Gibbon's caution.

With Custer's column rode, in addition to the 585 enlisted men and thirty-one officers of the 7th Cavalry, Autie Reed, Boston Custer, and Mark Kellogg, civilians; Charlie Reynolds, Mitch Bouyer, Frank

Girard, and two other white scouts, and twenty-five Arikaree and six Crow scouts, the latter being the ones detailed from Gibbon's command.

Immediately after the column had started, the letters written by the troops that morning, together with the others which had accumulated since they had left Fort Lincoln, were gathered by Captain Marsh and placed in a mail-sack to be conveyed to Fort Buford by skiff. Sergeant Fox and two privates of the escort were detailed by Captain Baker to carry the precious cargo down. Amid a chorus of hearty goodbyes from the people on the steamer, they started out. But they were totally unfamiliar with the handling of a small boat in the swirling current of the Yellowstone. Before they had gone fifty feet their skiff overturned. There, in full view of their comrades, who could not reach them in time to save, all three of the unfortunate fellows sank from sight, while the mail sack went to the bottom of the river.

When he saw the skiff go over, Captain Marsh put off boats with all speed, but by the time they reached the spot the soldiers were drowned. He then sent back to the steamer for boat-hooks and began dragging the river for the bodies and for the mail-pouch, though the army officers all discouraged the idea, believing nothing could be recovered. But the captain persisted, being especially anxious to find the mail, in which he knew was General Custer's last letter to his wife, and Boston's to his mother. He was too familiar with the perils of Indian warfare not to be conscious that some, at least, of those whose letters were in that pouch would probably fall during the next few days.

At length his patient efforts were rewarded, and a shout went up as the dripping pouch was hauled to the surface. It was taken back to the *Far West* and the letters spread out on the upper deck and dried. Not one was missing. They were then put back in the sack and a second start made with more experienced men, the skiff this time reaching its destination at Fort Buford without mishap. The bodies of none of the original party were ever recovered. In such times as those considerations of safety caused mails to be sent by water rather than overland, whenever possible. A large escort would be necessary as protection against Indians for the overland trip, while the few men required to handle a boat could hide themselves during the day time along the banks and make many miles progress every night, aided by the rapid current.

CHAPTER 35

The Messenger of Disaster

The despatch of the mail consumed most of the afternoon, and the *Far West* did not get away after Gibbon's command until the next morning, her departure leaving the camp-ground at the Rosebud deserted. When he did start, Captain Marsh ran slowly, and the troops had not yet been overhauled when darkness again compelled him to tie up. By four o'clock on the morning of the 24th he was off again and a half-hour later the boat steamed past the night's bivouac of Gibbon's infantry. But she did not stop, keeping on by the mouth of the Big Horn to the cavalry camp, two miles above old Fort Pease. The infantry soon came up to the same point and immediately after its arrival, eight days' rations were issued from the boat to the entire force for its march up the Big Horn.

At eleven o'clock Captain Marsh carried across the river, twelve Crow scouts, who, finding a recent Sioux trail, disappeared up the valley of Tullock's Fork, a small affluent of the Big Horn entering the latter near its mouth. About noon the boat began ferrying the troops over. General Gibbon had been taken severely ill on the up trip and was still confined to his cabin, unable to move, so General Terry superintended the passage. The cavalry crossed on the first three trips, Bradley's Crow scouts, Low's battery and part of the infantry on the fourth, and the remainder of the infantry on the fifth, all being over by four o'clock. The only force now left on the north bank was Company B, of the 7th Infantry, Captain Kirtland, which remained to guard the wagon-train.

General Gibbon being still too sick to leave the boat, the column started without him, marching about four miles up Tullock's Fork, where camp was made for the night. The following morning, before daybreak, Captain Burnett, of Gibbon's staff, came to Captain Marsh bearing orders from General Terry that the *Far West* attempt the ascent of the Big Horn, for the purpose of having reserve supplies within reach of the troops. The captain had not received any previous intimation that it was desired to push the boat up this stream, but though he saw that it would be a very difficult undertaking, he did not shrink from it. Ordering out all the crew to cut wood he kept them at this work until noon, by which time a good supply of fuel had been accumulated. Then he started.

The task assigned to the *Far West* was no ordinary one and probably no steamboat was ever called upon to contend with more obstacles. The river flowed through an extremely tortuous channel, obstructed with innumerable small islands and sandbars, taxing the pilot's dexterity to the utmost. The boat had scarcely more than cleared the mouth before rapids were encountered which she could not stem with her wheel alone. So the soldiers were put ashore and sent up the bank, carrying one end of a long warping cable. This they would wrap securely around a large tree, while the other end of the rope was fastened to one of the boat's capstans. The latter was then put in motion, rolling up the rope and dragging the boat slowly forward.

Now and then she reached a bit of smoother water where she could steam for a few hundred yards. Then another rapid would be met with and the whole process repeated. At times the river was found so swift and shallow that a party was put off on each shore with a rope and both capstans worked, the boat thus being pulled along in midstream. This method had never before been employed, for the breadth of most navigable streams would render it impracticable.

Through all that long, hot Sunday afternoon of June 25th the soldiers and the crew, sweating and weary, coaxed and hauled their cumbersome charge up the mountain stream, past dark, overhanging cliffs and through ranges of broken and naked bad lands. Throughout the day heavy columns of smoke were visible rolling up along the distant southern horizon. Everyone knew that they probably betokened the presence of the Sioux villages. But of the terrible scenes being enacted beneath the shadow of those smoke clouds during the early hours of the afternoon no one on the *Far West* could dream.

Nothing had been heard from Custer since he left the Rosebud, but nothing was expected yet. Terry's troops were now moving steadily up the east side of the Big Horn among the hills, having crossed over the watershed from Tullock's Fork. They had been delayed by encountering very rough bad lands, but the infantry camped about twenty-five miles up the Big Horn that night and the *Far West* stopped near them. General Terry, who had also observed the smoke clouds, pushed on with the cavalry through the night, endeavouring to reach the Little Big Horn.

It seemed as if the *Far West* had gone about as far as would be possible, but before dawn of the 26th Captain Burnett again appeared with orders that the boat endeavour to reach the mouth of the Little Big Horn. General Terry instructed Captain Marsh in making the attempt not to pass any point where the water was less than three feet deep, lest the river fall and imprison the boat, and he further directed that, in case the Little Big Horn could not be reached, the boat return to the point where the orders were received and there await further instructions. General Gibbon by this time was sufficiently recovered to be able to travel and before the *Far West* started he set out after the cavalry advance, which the infantry also soon followed.

During the forenoon the men on the steamer repeated their labours of the previous day and about twelve o'clock they were rewarded by arriving at the mouth of a considerable creek entering the Big Horn on the east. From the descriptions he had heard of the stream, as well as from the fact that for twenty miles up the east bank of the Big Horn ahead not a break appeared in the smooth crests of the bluffs to indicate an entering tributary, Captain Marsh was certain that this was the Little Big Horn. But for some reason Captain Baker did not concur in his opinion. After debating the question for some time and still remaining unsatisfied, he landed his company and marched up the tributary about four miles. He returned with the definite announcement that it was not the Little Big Horn, and desired that the boat continue up the main stream. Captain Marsh said nothing more, but complied.

After proceeding about fifteen miles further without discovering any creeks, they came to a place where the channel of the river was obstructed by two islands, breaking the water into three chutes. It was necessary to learn whether any of them contained three feet of water and, having an ulterior object in view, Captain Marsh himself took charge of the yawl and rowed up to sound through the chutes. On his return he informed Captain Baker that all of the channels were too shoal to be attempted. The army officer was much disappointed but nothing was to be done save give up a further advance or else disobey General Terry's orders.

Night now coming on, the boat tied to the bank where she was, but during the evening Captain Marsh confided with a quiet chuckle to George Foulk, the engineer:

"George, there is more than three feet water between those islands, but there's no use in our going above them, for that's the Little Big Horn fifteen miles back and you can bet on it."

At dawn the boat turned about and started back. In the meantime Captain Baker, having slept over it, had begun to think that he might have been mistaken and when the boat again arrived at the stream previously explored, with his sanction she stopped. In order to keep her safe from Indian attack she was tied to the shore of an island opposite the mouth of the tributary and the crew and escort then proceeded to pass the time as pleasantly as possible until tidings should come from the column.

From where they lay the valley of the Little Big Horn, as the stream later proved in fact to be, was visible for several miles extending back among the hills. Along both its shores spread dense thickets of willow brush, while about its mouth and over the island where the boat lay, large cottonwood trees, their leaves rustling pleasantly in the summer wind, afforded shelter from the heat. The waters of the Big Horn, rippling over their gravel bed, were clear and cold and teemed with pike, salmon and channel cat-fish, which had not yet learned through sad experience to be wary of the angler's bait. A number of the men therefore cut willow poles and, scattering along the shore of the island, devoted themselves with great success to fishing. A little after ten o'clock, Captain Marsh, Engineer Foulk and Pilot Campbell, together with Captain Baker and Lieutenant Carlin, strolled out from the boat, and, selecting a spot a little removed from the others, engaged in the general pastime.

The smoke columns noticed along the southern horizon on the two previous days had disappeared now, and the general opinion was that Custer and Terry had met the enemy and routed them, so little fear was felt of an Indian surprise. Nevertheless, as they sat there, George Foulk noticed how close they were to the dense willows on the main shore and remarked to the others that it would be very easy for Indians to creep up and fire on them. They were still idly discussing the suggestion when, without the least warning, the green thickets at which they were looking, parted, and a mounted Indian warrior, of magnificent physique and stark naked save for a breech-clout, burst through and jerked up his sweating pony at the brink of the water.

The fishermen leaped to their feet with startled exclamations, but before they could run back the Indian held aloft his carbine in sign of peace. They then paused and, upon scrutinizing him more closely, recognized from his erect scalp-lock that he was a Crow, and then, to their surprise, that he was Curley, one of the scouts who had gone with Custer. They had expected to hear from Terry and Gibbon, but not from Custer. Motioning to him to come to the boat they hurried there themselves while he forded the stream and joined them.

As soon as he was on board he gave way to the most violent demonstrations of grief. Throwing himself down upon a medicine-chest on deck he began rocking to and fro, groaning and crying. For some time it was impossible to calm him. When at length he had to some extent regained his self-control, the question arose as to how to communicate with him, for no one on board could understand the Crow language, while he spoke no English, so that all efforts at conversation failed. Finally Captain Baker produced a piece of paper and a pencil and showed the Indian how to use them.

Curley grasped the pencil firmly in his fist and dropping flat on his stomach on the deck, began drawing a rude diagram, while about him the army and steamboat officers gathered closely, waiting in silent suspense for his disclosures, for everyone guessed from his actions that he brought important news. The Crow drew first a circle and then, outside of it, another. Then between the inner and outer circles he began making numerous dots, repeating as he did so in despairing accents:

"Sioux! Sioux!"

When he had quite filled the intervening space with dots, he glanced up at the intent faces around him and then slowly commenced filling the interior circle with similar marks, while his voice rose to a yet more dismal tone as he reiterated:

"*Absaroka! Absaroka!*"

"By Scotts!" exclaimed Captain Marsh, "I know what *that* means. It means soldiers. That Englishman, Courtney, who runs the woodyard at the head of Drowned Man's Rapids, told me so. One time when I was there some Crow Indians started down river from the woodyard and Courtney told me they were going to see the *Absaroka* at Camp Cooke."

He was interrupted by Curley, who suddenly sprang to his feet, faced the listeners and flung his arms wide. Then, swinging them back, he struck his breast repeatedly with his fingers, exclaiming at each blow, in imitation of rifle shots:

"*Poof! Poof! Poof! Absaroka!*"

The white men stood in tense silence, searching each other's faces. For a moment no one dared confess that he understood. Captain Baker was the first to speak:

"We're whipped!" he said, hoarsely. "That's what's the matter." And he turned away.

Curley continued his pantomime by grasping his scalp-lock with one hand while with the other he described a circle around it, then made as if to jerk it off and hang it at his belt, meantime executing a Sioux war dance. But his absorbed observers already realized that they were receiving the first news of a great battle, in which many soldiers had been surrounded, slain and scalped by the Sioux. Having learned so much as a beginning, they were able to bring the sign language into use for acquiring further particulars. It was a very slow process but, by it, in the course of hours, they gradually gathered details from Curley, each one of which added to the appalling nature of the news.[1]

According to Curley, General Custer was killed and every man who had gone into action with him, excepting the Crow himself. He did not tell of the dividing of the regiment before the battle and evidently knew nothing of Reno's survival. So far as they could understand, he was trying to tell them that the whole 7th Cavalry had been annihilated. He declared that he had been in the thick of the fight, while the soldiers, surrounded by thousands of yelling foes, were falling in scores, the survivors struggling forward blindly in vain search for some spot among the waste of broken ravines where they might make a successful defence. Some of them had used their dead horses for barricades, and the remnant of one troop, E, under Lieut. A. E. Smith, had tried to cut its way out but was utterly destroyed.

At last Curley had seen that the battle must inevitably end in the annihilation of his white friends. He had then picked up two blankets and going to General Custer, who was still unhurt and fighting desperately in the centre of his little band of heroic followers, implored him to throw one of the blankets over his head and, thus concealed, attempt under Curley's guidance to escape in the confusion through

---

1. The word *Absaroka*, which is stated above to mean *soldier*, is generally understood to be only the Crow name for their own people. But Dr. W. J McGee, formerly in charge of the Bureau of American Ethnology, Smithsonian Institution, informs the author that it has a broader meaning, which is implied quite as much as *Crows* by the Indians when they use the word. The broader meaning is difficult of literal translation, but, liberally, it is, "the great warrior people." Hence, after the Crows had grown to know and admire the white soldiers, they came to apply their own flattering tribal name to the latter, out of compliment.—J. M. H.

the madly circling masses of the Sioux. As was to be expected, the peerless soldier rejected the proposal scornfully. He had no desire save to die with his men. But he bade Curley escape if he could and the latter, with bitter grief, looking his last upon the great white chief whom he loved and honoured, tossed one of the blankets over his own head to conceal his Crow scalp-lock, and, watching an opportunity, sprang into a *mêlée* of Sioux warriors as they crowded up to kill and mutilate some of the fallen.

The last man of the soldiers whom he saw to recognize had been Lieutenant W. W. Cooke, the regimental adjutant, whose tall form and long, flowing beard were plainly visible as he stood above his fellows, firing into the faces of the foe. Gradually working to the outer edge of the Sioux hordes, Curley had ridden northward into the sheltered valley of the Little Big Horn. Here he was partially concealed and was able, by using great caution, to make his way toward the mouth of the river, where he arrived forty-four hours after the battle, though the distance was only eleven miles.

The people on the boat could scarcely believe that the Crow's story was true in all its dreadful particulars, though his grief was too genuine not to force some credence. Captain Baker, after the first shock of the intelligence, was far from being convinced and endeavoured to persuade the scout to return to Custer with a despatch telling him where the supply boat lay. But Curley refused to leave the steamer, refused to take food and retiring to a corner of the deck, squatted on his haunches and began mourning for the dead after the manner of his tribe. There was nothing to be done, therefore, but wait for the arrival of some one else from the columns with news and orders, and the men on the *Far West* passed the remainder of the day in uneasy discussion of the possibilities suggested by Curley's story.[2]

---

2. Some few historians have sought to cast discredit upon Curley's story, assuming that he did not participate in the fighting at all, but secreted himself in a ravine before it began and escaped after nightfall, when it was over. Among these is Dr. Cyrus Townsend Brady, in his generally admirable and painstaking account of Custer's last campaign, in his *Indian Fights and Fighters,* (also published by Leonaur). There is no more warrant for doubting Curley's story than there would be for doubting the story of any other man whose assertions have no witnesses to support them. Curley's reputation for veracity, both before and since the battle, has been excellent. Lieutenant Bradley had found him a reliable scout and had assigned him to duty with General Custer as one of his "six best men." The account of the fight which he gave on board the *Far West* was subsequently borne out fully in all its main features. It was the first and for a long time the only, account of Custer's battle given to white men by an eye-witness. Curley, as he declared at (continued next page)

the time, was the sole survivor of the defending force, and the only other eye-witnesses were hostiles whose stories were not gathered until years later.

The Crow had been absolutely alone from the time he left the battlefield until he reached the *Far West,* and had therefore had no opportunity for comparing notes with anyone else and thus concocting a story. He was certainly present at the fight, else he would not have known facts, which, at the hour when he must have left the vicinity of the battlefield in order to reach the boat when he did, were still unknown to either Reno's survivors or to Terry's column. Lieutenant Bradley says in his journal that the Crow scouts from Reno's command whom he, with Terry's advance, encountered on the morning of June 27th, reported that Curley had been with Custer and was undoubtedly among the killed. He was, in fact, at that moment approaching the mouth of the Little Big Horn, where he arrived at 11 o'clock a. m. The sketch drawn by Curley on a piece of paper with Captain Baker's pencil, showing how Custer and his men were surrounded and killed by the Sioux, was extremely crude. But it presented the crucial features of the battle accurately, and antedated by more than eighteen years the drawing made by Rain-in-the-Face on the back of a hunting-shirt, in August, 1894, which has been frequently heralded as the first and only map of the field of the Little Big Horn ever drawn by an Indian participant.—J. M. H.

After reading the above footnote regarding Curley's story, General Godfrey wrote to the author: "Chief Gall pooh-pooh'd Curley's story of escape, said it was impossible for him to disguise and escape in the fight, and that he probably saw the fight from the high ridge north and made up his story."

Such may, of course, have been the case. But it must be remembered that Gall was a Sioux and hated the Crows as the hereditary foes of his people. He would naturally be loath to credit one of them with any act of bravery; savages are prone to voice contempt for their enemies, whether they feel it or not. Moreover, of the three Crow scouts who were with Custer in the battle, Lieutenant Bradley states that Curley's two comrades, White Swan and Half Yellow Face, were killed with Custer's men, while the other three, who were with Reno, remained with him and fought throughout the engagement, according to General Godfrey's *Century* article, though the twenty-odd Arikaree scouts fled ignominiously at almost the first fire of the Sioux and did not stop running until they reached Major Moore's camp at the mouth of the Powder, It seems reasonable to suppose that Curley was at least as resolute as his five companions, and that he went into the fight as they did and stayed in it until he saw that his only chance for life lay in escaping quickly.—J. M. H.

CHAPTER 36

The Squadron That Perished

The gray twilight of dawn was just creeping over the valley when the men of the *Far West* were roused from slumber by a sudden sputter of rifle fire, part close at hand and part far distant. Rushing out on deck, they found their boat guards firing excitedly, while from the hills to northward a single horseman could be seen galloping furiously into the dim valley of the Little Big Horn. He was waving his arms in frantic signals to the boat, but turning in his saddle every moment to fire into the faces of a party of Indians who were riding hard behind him. No sooner had the pursuers caught sight of the *Far West* than they gave up the chase and, wheeling off to the left, vanished again among the hills, while their intended victim came in unharmed.

He proved to be Muggins Taylor, one of Gibbon's scouts, on his way to Fort Ellis with despatches from his commander. He had set out for Captain Kirtland's camp on the Yellowstone, travelling along the Big Horn—Tullock's Fork watershed, but on his way had been discovered by Indians and compelled to run for his life. Though he had little hope of finding safety there, he had ridden in desperation toward the mouth of the Little Big Horn and by good fortune alone had chanced to stumble on the boat. Had he not done so he would soon have been killed, for his horse was completely winded and could not have borne him much farther.

As soon as he had recovered somewhat from his fatigue, Taylor gave them the first account of the battle they had received from a white man. He told of the difficult march of Terry's troops up the Little Big Horn and of their horrifying discovery, early on the morning of the 27th, of the hillsides on Custer's battlefield, strewn with the mutilated bodies of the slain, each bearing the Sioux death-mark, a slit to the bone from hip to knee. Custer was there and with him his whole family: Captain Tom, Boston, and Autie Reed. Poor Kellogg, the Bismarck *Tribune* correspondent, was there, his portfolio of manuscript on the events of the campaign still lying beside his body.

Then he told of the subsequent discovery of the exhausted remnant of the 7th Cavalry under Major Reno, who had lain for thirty-six hours on a barren hilltop, assailed by thousands of savages, blistered by the sun and half mad with thirst, barricaded with the putrefying carcasses of their dead horses and pack mules, and their position littered with dead comrades, and wounded who raved for the water which for many hours could not be obtained for them. Learning of the approach of Terry on the morning of the 27th, the Indians, he said, had raised the siege and retreated toward the Big Horn Mountains, taking their vast villages with them. The recital seemed appalling almost past belief, but it was only too true. Taylor was made comfortable on the *Far West*, having himself decided that, in view of his experience, it would be unwise for him to proceed alone on his journey with the hostiles so numerous in the vicinity. The boat's company, plunged into inexpressible gloom by his tidings, confirming the earlier ones brought by Curley, settled down to wait for whatever part they were to play in the later scenes of the drama of defeat.

From the mass of accurate and detailed information which has since been gathered concerning them, the operations of General Custer's command after it left the Rosebud may be briefly summarized, since some knowledge of them is necessary to a complete understanding of the later movements in the theatre of war. On the afternoon of the 22nd of June, Custer marched twelve miles and went into camp at four o'clock p.m. After a long night's rest, at five a.m. on the 23rd he moved forward again, marched thirty-three miles and camped at five in the afternoon in the valley of the Rosebud. On the 24th he marched twenty-eight miles between sunrise and sunset, halting often to permit of the scouts thoroughly examining the valley of Tullock's Fork to his right.

About midnight, after some four hours' rest, he started his command for the divide between the Rosebud and Big Horn valleys, about twenty miles distant, informing his officers that he wished to conceal the column near the divide and spend the day, the 25th, in reconnoitring the enemy's position, preparatory to attacking it on the 26th. The divide was reached at 10:30 in the morning and the troops dismounted in a ravine. These facts, given by Gen. Edward S. Godfrey,

U. S. A.,[1] who, as first lieutenant commanding Troop K, was present with the 7th Cavalry throughout the campaign, make it evident that Custer did not unduly hasten his march nor bring his men or his animals up to the Little Big Horn in an exhausted condition.

Shortly after reaching the divide, Sioux scouts were observed making deliberate inspection of the command from adjacent eminences, and it became obvious that its presence was discovered and that further attempts at concealment would be useless. The general therefore ordered his troops forward for immediate attack upon the Indian village to prevent the latter from scattering and making its escape. The regiment was divided into three battalions; the first, consisting of five troops, under General Custer himself; the second, of three troops and a company of Arikaree scouts, under Major Reno; and the third, of three troops, under Captain Benteen. One troop, under Captain McDougall, was detailed to guard the pack-train.

Benteen was instructed to move to the left and strike the Little Big Horn several miles above the supposed location of the village, in order to cut the latter off from the Big Horn Mountains. Reno was ordered to move straight ahead, cross the river immediately above the village and attack it from the south. Custer himself was to support Reno's attack. Benteen marched on his prescribed course for some miles and then was forced out of it by the ruggedness of the country into the trail of Reno. The latter, meanwhile, had gone ahead as ordered, passing down the face of the bluffs and across the river into the valley above the village. Here, encountering the enemy, he deployed.

His advance was shortly checked by the vigorous resistance of the Indians, who developed in far stronger force than was expected. Reno did not "charge the village," as ordered, but retired to a strip of timber along the river where he dismounted his men and stood his ground for a time. Then, growing faint-hearted, he retreated precipitately to the steep bluffs of the east bank, permitting his troops to become disorganized and panic-stricken in the movement and suffering heavy loss. The Indians who had been opposing him, relieved by his retreat of the immediate necessity of watching him, hurried northward across the river and joined with those who were just coming into contact with the advance of Custer.

The latter, after following Reno for some time, had moved off to the right with the evident intention of supporting Reno by a flank

---

1. In his *Century* article previously cited.

attack on the village from the east.² He finally reached a point where the valley of the river lay spread out below him. From this position, occupied just previous to his deployment, Custer could observe through breaks in the bluffs a number of the Indian lodges, though it is evident that, even then, he had no conception of the real extent of the Sioux encampments. Stirred at the sight, he had the adjutant despatch a messenger, Trumpeter Morton (or Martini), the last who went through, with the following hastily scrawled order to Captain Benteen:

> Benteen, come on. Big village. Be quick. Bring packs.
> P. (S.) Bring pac's. W.W. Cook.³

Relying upon Reno's vigorous co-operation, and not knowing that the latter was already suffering, or had suffered, a repulse, Custer then deployed for attack and went forward. In the broken and precipitous hills bordering the east bank of the river he was immediately

---

2. If there was any excuse for Reno's failure to press his attack vigorously, it lay in his misinterpreting what Custer meant by saying that he (Custer) would support him. He may have been disconcerted, after coming into action, by finding that Custer's battalion was not right behind him. General Godfrey has written to the author:
"Don't forget that Custer told Reno that the whole outfit would *follow* and *support* him. Reno had the advance, and Custer did follow to a point near the Little Big Horn and *then* branched off to the *right,* but that was not premeditated."
If Custer had assured Reno that he would *follow* the latter in order to support him, then the latter's misgivings may have been somewhat justified when he did not find Custer in his rear. It is, perhaps, a new point in Reno's favour. General Godfrey, in his *Century* article, wrote simply:
"Reno's command and the scouts followed them" (a few scattering Indians) "closely, until he received orders 'to move forward at as rapid a gait as he thought prudent, and charge the village afterwards, and the whole outfit would support him.'"
That Custer followed the spirit of his arrangement with Reno when he moved off to the right, Dr. Cyrus Townsend Brady succinctly demonstrates when he says, in *Indian Fights and Fighters,* (also published by Leonaur):
"Reno mistook the purpose of Custer's statement. In order to support an attack, it is not necessary to get behind it. A flank attack or a demonstration in force, from some other direction, frequently may be the best method of supporting an attack. Custer's plan was entirely simple. Reno was to attack the end of the village. Benteen was to sweep around and fall on the left of it, Custer on the right."
Custer, attended by his staff, appeared on the bluffs on the east side of the river and to Reno's right, after the latter had crossed the river and entered the bottom and just before he became engaged. Custer waved his hat toward them encouragingly and then disappeared, and Reno must have known from the incident that Custer was moving down river for a flank attack.—J. M. H.
3. Official report of Capt. F.W. Benteen.

assailed by practically all the Indians of the immense camp at once; by those streaming up from Reno's front as well as by those already on the east side. His struggle could not have lasted long; he was overwhelmed and wiped out.

All the Indians then returned to the attack on Reno, who had meantime been joined by Benteen and McDougall. They held these seven troops closely besieged until the evening of the following day, when, evidently aware of the approach of Terry up the valley, they raised the investment and retreated with all their impedimenta toward the Big Horn Mountains. Before they left they fired the grass in the bottoms to conceal their movements as much as possible behind the smoke clouds, but as they moved off in the red glow of sunset, Major Reno[4] declared that "the length of the column was full equal to that of a large division of the cavalry corps of the army of the Potomac, as I have seen it on its march."

With Custer died twelve other officers, 191 enlisted men and four civilians. Reno lost three officers, forty-eight men and five civilians and scouts killed, and fifty-nine wounded, of whom seven died on the field. As has been stated, Custer expected to encounter between 1,000 and 1,500 warriors, certainly not more than the latter number. He actually did encounter more nearly 3,000, and they were simply too many for his force. The Indians generally were much better armed than the soldiers, whose carbines, in addition to being of short range, had defective shell-ejectors which were always liable to clog during rapid firing and which, in the action, undoubtedly rendered many of the weapons useless.

In the hostile camps was a total of at least 12,000 souls, possibly 15,000,[5] consisting of Indians of the Uncpapa tribe under chiefs Gall, Crow King and Black Moon; of the Sans Arcs under Spotted Eagle; of the Minneconjoux under Hump; of the Brule; of the Northern Cheyenne, allied with the Sioux for this campaign, under White Bull, Two Moons and Little Horse; and of the Ogalalla under Crazy Horse, Big Road and Low Dog. The warriors of the latter tribe had joined the main camp shortly before the battle, their trail from the field where they had fought Crook on June 17th being found by Gibbon after the relief of Reno. Among all the chiefs engaged at the Little Big Horn, the real leaders were Crow King, Gall, and Crazy Horse. The

---

4. In his official report of the battle, Secretary of War, 1876-77.
5. *Custer's Last Battle*, by Wm. S. Brackett, in *Contributions to the Historical Society of Montana*, Vol. 4.

renowned Sitting Bull, though nearby, is said to have taken no part in the fight.

The Indians themselves esteemed him something of a coward, though they feared his power as a medicine man. During the battle he was *making medicine* in the village and afterwards, of course, he declared the Indian victory to be due solely to the strength of his necromancy. As usual, the superstitious savages believed him and his prestige received a corresponding increase.

Sitting Bull

CHAPTER 37

The Aftermath of Battle

Toward evening of the 28th, Henry Bostwick and another scout from Terry arrived at the *Far West*. They had been looking for the boat and had followed the Big Horn down for some distance in their search. They reported the general very solicitous concerning the safety and whereabouts of the steamer, as his supplies were nearly exhausted and most of Custer's pack animals had been killed in the fight on Reno's hill. Scouts had previously been sent, on the 26th, to find the boat, but had failed because she was up river on Captain Baker's mistaken quest, while they had searched for her at the mouth of the Little Big Horn and lower down. Bostwick and his companion at once returned to Terry with the information of her position and the next morning two more scouts reached her with orders that she be made ready to carry the wounded down to Fort Lincoln.

Here, at last, was something active to be done; the long period of idle waiting was over. The messengers reported that over half a hundred wounded were being borne down the valley from Reno's field. The crew and soldiers under Captains Marsh and Baker sprang to work with a will to prepare the steamer for their coming. The boilers of the *Far West* stood near the bow and between them and the stern was a wide, open space where Baker's men had made their quarters. This was turned into a hospital, and under directions from Doctor Williams, the army surgeon on board, the floor was completely covered to a depth of eighteen inches with fresh grass cut from the low marsh lands along the river. When it had been spread, enough new tarpaulins were taken from the quartermaster's stores on board to carpet the whole like an immense mattress. Around the sides were arranged the medicine chests, ready for use. After all was completed, Doctor Williams declared it to be the best field hospital he had ever seen.

Meantime, the men who were escorting the wounded down were having a hard time in the rough country along the Little Big Horn. During the greater part of the 28th, all the troops on the scene of battle had been engaged in *burying* the dead and in making litters with which to transport the wounded to the boat. An ingenious officer of the 2nd Cavalry, Lieut. G. C. Doane, undertook to construct mule litters out of the crude materials available. Two lodge poles taken from the abandoned hostile camp were used for each litter, and a piece of tent canvas was stretched between them and fastened with bits of rawhide and rope. They were then slung between two mules, but the animals proved so intractable that the attempt was abandoned and the wounded were placed on hand litters similarly made of canvas and lodge poles.

With the hand litters two troops of the 2nd Cavalry, acting as bearers in relays, started down the river about sunset. But so slow and exhausting was their progress through the rough country that they had covered less than five miles by midnight, and were then forced to stop. The next day, while the rest of the troops were destroying the abandoned property in the Sioux camps, Lieutenant Doane and his assistants resumed the construction of mule litters and by evening had built enough to accommodate all the wounded. A careful selection was made of the most docile mules in the train to carry them and the escort with their pathetic charges again started at six o'clock in the evening, four men accompanying each litter to keep the mules in order.

All worked so well now that instead of making the short march expected it was determined to attempt to reach the steamer that night in order that the suffering men might be placed in a comfortable resting place and given proper medical attention as soon as possible.[1] The night was dark and stormy and the way very rough, but about midnight they came to the low, marshy land some three miles above the mouth of the stream, where they found themselves unable to go on in the darkness.

But here they came upon some steamboat men who had been sent out by Captain Marsh when he saw the cavalcade approaching at dusk. They carried word to the boat of the condition of affairs, and Captain Marsh instantly ordered out his entire crew to build fires at frequent intervals along the trail and light the train forward. With such

---

1. Gen. John Gibbon in his official report of the campaign, Secretary of War, 1876-77.

timely assistance the march was resumed, and at two o'clock the head of the column, looming weirdly through the darkness in the flickering firelight, approached the boat. Here a hundred willing hands tenderly received the stricken men and placed them in rows on the grass-covered deck, where the surgeons, Doctors Williams and H. R. Porter, set about examining and dressing their wounds. There were fifty-two injured men brought on board.

Doctor Porter, who had come with them from the battlefield, was the only surviving surgeon of the three who had gone out with the 7th Cavalry. Doctor Lord had been killed with Custer, Doctor De Wolf with Reno, and Doctor Porter himself had accompanied the latter's command. When Reno's hurried flight from the bottom began, Porter was ministering to a dying soldier, and his experience in escaping was afterwards described in the following graphic language by a Western newspaper:[2]

> Porter was by the side of a dying soldier. His orderly and supplies were gone, and the command was off several hundred yards. He was alone. Bullets were piercing the trees and a terrific yell was sounding the alarm of universal death. Porter left his lost patient and led his horse to the embankment that protected the woods. He was startled by Indians dashing by him within ten feet. They were rushing along the foot of the little bluff. Their aim was so directed in the line of the flying battalion that Porter's presence was unnoticed. He was unarmed, and his powerful black horse reared and plunged as if he was mad. Porter saw the fate that was in the immediate future if that horse escaped before he was on his back.
>
> He held on with superhuman strength. He could hold him, but that was all. To gain the saddle seemed a forlorn hope. Leap after leap with the horse quicker than he. It was a brief ordeal, but in the face of death it was a terrible one. One supreme effort and, half in his saddle, the dusky charger bore away his master like the wind. He gained the full seat, and lying close upon his saviour's neck, was running a gauntlet where the chances of death were a thousand to one. The Indians were quick to see the lone rider and a storm of leaden hail fell around him. He had no control of his horse. It was only a half-mile dash, but it was a wild one. The horse was frenzied. He reached the river in

---

2. The *St. Paul Pioneer-Press*.

a minute and rushed up the bluff, where Reno had gone, and was then recovering himself. The horse and rider were safe.

All through that afternoon and the fearful hours of the next day, Doctor Porter had worked over the wounded and dying with unremitting heroism and total disregard for his own safety. After Terry's relief had come he still continued his devoted services, which did not cease even after his charges were safely on the boat. He was a man of Spartan mould, whose splendid adherence to duty has not often been equalled in medical history. When he came on board the *Far West,* Captain Marsh met him, and, after wringing his hand and congratulating him on his own escape, inquired anxiously for Charlie Reynolds.

"Captain," answered the doctor, sorrowfully, "Charlie Reynolds is dead. He fell at my side. I was tending a dying soldier in a clump of bushes, just before the retreat to the bluffs, when it happened. The bullets were flying, and Reynolds noticed that the Indians were making a special target of me, though I didn't know it. He sprang up and cried: 'Doctor, the Indians are shooting at you!' I turned to look and in the same instant saw him throw up his hands and fall, shot through the heart."[3]

It was sad news to the captain, who had learned a deep regard for the brave and modest scout during the years of their acquaintance. But there was no time to be wasted in grief that night, for a hundred duties called, and the captain turned away to look after the accommodation of another passenger brought down with the wounded, whose housing, in the now crowded condition of the boat, was no easy problem. The passenger in question was a horse, but with such tender interest and affection was he already regarded by every man on board that they

---

3. To obtain further particulars of Reynolds' death, the author wrote to Major Luther R. Hare, U. S. A., who, as a Second Lieutenant of the 7th Cavalry, was second in command of the company of Arikaree scouts under Lieutenant Charles A. Varnum, at the Little Big Horn. Major Hare replied, in part, as follows: "I saw him" (Reynolds) "after his death and my recollection is that he was buried by the detail that I was in charge of, or it may have been done by the detail that Wallace had charge of, for we were working together. At any rate he was killed in the bottom and buried there. I have no recollection of any conversation with Doctor Porter in regard to Reynolds' death. I saw him several times during the fight in the bottom and, of course, noticed and was impressed by his wonderful coolness and apparent indifference to the warm fire that was being poured in on us. It was my first fight and my recollections of such men as Benteen, Godfrey and Reynolds have flashed across my mind in startling vividness in the beginning of every engagement in which I have since been present."—J. M. H.

would almost rather have been left behind themselves than to have had him deserted. He had been the sole living thing found on the Custer field, two days after the battle.

Lieutenant Nolan, of Captain M.W. Keogh's troop, I, who had been on detached service with Terry's staff, was with the men gathering together the dead and discovered the horse standing in a ravine, covered with bullet and arrow wounds and half-dead from loss of blood. He was instantly recognized as Comanche, the *claybank sorrel* charger of Captain Keogh,[4] who, with his whole troop, had perished in the fight. Lieutenant Nolan caused the animal's wounds to be dressed as well as possible and brought him to the boat. Captain Marsh at length found a place for Comanche at the extreme stern of the *Far West*, between the rudders. Here a stall softly bedded with grass was made for him and his care and welfare became the special duty of the whole boat's company.

With the main column, which arrived at the river bank not long after the wounded, came a civilian contract veterinary surgeon, whom Captain Marsh describes as "the worst scared man I ever saw." The terror of the Indians had entered his soul, but the captain induced him by forcible persuasions to control his fears sufficiently to extract the bullets and arrow-heads from Comanche's body and to dress his wounds thoroughly. The horse began to mend rapidly, and reached Fort Lincoln in safety. After the 7th Cavalry returned from the field, special orders were issued regarding Comanche, by which he was made the particular charge of the regiment. It was ordered that from that time forth no one should ever ride him. One man from Troop I was detailed as his keeper, to feed and care for him and to lead him, bridled and saddled and draped in black, on all dress parades and other occasions of regimental ceremony. Wherever the 7th Cavalry went, Comanche went with it, first to Fort Meade, Dakota, in 1879; and then, in 1888, to Fort Riley, Kansas. When, at last, his time came, more than twelve years after the battle in which he bore so distinguished a part, Comanche died full of years and honours.

The wounded had scarcely been cared for on that early morning

---

4. General Godfrey writes to the author: "Comanche belonged to his" (Keogh's) "troop I, and was ridden by Captain Keogh when General Sully made his expedition against the southern Indians in September, 1868, to the Sand Hills on the North Fork of the Canadian, where Camp Supply was afterwards located. On that expedition the horse was wounded under Keogh during one of the many fights he had. Keogh christened him 'Comanche,' and always after that rode him in the field."—J. M. H.

First monument on the Custer battlefield in course of construction.

Graves of unknown dead on the Custer battlefield

of the 30th of June, when General Terry and his staff and Major Brisbin, travel-stained, weary, and utterly depressed by the events of the past few days, arrived at the boat and re-established headquarters on board, General Gibbon now being near the bank also with his own troops and the remains of the 7th Cavalry under Major Reno. The troops were to march down to the mouth of the Big Horn and rations for the journey were issued to them from the boat.

Dawn was now breaking and it was time for the *Far West* to start on the first stage of her long trip to Fort Lincoln, where the wounded were to be brought as soon as steam could carry them. Plenty of fuel had been stored up during the days of idleness, everything was ready and Captain Marsh was just preparing to have the lines cast off when he received a message asking him to come to General Terry's cabin. He found the general alone and, as he entered, Terry arose and closed the door. Then, turning, Terry said to him, with great earnestness:

> Captain, you are about to start on a trip with fifty-two wounded men on your boat. This is a bad river to navigate and accidents are liable to happen. I wish to ask of you that you use all the skill you possess, all the caution you can command, to make the journey safely. Captain, you have on board the most precious cargo a boat ever carried. Every soldier here who is suffering with wounds is the victim of a terrible blunder; a sad and terrible blunder.

The last words were spoken with a depth of emotion surprising to the captain, who had never seen his usually self-controlled commander so strongly moved. But the contrast to his usual manner only served to make his speech the more impressive. With equal feeling Captain Marsh assured him that he would use his best efforts to complete the journey successfully. He then left the cabin and returned to the pilot-house.

It was now full daylight. Down on the main deck George Foulk stood by his levers, waiting for the pilot's bell to start the engines. But as Captain Marsh stepped into the pilot-house and put his hand on the familiar spokes of the steering-wheel, a strange weakness such as he had never before felt, swept over him and he dared not pull the bell cord. He leaned back against the wall and looked out over the narrow river, rushing between the main bank and the islands below, while into his mind came the vision of all the helpless men lying on the decks under him. The thought that all their lives were depending on his skill alone, the sense of his fearful responsibility, flashed upon him and for a moment overwhelmed him. It seemed that he could never turn the boat in that restricted channel and head her down past the island. Dave Campbell and Mate Ben Thompson were sitting on the pilot's bench behind him. He turned to them, saying, weakly:

"Boys, I can't do it. I'll smash her up."

"Oh, no, you won't," answered Campbell, reassuringly. "You're excited. Cool off a minute and you'll be all right."

The captain took his advice. After a moment which seemed an hour, his strength began to return and presently he pulled the bell cord. The boat swung slowly around, headed down, clearing the island nicely, and after he had gotten her straightened out and had crossed a couple of bends, the captain recovered his composure. But he declares that never again does he want to experience such a sickening sensation of utter helplessness as gripped him that morning in the pilothouse of the *Far West*.

Aided by the swift current, the boat covered the fifty-three miles to the Yellowstone with all the speed it was safe to give her, dodging in and out among the Big Horn's multitude of islands, which the captain knew only from having passed them once before. It is said that a river pilot only half knows his river when he has run it but one way, for the landmarks he passes going up bear a totally unfamiliar aspect when seen again going down. But on that 30th of June, 1876, the *Far West* was brought safely through all the pitfalls of the Big Horn, and late in the afternoon tied up to the bank of the Yellowstone where Gibbon's wagon-train was parked.

From here, the next morning, Muggins Taylor left for his long, lonely ride of 175 miles to Fort Ellis, with the despatches of General Gibbon, General Terry intending to send his official announcement of the disaster down to Bismarck by the *Far West* for transmission to division headquarters. The young clerk of the *For West,* Walter Burleigh, was very anxious to accompany Taylor, but the captain dissuaded him, as the trip would by no means be without danger from roving parties of Sioux.

First headboard over the grave of Lieutenant James G. Surgis, 7th Cavalry on the Custer Battlefield.

First monument on the Custer Battlefield

CHAPTER 38

The "Far West" Races With Death

Though every instinct of humanity demanded that the suffering wounded be taken to Fort Lincoln without delay, military necessity required the *Far West* to await Gibbon's troops at the mouth of the Big Horn, whence they were to be ferried across to the north bank of the Yellowstone for rest and refitting. After their rough experience they were in no condition to continue the campaign and, even had they been in condition, the disaster to the 7th Cavalry had demonstrated that they would have to be heavily re-enforced before they would be able to deal effectively with the unexpected strength of the hostiles. The boat lay at the bank through Saturday and Sunday, July 1st and 2nd, waiting for the column. On Sunday evening it at last appeared and the next morning was carried over, leaving the south side of the river temporarily abandoned, save for the distant forces of Crook, from whom not a word had been received and whose whereabouts were a subject of grave speculation.

From the capacious hold of the *Far West,* Gibbons' men were furnished with many supplies of which they stood in immediate need. But she could not replace the pack-mules or the cavalry horses killed in action, whose loss had paralysed the column as an offensive force. When all the troops had been taken over to the north bank, Captain Baker's company of the 6th Infantry was relieved from duty on the steamer and put ashore also, General Terry having determined to concentrate all his available forces in the camp opposite the Big Horn. In pursuance of his plan, he soon sent orders to Major Moore to evacuate his position at the mouth of the Powder and march up to the main camp. The places of Captain Baker's men on the boat were partly filled by seventeen dismounted troopers of the 7th Cavalry, who had lost their horses in the battle. The cavalrymen came aboard in a rather indefinite capacity.

Without their mounts they were temporarily useless in the field and were permitted, though not ordered, to accompany the steamer to Fort Lincoln, since they could be of assistance in caring for their wounded comrades. They were from several different troops and had no officially appointed commander, though virtually they were in charge of the senior non-commissioned officer among them, Sergt. M. C. Caddie. Under his leadership they not only rendered good hospital service but aided Captain Marsh greatly by helping with the wooding and by performing other work on the boat not required of them as military duty, but for which they cheerfully volunteered.

By the time the *Far West* was ready to start down the river fourteen of the wounded men were so far recovered as to be able to remain at the camp. They went ashore, as did General Terry and Major Brisbin, and at five o'clock on the afternoon of July 3rd the steamer, followed by the cheers and fervent good wishes of the assembled troops, backed away from the bank and started her paddles for Bismarck and Fort Lincoln, 700 miles away. Thirty-eight sorely wounded soldiers were still in her deck hospital, and in her cabin travelled Capt. E. W. Smith, *aide-de-camp* to General Terry, on his way to Bismarck with despatches for Division Headquarters at Chicago, and carrying, besides, a bag full of letters from other members of the expedition and a great number of messages to be put on the wire for distant friends.

The boat had scarcely left the bank before she was under full head of steam. There was to be no tying up for darkness that night. Captain Marsh's orders were to reach Bismarck in the shortest possible time and, as always, he took them literally. Every man on board was steeled to do his utmost and nobly each performed his part. The river was fortunately high, but, even so, it was perilous work driving a steamboat at top speed down such a channel. Through the hours of the short midsummer night and the glaring sunlight of the next day the *Far West* rushed on, Foulk and John Hardy crowding on the steam until a glance at the gauge turned them dizzy; Marsh and Campbell, in four-hour reliefs *on the roof*, holding the wheel with iron grip as they strained their eyes over the narrow channel ahead and spun the boat in and out between islands and rocks.

On the *Far West* few thoughts were given to the significance of the day, that Fourth of July. Thousands of miles away in the palaces of the Centennial Exposition at Philadelphia, vast throngs were bidding wel-

First monument over the grave of Captain Myles W. Keogh on the Custer battlefield.

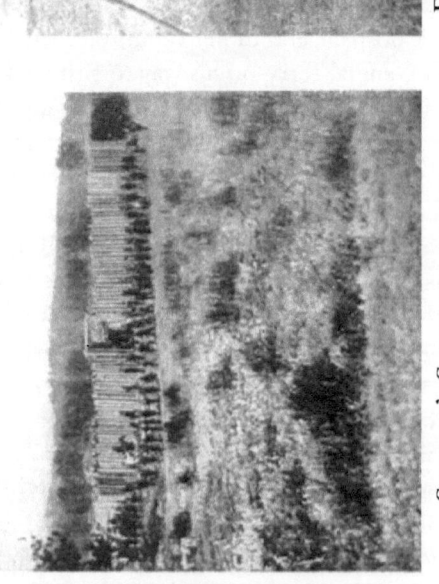

Stanley's Stockade on the Yellowstone, 1873

come to the one hundredth anniversary of the Nation's birth. From the peaceful hamlets nestled among New England's hills to the mining camps of the Sierra Nevada, the freemen of Columbia were giving themselves over to joyous celebration of the great event. Yet surely nowhere beneath the shadow of the Stars and Stripes were men engaged in more patriotic duty than those who trod the decks of the *Far West*. From bow to stern her timbers were quivering to the incessant clang and cough of the machinery as shirtless firemen, sweating and grimy, stood before the furnaces, cramming fuel into the hungry flames.

Now and then the hoarse bellow of the whistle sent its echoes reverberating along the bald cliff sides, startling the grazing herds of buffalo and elk to wild stampede from the fiery monster that came tearing, like a demon of destruction, into their solitudes. Now and then the keel scraped along a projecting bar and sheered off violently, throwing the men to the deck like tenpins. A hundred times it seemed as if she would be dashed to pieces, but each time the skill of the pilots saved her and she sped on with her message of disaster to a waiting nation and her burden of suffering humanity groaning for relief. General Godfrey says of the run of the *Far West:* "I remember how thrilled we were to hear Colonel Smith, assistant adjutant-general of the expedition, when relating his experiences of the down river trip; how the boat would skim over a bar; how, in turning a bend, the treacherous current would push her bow over so as to run her nose into the bank, but more often would carrom her hull against it. But Grant Marsh never hesitated to take reasonable chances to save distance or to make speed, and he made good."

The heroic Doctor Porter, working without interruption, lost one of his patients in the early morning hours of the 4th, Private William George, of H Troop, shot through the left side on Reno's Hill. At Powder River the boat stopped long enough to have his body interred and to confirm the news of battle to Major Moore's little garrison, still encamped there, who had hardly believed Reno's stampeded Arikaree scouts. Then, after taking on board the private property of the officers killed on the Little Big Horn, which had been left at the Powder with the wagons, she was off again. Near old Stanley's Stockade she passed the *Josephine,* Captain Mart Coulson, upward bound with supplies for Terry's column, but the *Far West* merely hailed as they hauled abreast without abating her speed.

Then out of the Yellowstone she shot into the Missouri, whose channel seemed spacious indeed after the mountain stream she had been threading. At Fort Buford there was a momentary stop to put off a wounded Arikaree scout. The garrison went wild with excitement. Men crowded upon the boat, shouting and begging for news. Their questions were not half answered when they were cleared from the decks and the boat was out in the stream again. At Fort Stevenson, during the afternoon of the 5th, she halted once more, and again leaving a garrison convulsed with unsatisfied anxiety, she leaped out on the last lap, straight away for Bismarck. After leaving Stevenson, Captain Marsh, in accordance with General Terry's order, draped the derrick and jack-staff of the boat with black and hoisted her flag at half-mast, in honour of the dead and wounded.

Night and day all had been the same on the *Far West*. But when through the darkness the lights of Bismarck loomed ahead, men looked at their watches and saw that it was eleven o'clock as her bow touched the bank and she came to rest at her journey's end, just fifty-four hours out from the mouth of the Big Horn. She had covered 710 miles[1] at the average rate of thirteen and one-seventh miles per hour and, though no one stopped to think of it then, she had made herself the speed champion of the Missouri River, with a record unequalled by any other craft that had ever floated on the turbulent stream or its tributaries, from St. Louis to Fort Benton. Her accomplishment had been performed in the line of duty alone, with no desire for the winning of laurels other than the gratitude of those she served.

The boat had barely touched the bank when her officers and men were off, running up the streets and rousing the sleeping town. It was like the night that Concord was startled from slumber by the hoof-beats of Paul Revere's horse, galloping down the elm-shadowed streets on his mission of warning.

Men ran from their houses half-dressed and dishevelled, in every direction lights flashed at the windows. The first men routed from their beds were C. A. Lounsberry, the editor of the Bismarck *Tribune,* and J. M. Carnahan, the telegraph operator. They, together with Captain Marsh, Doctor Porter, Captain Smith, and a number of others from the boat, hurried to the telegraph office and Carnahan took his seat at the key, from which he scarcely raised himself for twenty-two hours.

Editor Lounsberry, who was also the accredited correspondent of the New York *Herald,* prepared copy, handing it over to Carnahan as

---

1. The Missouri River Commission's Report for 1897 makes the distance 920 miles, but this is not borne out by the distance tables.

fast as the latter could send it.² None of them thought of tiring, for it was the most thrilling work they had ever done. The words they were sending would soon be flashing around the world. The first message was a brief bulletin to the New York *Herald,* reading as follows:

> Bismarck, D. T., July 5, 1876:—General Custer attacked the Indians June 25, and he, with every officer and man in five companies, were killed. Reno with seven companies fought in entrenched position three days. The Bismarck *Tribune's* special correspondent was with the expedition and was killed.

Then the little party in the telegraph office settled down to work in earnest, Lounsberry's hand flying over sheet after sheet as he wove the tremendous story poured into his ears by the participants. There was over a column of notes on the campaign up to the day of battle, written by Mark Kellogg and rescued by General Terry himself from the pouch beside the correspondent's body. There were two columns of comment and description sent down by Major Brisbin. Then came interviews with Captain Smith, Doctor Porter, Captain Marsh, Fred Girard, and the stories of General Terry, of Curley, of some of the wounded, and of the death of Charlie Reynolds. During a lull when Carnahan's key for a moment ceased clicking, Lounsberry flung over to him a copy of the *New Testament,* exclaiming:

"Take this! Fire it in when you run out of copy. Hold the wires. Tell 'em it's coming and to hold the key!"

Now followed the full list of the killed and wounded, and now, in the early morning hours, the message written by Captain Smith for the widows at Fort Lincoln, which was being carried to them by the *Far West,* dropping down to the fort with the wounded. Through the day the story grew until, when it was finished, more than 15,000 words had been transmitted. It cost the New York *Herald* $3,000 but it was worth the money, for it was the biggest *beat* in newspaper history. The *Herald* at once adopted Kellogg as having been its special correspondent. That it did so was well for his widow and children, for the great metropolitan daily sent $2,000 to them. But it was not strictly true. Colonel Lounsberry was the *Herald's* correspondent and up to the moment when Custer's column left for the field he had ex-

---

2. The details of the work done that night, as well as the facts relating to the question of whether the *Far West* brought the first authentic news of the battle, have been largely gathered from Col. C. A. Lounsberry who, in correspondence with the author, has kindly furnished him with full information.—J. M. H.

pected to accompany it. Then his wife fell ill and Kellogg, a reporter employed by him on the *Tribune,* went instead.

The tidings fell on the outer world like a thunderbolt. No previous news of a credible nature had reached the country that such a disaster had befallen. Before the official despatches from General Terry to General Sheridan had been given out, the press of the whole nation was demanding that the government prosecute the campaign against the Indians until every hostile should be either dead or disarmed. And as will be seen, the government obeyed the demand.

It has been claimed at different times and by various authorities[3] that Captain Marsh and the *Far West* did not bring the first news of the battle of the Little Big Horn to the outside world, the credit being given instead to Muggins Taylor. Such claims are without foundation in fact. The *Far West* brought the first news of a credible nature, though from Montana emanated at about the same time a few garbled rumours which received publication but no credit from persons in a position to judge of their value. As has been seen, Taylor left the *Far West* on the morning of July 1st, at the mouth of Big Horn, having 175 miles to travel before he could reach Fort Ellis and Bozeman, the nearest telegraph stations.

On July 2nd he came to Stillwater Creek, where he overtook a discharged wagon-train returning from Gibbon's column to the settlements. To the men with it he gave some news, and one of them started with it for Bozeman, arriving there on the same day as Taylor, July 5th, in the evening. Taylor was seen in Bozeman by reporters, who gathered from him enough to transmit brief reports to some Helena, Montana and Salt Lake City, Utah, papers, which appeared in their morning editions. The nature of these reports may be gathered from the following, which was published as an extra by the Helena *Independent* on the morning of July 6th, and which is a fair example of the rendition given to Taylor's story by the few papers using it:

> Advices just received from the Diamond R outfit with Gibbon report a terrible battle with the Indians on the Little Big Horn River. Custer attacked a camp of 4,000 Sioux and after a desperate battle defeated them. Three hundred soldiers and fifteen officers were killed and Custer himself, as reported in another dispatch, is slain. The battle ground is literally covered

---

3. See *History of Early Steamboat Navigation on the Missouri River,* by Col. H. M. Chittenden, U. S. A., for example.

with slain. The Indians retreated. Gibbon was thirty-six hours too late for the battle."[4]

On the same morning the Bismarck *Tribune* published an extra containing an accurate and complete account of the battle of nearly 2,500 words, to which was appended a complete list of the killed and wounded, detailing in the case of the latter the nature of their injuries. It was one of the best pieces of newspaper composition ever produced in the West and few of the subsequent histories of the fight possess the vivid dramatic power of this first story, written under the impulse of intense excitement. Taylor's report, which came from Gibbon and contained, at best, no news whatever of Terry, was telegraphed from Salt Lake City during the day and received publication in some eastern papers. General Sheridan was interviewed and commented upon it as follows, as reported in the New York *Herald*:

> It comes without any marks of credence; it does not come to Headquarters; it does not come to the leading papers from special correspondents; it is not given to the press for telegraphing, but appears first in a Salt Lake and Montana paper. These scouts on the frontier have a way of spreading news, and all frontier stories, especially about Indian wars, are to be carefully considered.

Everyone in authority concurred in Sheridan's opinion, and the news of battle was not believed in the East until the full accounts from Bismarck, *via* St. Paul, came in on the 7th. St. Paul itself had meantime learned all about events on the 6th, from the same accounts, but the latter did not get further on that day because the Bismarck wire only worked direct as far as St. Paul. But even under such conditions the military authorities received no official confirmation of the reports, either from Bismarck or from Fort Ellis, until after the newspaper stories had been published everywhere.

After her arrival at Bismarck, the *Far West* lay there only a few hours. Then Captain Marsh returned on board, and she started for Fort Lincoln with the wounded and Captain Smith's message to the widows. In the twilight just before sunrise she arrived. General Godfrey, in a letter to the author, says:

> I have heard the women, wives of officers, tell of their intense excitement when they heard the whistle blast of the *Far West* as

---

4. *Contributions to the Historical Society of Montana*, Vol. 4.

Original copy of the extra of the *Bismarck Tribune* July 6, 1876. Giving the first published news of the Battle of Little Big Horn.

she approached Bismarck on that July evening; how they waited and waited for tidings, each afraid to tell her thoughts and anxieties, till near midnight, when, with heavy hearts, almost with sobs, they separated and went to their homes. My wife told me how she tossed with restlessness till dawn, when she was startled from a doze by a tap on her window and instantly, suppressing a scream, exclaimed:

'Is my husband killed?'

She was answered by a voice choked with emotion:

'No, dear, your husband is safe and Mrs. Moylan's is safe, but all the rest are killed.'

Then came the heart-breaking task of telling the news to the widows.

Lieut. C. L. Gurley, 6th Infantry, has narrated what followed:[5]

The news came to me about 2 A. M. William S. McCaskey, 20th Infantry, summoned all the officers to his quarters at once, and there read to them the communication he had just received—per steamer *Far West,* from Capt. Ed. W. Smith, General Terry's adjutant general. After we had recovered from the shock, Captain McCaskey requested us to assist him in breaking the news to the widows. It fell to my lot to accompany Captain McCaskey and Dr. J. V. D. Middleton, our post surgeon, to the quarters of Mrs. Custer, immediately east of those occupied by myself. We started on our sad errand a little before seven o'clock on that 6th of July morning. I went to the rear of the Custer house, woke up Maria, Mrs. Custer's housemaid, and requested her to rap on Mrs. Custer's door, and say to her that she and Mrs. Calhoun and Miss Reed were wanted in the parlour.

On my way through the hall to open the front door, I heard the opening of the door of Mrs. Custer's room. She had been awakened by the footsteps in the hall. She called me by name and asked me the cause of my early visit. I made no reply, but followed Captain McCaskey and Doctor Middleton into the parlour. There we were almost immediately followed by the ladies of the Custer household, and there we told to them their first intimation of the awful result of the battle on the Little

---

5. From a clipping of a newspaper interview contained in the scrap-book of the late Dr. H. R. Porter, kindly loaned to the author by his son Mr. H. V. Porter, of Bismarck, N. Dakota.

Big Horn.

Imagine the grief of those stricken women, their sobs, their flood of tears, the grief that knew no consolation. The fearful depression that had hung over the fort for the past two days had its explanation then. It was almost stifling. Men and women moved anxiously, nervously, straining their eyes for the expected messenger, listening as footsteps fell. There was whispering and excitement among the Indian police. There were rumours of a great battle. Those who saw the Indians and witnessed their movements knew that something unusual must have happened. But what? Who would not give worlds to know just why all this excitement among the Indians? Fleet-footed warriors, mounted on still fleeter animals, aided perhaps by signals, had brought the news even before the *Far West* came, but no white man knew. That it brought joy to them was reason enough why it should have brought depression to the whites.[6]

There were twenty-eight widows in stricken Fort Lincoln that morning, and Captain Marsh never witnessed such a scene as followed the announcement of the awful tidings. Everyone in the post was frantic, and men, women, and children came running to the boat, sobbing and moaning as they begged for news. Some of the poor, frightened families of the men in ranks received the blessed assurance that their dear ones were safe, but to many the only answer could be a sad confirmation of their fears, from which they turned away with breaking hearts. Two days after the arrival of the *Far West,* when the wounded had been made comfortable in the post hospital, Mrs. Custer sent Doctor Middleton in her carriage to the boat landing with the request that Captain Marsh come up and see her and the other bereaved women. But he could not bear the thought of witnessing their grief, and declined. He never saw one of them after that bright May morning when, happy and light-hearted, they had lunched with him in the cabin of the *Far West,* little anticipating the sorrow which was

---

6. As witnessing the rapidity with which the Indians could transmit intelligence to distant points, General Godfrey wrote to the author after reading the above: "Among papers sent out to the command that summer, I remember to have read in a Cincinnati paper (the *Commercial,* I think) a little paragraph in a rather obscure place dated Omaha, *June* SO, stating that a despatch from Camp Robinson (or Camp Sheridan) said that runners from the hostile camp had arrived with news that the hostiles had had a big fight with soldiers and been whipped and that the soldiers were not of General Crook's command. I think this despatch located the fight on the 'Greasy Grass.'"

so soon to be theirs.

So ended, in gloom and failure, the campaign for which such high hopes had been entertained. Though much still remained to be done, though troops were already mustering to prosecute to a successful conclusion the work begun, the Custer campaign proper, in which Captain Marsh and his stanch craft had borne so conspicuous a part, was over. When a soldier's work is completed, it is one of his chief ambitions to find his name honourably mentioned by his commander in "official reports." In Captain Marsh's portfolio of treasured documents is a paper, inscribed by an army officer for his old friend, "the army's steamboat captain." It is written with the ornamental lettering and the underscorings of red ink characteristic of engrossed copies. It reads as follows:

EXTRACT FROM GENERAL TERRY'S ANNUAL REPORT, DATED SEPTEMBER, 1876:

When Colonel Gibbon's column left the Yellowstone, the Supply Steamer *Far West,* upon which was Company 'B' of the 6th Infantry, was directed to make the attempt to ascend the Big Horn as far as the mouth of the Little Horn, in order that supplies might be near at hand to replace the scanty amount of subsistence which Colonel Gibbon's pack-animals were able to carry. Thanks to the zeal and energy displayed by Captain Grant Marsh, the master of the Steamer, the mouth of the Little Horn was reached by her, and she was of inestimable service in bringing down our wounded. They were sent upon her to Fort Lincoln.

The tribute to Captain Marsh was a high one, but surely it had been well earned.

Custer Monument

CHAPTER 39

The Battle at Powder River

The telegraph wires had not yet ceased to vibrate with the details of the tragedy on the Little Big Horn, when General Sheridan, with characteristic promptitude, began to bend his energies to the task of retrieving the disaster. He despatched a message to General Terry, bidding him hold his ground and be of good courage, for all the reinforcements he could possibly need were being sent to him as fast as railroads and steamboats could carry them. To General Crook he conveyed similar assurances, instructing him, further, to join Terry without delay. On July 11th, Lieut.-Col. Elwell S. Otis with six companies of the 22nd Infantry, which had been relieved from duty in the Department of Dakota only a few months before, departed from Detroit *en route* to the Yellowstone. A few days later six companies of the 5th Infantry, under Colonel Nelson A. Miles, left the Department of the Missouri for the same point. To the assistance of Crook, still in the camp on Goose Creek, where he had laid since the battle of the Rosebud, was sent the 5th Cavalry, under its new colonel, Wesley Merritt, the brilliant cavalry leader of the Civil War.

All of these fresh troops were in motion at once for the seat of war in the buffalo country.[1] But long before the first of them arrived, the *Far West* was back at the lonely camp by the Big Horn's mouth, where the pall of gloom had not yet lifted and where the terror of the dusky foe, unconquered and unnumbered, still chilled every heart. Captain Marsh left Bismarck on the 9th of July with a cargo of supplies and sixty cavalry horses, ordered up by General Terry to partially remount the 7th Cavalry, which had been reorganized into a regiment of eight troops under Major Reno. He reached camp on the 25th, to meet with a warm welcome from his old comrades, who were eager for his

1. *Report of the Secretary of War, 1876-77* and *The Army of the U. S.*

news from Fort Lincoln and the East.

He found the camp in much better order than when he had left it three weeks before. The soldiers were comfortable physically, for the log huts of old Fort Pease had been utilized as quarters for many of them, while the *Josephine,* which he had passed on his trip to Bismarck, had brought up a large quantity of supplies. General Terry, however, was now preparing to break camp and move his men down to a point opposite the mouth of the Rosebud. The General had visited the place in person on the *Josephine* and had determined to establish a new depot there, since it would furnish a convenient base from which to march south for the junction with Crook when the time should be ripe.[2] He had ordered the abandonment of the Powder River depot and instructed Major Moore to bring his troops and supplies to the Rosebud.

On the afternoon that the *Far West* reached Fort Pease, an incident occurred remarkable enough to arouse the enthusiasm of even Terry's men, grown accustomed to deeds of valour. The general had come on board the boat and was discussing the situation and future plans with a number of officers, including Captain Marsh, when three men were discovered approaching across the wide prairie bottom to the southward. The sight of them caused a flurry of excitement, for as they drew near it became evident that they were white men, whose appearance from the regions abandoned to the Sioux seemed almost incredible. When they reached the boat, travel-stained and weary, they proved to be three soldiers of General Gibbon's 7th Infantry, bearing despatches from General Crook. Their comrades received them with wild enthusiasm, for no one had expected, when they had set out for Crook's camp a few days before, to ever again see them alive. General Terry the next day published a special order to the command praising the courage of these men, and his language very fittingly details the nature of their exploit and the admiration with which he and all his followers regarded it:

> The Department Commander has recently had urgent occasion to communicate from this camp with Brigadier-General

---

2. The record of events transpiring during the absence of the *Far West* is largely based upon the *Diary of Matthew Carroll, Master in Charge of Transportation for General John Gibbon's Column,* contained in the *Contributions to the Historical Society of Montana,* Vol. 2. Mr. Carroll's diary has also been referred to frequently for confirming dates in the account of the operations succeeding the battle of the Little Big Horn.—J. M. H.

Crook, commanding a force on the headwaters of Powder River. The duty of carrying despatches between these points, through a country occupied by a large force of hostile Sioux, was one of the most perilous and arduous nature. A scout, inspired by the promise of a large reward, made the attempt, but soon abandoned it as hopeless. As a last resort, a call was made upon the troops of this command for volunteers, in response to which not less than twelve enlisted men promptly offered their services.

From among them the following named soldiers were selected: Privates James Bell, Benjamin H. Stuart, and William Evans, of Company E, 7th Infantry. On the 9th day of July they set out for General Crook's camp, which they reached on the 12th, delivered the despatches and returned, arriving in camp on the 25th. In making this public acknowledgement of the important service voluntarily rendered by these soldiers at the imminent risk of their lives, the Department Commander desires to express his deep regret that at present it is not in his power to bestow the substantial reward which has been so well earned, but he is confident that an achievement undertaken in so soldier-like a spirit and carried so gallantly to a successful issue, will not be permitted to pass unrewarded.

The exploit is one calculated to establish in the public mind a higher and more just estimate of the character of the United States soldier. The Department Commander, on his own behalf, and on behalf of the officers of this command, desires thus publicly to thank Privates James Bell, Benjamin H. Stuart, and William Evans, Company E, 7th Infantry, for a deed which reflects so much credit on the service.[3]

After they had delivered their despatches from General Crook, Captain Marsh took the tired and hungry messengers into the cabin and caused to be set before them as appetizing and bountiful a supper as the steward of the *Far West* could provide. The gallant fellows, each of whom was afterwards granted a Medal of Honour by Congress, had brought important information to General Terry, for which he had been anxiously waiting. General Crook forwarded by them the first accurate news of his position on Goose Creek which Terry had yet received. He also reported the position of the main body of the

---

3. *The Army of the United States*, sketch of the 7th Regiment of Infantry.

hostiles near the base of the Big Horn Mountains, whither they had retreated after their victory over Custer. He further stated that he was striking his camp and preparing to move down Rosebud River for a junction with Terry.

The latter, on receipt of the news, hastened the transfer of his own force to the mouth of the Rosebud. On the morning of the 27th he evacuated the camp at Fort Pease and, after seeing the column set in motion under General Gibbon, himself came on board the *Far West* with his staff and the boat turned her head downstream toward the new rendezvous. The road along the river bottom was heavy from recent rains, but as the troops swung into route step much of their old-time enthusiasm came back to them, for, as always, the prospect of active service roused their drooping spirits and restored their confidence.

At the time of the organization of Terry's column at Fort Lincoln in the spring, some of the higher officers of the Commissary Department had been of the opinion that the expedition was large enough to warrant the appointment of at least a colonel or major from among their number to act as chief commissary of subsistence. They endeavoured to have such an appointment made, but General Terry, who usually knew quite well what he wanted and never hesitated to state it, designated for the position Lieut. R. E. Thompson of the 6th Infantry, a junior officer in whose integrity and ability he had implicit confidence. The gentlemen of the Commissary Department did not relish this proceeding, but they were powerless to prevent it. After the battle of the Little Big Horn, however, when heavy reinforcements began pouring into the Indian country, the position of chief commissary became one of such importance that the officers of the department could no longer bear with equanimity the idea of a lieutenant of infantry usurping their prerogatives.

So early in July a major from among them betook himself to Fort Lincoln and, boarding one of the upward-bound steamers, made his way to General Terry's camp to claim the position. Upon his arrival he sought out the general at the latter's headquarters on the *Far West,* and in a somewhat pompous manner made known his mission. Terry received him courteously and heard him with patience, but Captain Marsh, who was standing near, listening in silent amusement to the interview, felt sure that the major would meet with a surprise before long. Nor was he disappointed. When the new arrival had finished speaking, Terry looked up and in his quiet, decisive manner, said:

Major, I am sorry you have taken such a long trip for nothing. Lieutenant Thompson has been filling the position of commissary of subsistence for this expedition to my entire satisfaction. I am sure he will continue to do so and I could not think of removing him at this time. I thank you for your offer, but Lieutenant Thompson must remain. Good-day, sir.

There was nothing further to be said and the crestfallen major returned to St. Paul by the next boat, having received a brief but conclusive demonstration of the manner in which the commander of the Department of Dakota conducted the affairs of his administration.

On July 30th, after three days of hard marching, Gibbon's troops went into camp opposite the mouth of the Rosebud, finding when they reached there that Major Moore and his men had already arrived. The latter had brought with them all the supplies from the abandoned Powder River depot excepting a quantity of sacked oats which they had been unable to carry owing to insufficient transportation. Though the main body of the Indians was known to be many miles distant to the south-west, numerous small parties of warriors were scouring the country in every direction, seeking opportunities to run off stock or to murder any white men who might unwittingly cross their paths. It was feared that some of the marauding bands would visit the mouth of the Powder and destroy the stored forage, and as soon after his arrival at the Rosebud as possible, General Terry ordered Major Moore to take such a force as he deemed necessary on board the *Far West* and proceed to the Powder to recover the oats and drive away any Indians who might be prowling in the vicinity.

One cause and another delayed the start, but on the afternoon of August 1st the boat got under way for her sixty-five-mile run. Before she left the troops on board were able to join their cheers to those of their comrades on shore as they welcomed the steamer *Carroll*, bringing in Col. Elwell S. Otis and his six companies of the 22nd Infantry, the first of the promised reinforcements to arrive from the East. The *Carroll* brought information that when she had passed the mouth of the Powder two days before, she had been vigorously attacked from the hills by a considerable body of Indians. Troops had been landed who had driven the enemy from his positions and several soldiers had been wounded in the encounter.

From such news it was evident that the *Far West* might expect trouble when she reached her destination. But to the brave men she carried, the prospect of a brush with Custer's slayers was more than welcome, and once she was under way she could not steam fast enough to suit them. On the downward voyage she passed the steamer *E. H. Durfee,* bringing up Colonel Nelson A. Miles and six companies of the 5th Infantry.

Besides Captain Marsh and his crew and Sergeant Caddie with his sixteen dismounted troopers, who were still on the boat, the *Far West* carried Companies D, Captain Murdock; and I, Lieutenant Walker, both of the 6th Infantry; Company C, Captain McArthur, 17th Infantry; one Gatling and one twelve-pound Napoleon gun, commanded by Lieutenant Woodruff, 7th Infantry, and three civilian scouts, Messrs. Brockmeyer, Morgan and Smith.[4] Major Moore, the officer in command, bore an enviable reputation for bravery, for in at least one engagement of the Civil war his courage had received such conspicuous demonstration as to excite universal admiration, even in that epoch of daily battles. One summer day in 1863 Moore, who was then colonel of the Twenty-fifth Regiment of Michigan Volunteers, was at Tebb's Ferry, Kentucky, with five companies of his command, guarding the bridge across Green River. His men, only 200 in number, were occupying the small entrenchment at the bridge-head, when at dawn their position was suddenly surrounded by two regiments of Confederate cavalry under General John Morgan, then moving north on his famous raid into Ohio and Indiana.

Morgan sent in a peremptory demand for the surrender of the garrison, and, indeed, it seemed that it would be madness for such a handful to resist. But it was the morning of the Nation's birthday and Moore instantly sent back the spirited reply, "The Fourth of July is not a proper day for me to entertain such a proposition." Morgan, much incensed, thereupon made a desperate assault all along the line. He was repulsed, with a loss of fifty killed and 250 wounded, including some of his best officers, and was compelled to seek a crossing of Green River elsewhere, leaving the gallant Michiganders in undisputed possession of the ground they had so well defended.

It did not seem likely that a man of such metal would hesitate when it came to trying issues with the Sioux. The *Far West* drew abreast the wide mouth of the Powder in the early morning of the 2nd of August. The sky was cloudless and the first rays of the rising sun brought with them a heat presaging one of the warmest days of the summer. Not an Indian was in sight as the steamer, with engines backed, floated slowly

---

4. Official report of Maj. Orlando H. Moore.

THE CROW SCOUT, CURLEY
Sole survivor of Custer's column at the
Battle of Little Big Horn.

past the mouth. But over the rugged Bad-Lands to the east and west and up the shallow valley of the tributary, numerous signal fires were sending their columns of smoke wavering toward the zenith, betokening as certainly as rifle shots the presence of watchful enemies among the protecting ravines.

Under instructions from Major Moore, Captain Marsh steamed on around the bend into the fretful current of Wolf Rapids, but still the keen eyes of neither pilot nor scouts could detect Indians anywhere over the wide landscape. So the boat was turned about and headed back to the landing where the oats had been stored, some distance below the mouth of the Powder. To the surprise of everyone the forage was still there, though the sacks had all been removed and the grain, amounting to about seventy-five tons, scattered in a loose pile on the ground. It had not been expected that the Indians would remove it, for an Indian pony would no more eat oats than he would gravel, but it seemed strange that they had not prevented its recovery by burning it. Nevertheless, there it was, and the work of taking it on board began at once.

At some little distance from the river a circular ridge surrounded the landing, forming a strong defensive position, and upon arrival Major Moore ordered the troops to occupy it. They did so none too soon. Scarcely were they in position when a mass of Indians poured over the crest of the river bluffs who, lashing their ponies to a furious gallop, swept down on the ridge. Such a reckless approach was just what the soldiers wanted. Rushing out all of his troops, excepting ten men who were left to guard the steamer, Major Moore ordered them to lie down and conceal themselves, hoping to draw the hostiles within range. But unfortunately the crafty savages discovered the ruse in time to save themselves and, abating their speed, halted just beyond range of the infantry Springfields.

Major Moore now decided to treat them to a little surprise by bringing Lieutenant Woodruff's Napoleon gun into action. The piece was hauled up on the bank and while all hands on board suspended work to watch the result, it opened fire with spherical case percussion shell upon a party of warriors far off to the right, toward Powder River. As the roar of the discharge reverberated among the hills and the singing projectile circled down and burst in front of them, the Indians leaped to their ponies' backs and fled in wild terror, never stopping until they had put the bluffs between themselves and the steamer. Firing rapidly, Woodruff ranged his piece toward the left with each successive shot, until the shells had searched every ravine in the bend between Powder River and Wolf Rapids and sent the skulking occupants scurrying out of range, followed by the laughter and cheers of soldiers and steamboat men.

The Indians apparently having now been all driven out, the work of carrying the oats aboard was resumed and kept up for several hours. But the air grew more and more sultry as the morning passed and by two o'clock in the afternoon, when most of the forage was on board, the men were thoroughly exhausted. All who could do so stopped work and sought shady places to rest until the air should grow cooler, and an almost unbroken silence settled over the boat. The Indians had all disappeared from the ridges shimmering in the distance, the troops on the skirmish line were still, and the only sounds that broke the hush were the slow, half-smothered puffs of the exhaust-pipe and the occasional clatter of a grasshopper out on the sun-baked prairie.

But in the midst of this period of rest there came to the scouts Brockmeyer and Morgan, and to Pilot Dave Campbell, the idea that the whereabouts of the Indians should be learned. Securing their horses before anyone else realized what they were about, they mounted to ride down the river. Captain Marsh then saw them and asked what they meant to do. Upon being informed he remonstrated strongly, saying that such an attempt would be perfectly foolhardy, since the Indians were undoubtedly concealed only a short distance away on all sides. While he was talking, Major Moore came up and added his protests to those of the captain. But the men were reckless fellows and not being bound in such a case to take orders from any one, they made light of the danger and rode away, disappearing over the low ridge toward Wolf Rapids.

Again silence settled upon the boat while Captain Marsh and the others who knew of the scouts' departure anxiously waited for what they feared would be the certain result. In a few moments, several rifle shots rang out in rapid succession down the river. With throbbing pulses the steamboat men leaped to their feet and seized their weapons. There was a brief pause and then from the ridge where the skirmish line lay a soldier sprang out and ran toward the boat, shouting that the scouts were attacked.

As he came on, over a swelling hillock in the distance the three men appeared, lying low on their horses' necks and galloping furiously, while close behind them followed a yelping pack of twenty-five or more Indians. Instantly Captain Marsh, Doctor Porter, and several others, including Night Engineer George Foulk, half-dressed just as he had jumped from bed, rushed out on the bank and down the river. They were the only hope of rescue for the scouts, for Major Moore, quite properly, would not order his troops forward and thus expose the boat to possible attack from the other direction. Even at this moment another large body of Indians made its appearance further down the river, upon which Woodruff opened with shell, quickly dispersing it.

As they crossed the ridge nearest to the boat, Captain Marsh and his companions saw the horse of the rearmost of the three fugitives stumble and go down, pinning his rider to the ground. The Indians, who had discovered the rescuers approaching, were already halting, but one of them, bolder than the rest, galloped on to the fallen man, who later proved to be Brockmeyer, placed the muzzle of his rifle almost against the latter's breast, and fired. Then he turned and dashed away. But Morgan and Campbell had also halted now. They began to shoot at the escaping savage and a bullet from Morgan's rifle knocked him from his pony, stone dead. A moment later the men from the boat reached the scene. Brockmeyer was gnawing the earth and writhing in agony as Doctor Porter knelt over him and tried to stanch the blood from the terrible gap in his breast. Under the direction of the surgeon, the injured man was borne back to the steamer, but his wound was mortal and he passed away in a few hours.

Just before he died, Brockmeyer sent for Captain Marsh and asked the latter to sell his rifle, revolver, field-glasses, saddle, bridle and horse, all his earthly possessions, for what they would bring, and send the money to his sister in Marion County, West Virginia. She was a poor woman and the captain desired to realize for her every dollar possible from the dead scout's possessions. That evening he suggested to the army officers that a game of *freeze-out* poker should be played for the articles. The idea was received with enthusiasm, for poker in those days numbered among its devotees practically everyone on the frontier, and to this game, moreover, would be added an object which appealed to the hearts of all these generous soldiers.

So through the summer night, almost until break of day, they sat in the cabin of the *Far West,* cards in hand, fighting mosquitoes and fortifying themselves with such liquid refreshments as the mess chests of the officers could provide. When they finally arose from the table, Captain Marsh had a roll of several hundred dollars ready to transmit by the next mail, together with the sad news of her brother's fate, to the sister of poor Brockmeyer, far away among the foothills of the Alleghenies. The pathetic little incident, revealing the noblest philanthropy masquerading behind the mere love of gaming, was a curiously illuminating sidelight on the virtues and vices that so often commingled along the old military frontier.

The body of the unfortunate Brockmeyer was buried by his comrades next morning in a spot overlooking the broad valley and the restless waters of the Yellowstone. To this day the place is known as "Scout's Grave." After the skirmish in which he had met his death, the Indians did not again appear. The oats having all been loaded the day before, immediately after the brief ceremony over the scout's remains, the *Far West* cast off her lines and started for the Rosebud.

CHAPTER 40

Terry Takes the Field

On her way up the Yellowstone the *Far West* passed the *Carroll* going down to Buford, and the next morning arrived at camp to find everything there in commotion. During her absence the *Josephine* had brought down the last supplies left at Fort Pease, and General Terry was now using her for ferrying his troops to the south bank, preparatory to marching up the Rosebud in search of Crook. Captain Marsh's vessel was at once pressed into service, also, and by the 7th of August the entire force was assembled on the south shore.

The column had been reorganized and now consisted of a brigade of infantry commanded by General Gibbon and made up of four battalions, one each from the 5th, 6th, 7th and 22nd Infantry; a cavalry force embracing the entire 7th Cavalry and four troops of the 2nd Cavalry, all under Major Brisbin, and a battery of one twelve-pound and two ten-pound rifled field-guns commanded by Lieutenant Low.[1]

Accompanied by a wagon train carrying an ample supply of rations and forage, this formidable force started up the Rosebud valley next morning, leaving the steamers and the depot guarded by one company of the 17th Infantry under Captain Sanger, a few dismounted cavalrymen and the Gatling gun battery.

To all appearances, Captain Marsh and the other boat men were about to experience a long period of inactivity while the troops were away scouring the country for the evasive Sioux. But the crew of the *Far West* found plenty to do. Game was, of course, abundant, all over the country. As in earlier years the islands were full of elk, the prairies were dotted with antelope and herds of buffalo, while over the low

---

1. Official report of General Terry.

sandbars wild geese and ducks were flocking in myriads. Surrounded by such plentiful opportunities for sport, the ordinary practices of hunting palled upon the men of the *Far West,* and at length they struck upon a method for the wholesale destruction of the wild creatures of the plains and river the like of which had never been used before and probably never will be again.

At the time when General Terry retired from the field of the Little Big Horn, one of the Gatling guns with his command had become disabled and had been placed on board the *Far West* for safekeeping. It had been stowed away in a corner of the deck, together with a plentiful supply of ammunition, and still remained there undisturbed. One day when time was hanging heavily on his hands, John Dark, an ingenious member of Sergeant Caddle's contingent of *horse marines,* hauled the gun out and finding that its running-gear only had been injured and not its firing mechanism, he made such repairs as were necessary to render it available for use on the boat. Then procuring a bucketful of cartridges, he and a comrade trained the gun down river at a flock of unsuspecting geese seated quietly on a sandbar, far beyond rifle range, and began grinding. Before the unfortunate waterfowl could comprehend that a great and mysterious disaster had come upon them, their ranks were decimated, and as they rose to fly in squawking terror they left the sandbar ploughed, like a battlefield, by bullets and strewn with the bodies of the fallen.

Encouraged by their success, the amateur artillerymen extended their target practice as opportunity offered, slaying buffalo, antelope and elk at discretion, for the Gatling gun could bring down any of these animals at such ranges that they had no chance to escape. Since frequently during the summer and fall all the experienced scouts and hunters were away with the campaigning troops, the spoils of the Gatling gun were very welcome to the men on the boat. It kept them better supplied with fresh meat than they could have been by even the redoubtable rifle of *Yellowstone* Kelly, or that of the lamented *Lonesome* Charlie Reynolds.

The march of General Terry's column through the rough country along the Rosebud was much impeded by the long wagon train, but after travelling for three days it had covered a distance of about twenty-eight miles. Then, one morning, the Crow scouts in front came galloping madly back to the advance guard, chanting their war songs and shouting that the Sioux were coming. Their report was verified by the appearance of a few horsemen far in the distance ahead, and

Terry closed up his column and deployed skirmishers for action. But in a few moments one of the strangers rode boldly down from the hills, waving his hat. His action made it evident that he was a white man, and Captain Weir, of the 7th Cavalry, went forward to meet him. Upon coming up, the captain found him to be a scout whose name was already famous all over the West. He was conducted inside the lines, where Captain Weir introduced him to the troops by shouting:

"Boys, here's "Buffalo Bill". Some of you old soldiers know him. Give him a cheer!"

The injunction was heartily obeyed, not only for, the sake of the renowned Indian fighter himself, but because when discovered, he was scouting in advance of Crook, and brought news of the latter's near approach. A short time later the two forces, so long held asunder by the strong arm of the common enemy, united and went into camp together, while their commanders began the discussion of plans for the future.

The united commands numbered quite 3,600 men,[2] enough to destroy all the Indians in the country if they could only be brought to battle. General Crook brought word that the hostiles had left the base of the Big Horn Mountains, and, passing around his right, had descended the Rosebud for a distance and then turned eastward toward the Tongue. They had left the Rosebud at the point where the columns met and here their trail was broad, distinct and trampled flat by the passage of a myriad of horses and *travois*. It was quite fresh and had plainly been made but a few days before. Terry and Crook at once decided to follow it with all possible speed. But one difficulty presented itself. The Indians as a body would certainly not keep on eastward indefinitely, for that course would lead them to the Missouri River and the forts, where they knew that they would soon be surrounded. It was much more likely, therefore, that they would turn toward the Yellowstone, cross it, and keeping on northward would ford the Missouri and effect their escape into the British Possessions, where they would be safe from pursuit.

To frustrate any such design, General Terry determined on sending a part of his forces back to seize and guard the various fords of the Yellowstone. For this important work he selected the battalion of General Miles. The latter was instructed to return to the mouth of the Rosebud, taking the artillery with him, and there board the *Far West* and run down river, establishing detachments wherever he deemed neces-

---

2. Diary of Matthew Carroll.

sary along the north bank. After accomplishing these dispositions he was instructed to employ the boat in patrolling the stream. The supply train could not be taken with the main column across the precipitous ridge between the Rosebud and the Tongue, so fifteen days' rations were transferred from it to pack-mules and the wagons made ready to go back to the depot, under escort of the returning troops.

Lieut-Gen. Nelson A. Miles.

CHAPTER 41

Patrol Duty With Miles and "Buffalo Bill"

General Miles started for the mouth of the Rosebud on the same night that he received his orders. With characteristic vigour he made a forced march, coming into the depot at daybreak, his men tired and footsore. Their appearance was a surprise to the garrison, but almost before they had time to realize it, Captain Marsh had steam up on the *Far West,* Miles' troops had embarked, and the boat was skimming downstream between the islands toward Powder River. It was an exciting run from the first turn of the wheel, for the power of steam was now pitted against the nimble feet of Indian ponies. At every bend they rounded, the pilot and the army officers gathered in the little house on the roof peered anxiously ahead through the dismal rain that was falling all that day, half expecting to see the banks lined with dusky warriors and the paraphernalia of savage camps. The river was quite low and none too easy to navigate, but Marsh and Campbell knew every foot of it and no accidents occurred.

General Miles was frequently in the pilot-house during this voyage and the ones succeeding it, constantly observing the country and seeking information, however trivial, which might prove of future military value. Thus it was that a friendship sprang up between him and Captain Marsh which lasted through the years of Indian warfare and continued unbroken long after the colonel of infantry had risen to be the commanding general of the United States Army. When the name of Nelson A. Miles is mentioned, the captain can scarcely find words strong enough in which to express his admiration and affection for the man, who, through all his campaigns in the Northwest, never found any work too hard to be performed, any danger too great to be faced, when duty demanded it; who gladly shared with his men every privation and peril to which they were exposed, and whose watchful care for their welfare knew no relaxation.

The brilliant career of General Miles in the war of the Rebellion and on the southern plains had appealed to the captain's imagination long before they met. The expectations thus aroused in his mind were more than fulfilled during their association by the General's courage and tireless energy as a soldier and by his noble character and unfailing kindliness as a man. That the captain's admiration for the distinguished soldier was reciprocated, is evident from the following tribute recently paid to him by General Miles:[1]

> I found him a resolute, active, brave, intelligent commander, a skillful navigator, and a strong man mentally and physically; in fact, he would be a marked man in any community, as he was a natural leader among men. His services were exceedingly valuable at that time, during the serious hostilities of those large tribes of Sioux Indians which occupied that extensive section of country. In clearing the way for civilization and occupation by the white race, Captain Marsh contributed his full share and is entitled to much credit for the splendid work in which he was engaged.

The first point below the Rosebud where the Yellowstone could be readily forded in the stage of water then prevailing, was at the mouth of Tongue River. The *Far West* arrived at this point on the afternoon of the day she started. After putting off a company to encamp and throw up entrenchments, she sped on toward the Powder. No Indians had yet been encountered when, on the 13th of August, she came in opposite the scene of the engagement of eleven days earlier and debarked Captain Burnett's company. As she touched the bank, the men who were responsible for the success of her trip felt a great load lifted from their minds, for it was evident from the appearance of the shores that the enemy had not yet crossed there and effected his escape northward. But, stopping only long enough for the troops to land, she turned about and went back to the Tongue that night.

Next morning as she lay there, the soldiers who were vigilantly watching the bluffs across the river for Indians, saw, instead, two white scouts approaching, who came down to the bank and signalled to the boat. They were from General Terry, and reported that his column

---

1. Contained in a letter written by General Miles to the author.

had marched across the ridge from the Rosebud and was now in the Tongue valley. The troops had failed to overtake the Indians, having suffered much discomfort and delay by reason of the heavy rains. The scouts had been sent to ascertain the whereabouts of the boat and they returned to their command that night.

After they had gone, the *Far West* began patrol duty, going down to the Powder again and thence on through Wolf Rapids. A few Indians were now to be seen and it was feared that they might be crossing further down the Yellowstone. Steam was crowded on, and after a run of a few hours the mouth of Glendive Creek came into view. Still there were no signs that heavy bodies of the enemy had recently been along the river bank, though signal smokes and Indians themselves were occasionally discernible among the hills to the south. General Miles therefore set ashore a company, together with one of the field-pieces, under Captain Rice, to entrench and guard the crossing. The steamer then put about and returned to the Powder.

On the 17th, Terry and Crook came down to that point, having hesitated to follow the Indian trail further among the bad-lands without fresh supplies. The trail still tended eastward and General Terry had despatched orders to Captain Sanger at the Rosebud to evacuate the depot there and bring the reserve supplies down to the Powder, where they would be more readily accessible to the main column. The *E. H. Durfee,* the only boat beside the *Far West* now left in the upper river, was busily engaged for the next week in bringing down the supplies, while the wagon train, which had been parked at the Rosebud, marched overland to the new position.

When the troops arrived at the mouth of the Powder, General Crook's chief scout, William F. Cody, much better known as "Buffalo Bill", was still with them, and here Captain Marsh received his first introduction to the noted frontiersman. Colonel Cody was ever a picturesque personality and never more so than on this campaign, during which he performed some of his most daring exploits. He was a young man then, barely thirty years of age, strong, graceful, and of splendid physique. Dressed in an elaborate, fringed buckskin hunting suit, with revolver and Bowie-knife at belt, high riding-boots and broad sombrero, he was a figure to attract attention anywhere, while his forceful manner, his readiness of resource in any emergency and his utter disregard for danger, would have marked him as a phenomenal man, without any embellishments of attire.

Just a month to the day before his arrival at the Powder, while marching southward with Crook to meet the 5th Cavalry under Merritt, "Buffalo Bill" had met with a thrilling experience. A large body of Indians had been encountered and he, riding with his usual daring in front of the command, had suddenly come face to face with Yellow Hand, a noted Cheyenne chief. They engaged in a spectacular duel, which was ended by the scout slaying Yellow Hand with his knife. "Buffalo Bill" then scalped him and swinging the scalp, with the war-bonnet still attached to it, in the faces of the oncoming Indians, shouted:

"The first scalp for Custer!"

He and Captain Marsh had often heard of each other before, for the name of each was familiar all along the frontier, and their first greeting was like that of old acquaintances. Colonel Cody, at the moment of their meeting, chanced to be in the company of Gen. E. A. Carr, second in command of the 5th Cavalry, an officer of Crook's command. Carr himself, a distinguished veteran of the Rebellion, for some reason was not deeply impressed with the progress which was being made in the campaign by the various officers above him, and when Cody presented him to Captain Marsh, he stepped forward and grasping the latter's hand, exclaimed, earnestly:

"Captain, I've heard of you and the way you do things and I told Bill I wanted to meet you. I'm mighty glad, sir, to know *one live man* up in this country. They seem to be extremely rare!"

Though it was pleasant to lie before the camp, surrounded by so much life and activity, Captain Marsh was not permitted to enjoy such a situation for long. He soon received orders to make the *Far West* ready for another down-river scout, in which General Miles and "Buffalo Bill" were to participate. Before they started, General Terry came on board and took the captain aside to speak about a matter which had been brought to his attention. Though most of the crew and all of the officers of the *Far West* thoroughly enjoyed the exciting service in which they had been and still were engaged, some few of the deck hands, more timid than their comrades, objected to the work, complaining that they had not been employed by the steamboat company to place their lives in danger like soldiers, and that they were drawing wages for working on the boat, not for fighting Indians.

Their complaints had reached the ears of General Terry and he now came to Captain Marsh and, in his usual brief manner, referred to them. He said that the men were undoubtedly within their rights in protesting. They could not be expected to undergo danger if they objected and, though he would always instruct the troops to shield them as much as possible, at the same time he had no authority to order them to go anywhere simply because the army went.

Captain Marsh was very indignant when he heard of the position taken by a few malcontents among his men. It had never occurred to him that any of them could be dissatisfied with the work they were doing on account of its perils.

"Well, I'll tell you, general," he said, when Terry had finished speaking, "you have always given me a big salary and the preference over all other steamboat men in government work. So have the other army officers for the last ten years. I consider it a compliment to be called on for this kind of service and I prefer that you consider my boat a soldier and send it just where you want it until you get through with it. Anybody among my crew who don't like it, can quit and go ashore."

The general answered not a word, merely bowing his head in assent as he turned and walked away. But that he understood and appreciated the action of the captain was evident from the favour he continued to show the latter so long as he continued in command of the Department of Dakota.

The incidents of the scout down the river now begun by the *Far West* are detailed with so much spirit by Colonel Cody in his volume of personal recollections, entitled, *The Adventures of Buffalo Bill*,[2] that the account cannot be improved upon. It is therefore inserted here in its entirety:

> One evening while we were in camp on the Yellowstone at the mouth of Powder River, (says Colonel Cody,) I was informed that the commanding officer had selected Louis Richard, a half-breed, and myself to accompany General Miles on a scouting expedition on the steamer *Far West,* down the Yellowstone as far as Glendive Creek. We were to ride on the pilothouse and keep a sharp lookout on both sides of the river for Indian trails that might have crossed the stream. The idea of scouting on a steamboat was indeed a novel one to me, and I anticipated a pleasant trip.
>
> At daylight next morning we reported on board the steamer to General Miles, who had with him four or five companies of his regiment. We were somewhat surprised when he asked

---

2. Harper & Brothers, Publishers, 1904.

us where our horses were, as we had not supposed that horses would be needed if the scouting was to be done on the steamer. He said we might need them before we got back, and thereupon we had the animals brought on board. In a few minutes we were booming down the river at the rate of about twenty miles an hour.

The steamer *Far West* was commanded by Captain Grant Marsh, whom I found to be an interesting character. I had often heard of him, for he was, and is yet, one of the best-known river captains in the country. He it was who, with his steamer, the *Far West,* transported the wounded men from the battle of the Little Big Horn to Fort Abraham Lincoln on the Missouri River, and on that trip he made the fastest steamboat time on record. He was a skilful and experienced pilot, handling his boat with remarkable dexterity.

While Richard and myself were at our stations on the pilothouse, the steamer, with a full head of steam, went flying past islands, around bends, over sandbars, at a rate that was exhilarating. Presently I thought I could see horses grazing in a distant bend of the river, and I reported the fact to General Miles, who asked Captain Marsh if he could land the boat near a large tree, which he pointed out to him.

'Yes, sir; I can land her there, and make her climb the tree if necessary,' said he.

On reaching the spot designated, General Miles ordered two companies ashore, while Richard and myself were instructed to take our horses off the boat and push out as rapidly as possible to see if there were Indians in the vicinity. While we were getting ashore, Captain Marsh remarked that if there was only a good heavy dew on the grass he would shoot the steamer ashore, and take us on the scout without the trouble of leaving the boat.

It was a false alarm, however, as the objects we had seen proved to be Indian graves. Quite a large number of braves, who had probably been killed in some battle, were laid on scaffolds, according to the Indian custom, and some of their clothing had been torn from the bodies by the wolves and was waving in the air.

On arriving at Glendive Creek we found that Colonel Rice and his company of the 5th Infantry, who had been sent there by General Miles, had built quite a good little fort with their trowel-bayonets, a weapon which Colonel Rice was the inventor of, and which, by the way, is a very useful implement of war, as it can be used for a shovel in throwing up entrenchments, and can be profitably utilized in several other ways. On the day previous to our arrival Colonel Rice had a fight with a party of Indians, and had killed two or three of them at long range with his Rodman cannon.

The *Far West* was to remain at Glendive over night, and General Miles wished to send despatches back to General Terry at once. At his request I took the despatches, and rode seventy-five miles that night, through the Bad Lands of the Yellowstone, and reached General Terry's camp next morning, after having nearly broken my neck a dozen times or more.

Captain Marsh was alarmed when he heard that "Buffalo Bill" was about to undertake this ride back to the camp at the Powder. Going to him as he was making his horse ready on the main deck, the captain exclaimed:

"Bill, don't try it. You'll never get through alive." The scout merely laughed and mounted his horse, and as he rode away in the gathering darkness the captain watched him out of sight regretfully, fully convinced that he would never again be seen of men. He was pleasantly surprised, therefore, when, late in the following night, he was awakened by someone coming to his bunk and grasping him by the shoulder. Opening his eyes he looked into the smiling face of Cody, who remarked: "Captain, have the steward get me something to eat, can you? I'm hungry."

The daring fellow had not only gone safely through to Terry, but had returned by the same route. After that the captain ceased to worry about the doings of a man whose life seemed to be under a charm.

The *Far West* now returned to the Powder, where General Miles was to leave the boat for a time. Before going he presented to the captain the following letter of thanks for services rendered:

Headquarters Yellowstone Line,
near Mouth of Powder River, M.T.
August 19, 1876.

Captain Grant Marsh,
    Commanding Steam-Boat *Far West:*
Before leaving your boat, I wish to express my acknowledge-

ment of your zealous assistance in the movements that have been made by my command in the past seven (7) days, during a period of active operations against the hostile Sioux Indians. I wish to say that the disposition of troops, and the transportation of stores, that have been made, could not have been made had it not been for your energy and skill in the management of your Steamer and command. You have done all in your power, and more than was expected, for the interests of the Government and to promote the enterprise in which we are engaged, and are sincerely deserving of my thanks.

 Very respectfully,
  (Signed)   Nelson A. Miles,
   Bvt. Major Gen'l., U. S. A."

On her way back to the camp, the *Far West* passed the steamers *Yellowstone* and *Carroll,* loaded with supplies, below Wolf Rapids, which they were unable to ascend owing to the falling river. The *Yellowstone* had a cargo of sutler's goods and the *Carroll* sixty tons of freight, and both of them lay too low in the water to carry over the rapids. Several days elapsed before they could be lightened so as to go through. At the depot it was found that the troops were preparing to take up the Indian trail again. Many of the cavalry horses on their long, hard marches through the hills, had become so weak from lack of grain that they had been held in camp longer than would otherwise have been necessary, in order that they might recuperate. Crook returned to the trail August 24th and Terry followed the next day. It seemed rather a hopeless proceeding to resume the pursuit after such a long delay, but it was a question of either doing that or doing nothing.

Shortly after starting, General Terry received from General Miles, who was again patrolling the river on the *Far West,* such decisive reports of the increasing numbers of Indians appearing near Glendive, that he abandoned his eastward march and returned to the Yellowstone at the mouth of O'Fallon Creek. Crook kept on, moving toward the Black Hills, and on September 9th his advance, commanded by Captain Mills, overtook and captured a large village under American Horse, near Slim Buttes, Dakota. The main body came up and a few hours later, while all were engaged in packing up the captured provisions which were sorely needed by the troops, another and much larger force of Indians under Crazy Horse attacked them, but were repulsed.

Though in reality the majority of the savages who had been engaged in the Custer battle had gone eastward, they had not done so in a body. Immediately after crossing the Little Missouri they had broken up into bands and innumerable small parties. The latter straggled back to the agencies gradually and quietly, hoping thus to avoid the notice of the military. True to their racial instincts, they had been satisfied with striking one decisive blow and could not long be held together by their chiefs after doing it. Crook swept aside all the organized opposition there was left in the country he was traversing and then returned to that portion of his own department whence he had marched northward in the spring.

After he had ceased active operations the only considerable bodies of hostiles left south of the Yellowstone were those in the camps of Crazy Horse and Dull Knife, about 600 lodges, all told. They swung off westward after Crook had passed them and returned to the neighbourhood of the Big Horn Mountains, intending to spend the winter there. But they did not camp together, and in November a column organized by Crook for a winter campaign and commanded by Colonel Mackenzie, 4th Cavalry, located and attacked the Cheyenne village of Dull Knife, in Willow Creek Canon of the Big Horn Mountains. The village was destroyed and its occupants driven out into the bitter weather, where many of them froze to death, while the remainder were hopelessly dispersed.

General Terry, after parting from Crook, began vigorous endeavours to run to earth such scattered fragments of the Indian army as had turned toward the Canadian line. A well-defined trail existed between the fords of the lower Yellowstone and the Missouri near Fort Peck, Montana, and it was feared the enemy might be making use of it on his flight. Terry crossed the Yellowstone on August 27th on the steamers *Carroll* and *Yellowstone,* and struck off north-westward through an unknown and very barren country toward the Big Dry Fork of the Missouri and Fort Peck.

Before leaving the river on his difficult march, Terry received advices from Lieutenant-General Sheridan that it had been determined to occupy the Yellowstone Valley with a military force during the coming winter. For this purpose Terry was instructed, as soon as field operations should close, to send the battalions of General Miles and Colonel Otis to the mouth of Tongue River to establish a temporary cantonment, it being already too late in the season to build a permanent fort before winter. Three steamers, loaded with building materials and supplies for the new post, reached Wolf Rapids almost at the same time that the Lieutenant-General's despatch came in. The river was now very low and General Terry went to see them.

The masters of two of the steamers refused absolutely to go any further, declaring that they would be wrecked in the rapids. The cargoes of their boats were therefore unloaded, hauled around the obstruction, and placed upon the *Far West,* which conveyed them to their destination. But plucky Mart Coulson, of the *Josephine,* was undismayed by the rapids. His boat had been vigorously attacked by the Indians forty miles below Glendive Creek, and after such an experience, he was not to be thwarted by so small a matter as low water. Boldly steaming ahead with his vessel, on which he was bringing up two additional companies of the 5th Infantry under Lieutenant-Colonel Whistler, he went through safely and proceeded to the Tongue.

The mouth of this stream had been indicated by General James W. Forsyth in 1875 as a favourable location for a post. It had been the desire of the military authorities for more than a decade to establish a permanent garrison somewhere in that country to hold the Indians in subjection. But the accomplishment of the project had been postponed from year to year, partly because of the isolated position which such a garrison would occupy, and the almost insurmountable difficulties that would be encountered in supplying it. But the chief cause for the delay had been the refusal of Congress to appropriate the necessary funds for the work. When Terry moved out in the spring of 1876, it was hoped that he would be able to leave a part of his troops in the country for the winter, but the hope had seemingly been crushed by the result of the battle of the Little Big Horn. That unfortunate event, however, had really rendered the founding of such a post imperative. Late in July, Congress had appropriated $200,000 for the enterprise and it was now about to become an accomplished fact.

For nearly a week Terry's troops scouted over the desolate uplands between the Yellowstone and the Missouri, making long marches, suffering much from lack of water, and finding no Indians, for the few who had actually crossed the river, principally followers of Sitting Bull, had broken up into small parties after reaching the north side. Having covered a wide circle of country, Terry returned to the river at Glendive Creek, on August 31st. He found in front of Captain Rice's camp the steamer *Silver Lake,* low-water bound with a cargo of supplies for the new cantonment, while three other boats, similarly loaded, were at a standstill eighteen miles below.

One of them, the *Benton,* had burst a steam-chest and was temporarily helpless to go either forward or back. Colonel Moore's detachment, with a large wagon train, had come down from O'Fallon Creek, where they had crossed at the same time as the troops, and they were able to handle some of the stranded supplies. But all of the boats, now so sorely needed above Wolf Rapids, had come out of the upper river and gone to Fort Buford or beyond.

CHAPTER 42

The Fruits of Struggle

During all the weeks of late summer, while other steamboat men were experiencing such perplexities in navigating the Yellowstone, Captain Marsh was taking the *Far West* wherever she was needed. Up or down river, over shoals, through rapids or chutes— it made no difference where.

He knew every foot of the river like the palm of his hand and could apparently run the *Far West* as long as there was water enough to keep the bottom damp. Sometimes General Miles was on the boat and sometimes on shore, though all of his troops not in the observation camps had gone with Terry's column when it moved out north of the river. But he kept the *Far West* constantly on patrol duty, alert for signs of the enemy.

She often conveyed from one shore to the other the scouts, white and red, who were engaged in similar work back on the prairies and in the Bad-Lands and who were likely to be encountered anywhere along the banks.

But at length General Miles temporarily relieved the boat from this service in order that she might run down to Buford after a cargo of supplies for the troops in the field. Before she left, Captain Marsh had the pleasure of greeting an old friend whose sudden appearance there was a welcome surprise to everyone. This was no less a person than "Yellowstone" Kelly. Through the summer he had been hunting and trapping in the Big Hole Basin in northern Montana, and had not known of the stirring events which were taking place along his favourite river.

But when, by chance, he heard of them and that Captain Marsh was on the Yellowstone, he hastened down to join the troops. General Miles at once employed him as a scout and he remained until the close of the year's work, doing valuable service.[1]

The *Far West* left for Fort Buford just before Terry's column came into Glendive, and the general was disappointed to find her gone, while so much transhipping was waiting to be done above the rapids. "Buffalo Bill", who had experienced enough adventures to satisfy him for the time, had ridden into camp ahead of the column, and he went down with Captain Marsh, on his way to join his family in the East.

When the steamer reached Fort Buford the supplies were found to be ready and they were promptly taken on board. The fort at this time was in charge of Gen. W. B. Hazen, commanding the 6th Infantry. He was a fine soldier and a distinguished one, but so strict a disciplinarian that the men of his command sometimes thought his rule too harsh. Just as the *Far West* was about to cast off her lines, General Hazen and his wife came on board, accompanied by a young officer whom they introduced to Captain Marsh as Lieutenant John C. Gresham, 7th Cavalry. He was going up on the boat to join his regiment. It was military custom that whenever an army officer came on board a boat on which soldiers were serving, he should assume command of them.

On the *Far West,* Sergeant Caddle and his men were still employed, never having been ordered back to the colours. It happened that no officer, excepting Lieutenant Gresham, was to make the trip, and as he was only some two months out of West Point and had never seen field service, General Hazen, on parting from him, gave him very explicit and detailed instructions regarding his duties as commanding officer, being particularly careful to impress upon him just how guard duty ought to be performed.

Sergeant Caddle and his sixteen faithful followers heard the General's formidable directions with trepidation, for they had grown ac-

---

1. Major Kelly, in a letter to the author referred to in a previous chapter, has something to say regarding the services of Captain Marsh in the campaign of 1876, which indicates that the frontier scouts held much the same opinion of him as did the soldiers.

"It took a daring man," Major Kelly writes, "to navigate the Yellowstone in the '70s, and the fact that Captain Grant Marsh was the man selected shows the favour in which he stood with army men. I think that he is the greatest steamboat captain living, and his 'Go ahead' when we came to a bad place rings in my ears yet, after all these years. He had great regard for all genuine hunters and mountain men and they admired him.

"I do not think that any other man would have dared to push his boat up the Big Horn River when the army was in dire need of such service, in the time when Custer and his men were surrounded and killed. I was in the country that year, 1876, and know the peril of it, and the terror that struck many good men."

customed, when alone on the boat, to performing guard duty in a very simple, though effective, manner. Captain Marsh was much more desirous that the soldiers should always have a good night's rest so as to be able to help in cutting and loading wood during the day, than he was that they should mount guard strictly according to the drill regulations. So it had been usual, when the boat tied up for the night, to pull the landing-stage on board, set her off from the bank with a spar, and station a single sentinel on the hurricane deck to give the alarm in case Indians should appear.

But this method did not suit the exacting views of General Hazen. He instructed Lieutenant Gresham to post a line of sentinels 200 yards out on the bank when the boat landed, and to maintain it by regular reliefs throughout the night. Having given the young officer all the good advice he could think of, the General then departed with his wife and the *Far West* got under way.

Near Forsyth's Butte she stopped for the night and Lieutenant Gresham proceeded to put his orders into practice, much to the disgust of the men. They dared say nothing, but determined if possible to frighten their inexperienced commander into bringing them back on board. The boat had made her landing beside a low bank, covered with dense willow thickets, through which a recent freshet had swept and, subsiding, had left a deposit of mud adhering to the bark of the trees. It was a disagreeable place in which to spend the night, but the Lieutenant conscientiously posted his sentries 200 yards out in the brush.

They had not been on duty long when several shots rang out, and Trooper John Dark, the same resourceful individual who had repaired the Gatling gun, came rushing breathlessly back to the boat, crying that he had just killed the biggest Indian he had ever seen. He expected the lieutenant to become pale with terror, but the lieutenant did not. Instead, he seized a lantern and plunging out into the black night through the willows, bade John take him to the Indian. The trooper was thoroughly crestfallen at this turn of affairs, for, of course, there was no Indian, and after crawling about among the willows for a while, Gresham gave him a severe reprimand and put him back on his post. There was no sleep for the sentinels that night, but when morning dawned the young officer was a sorry sight. He had been dressed the previous evening in all the spotless glory of his first new uniform of *army blue*; at daylight he was covered from head to foot with a crust of mud, accumulated from contact with the willows during his frequent tours of inspection through the night. But he had carried out his instructions to the letter.

During the day, however, he consulted with Captain Marsh and learned from him how guard duty had previously been performed, and ought to be performed for the good of the boat. The information was as a great light to him, and after that the methods previously in force were resumed. The conscientious young cavalryman went with his regiment through the remainder of the campaign and is today an officer of high rank in the service.

The *Far West* passed up through Wolf Rapids about September 5th and resumed her work of hauling supplies and patrolling the stream. Field operations had closed and the troops were breaking up and moving to their several stations. General Gibbon, with his detachments of the 7th Infantry and 2nd Cavalry, had started back to Fort Ellis. Major Reno with the 7th Cavalry had marched for Fort Buford, and General Terry, accompanied by all of Colonel Moore's troops excepting Captain Baker's Company B, had gone down to the same point on one of the boats, all of which were leaving the lower Yellowstone as fast as possible. A force was still at Glendive Creek, guarding and moving supplies, but General Miles had taken his troops to the cantonment on the Tongue. At this point the *Far West* now made her headquarters, with Company B, 6th Infantry, again on board.

General Miles was often on the boat, and one day he was desirous of sending a despatch down to Fort Buford. He had no scouts excepting "Yellowstone" Kelly, and him he could not spare. But in Captain Baker's company was a private named Cassidy, who modestly came to Captain Marsh and said:

" If you will speak to Captain Baker for me, I will take the general's despatch to Buford."

The captain did so, and the soldier was taken to General Miles and started that night on his perilous journey. As was usual on such trips, he travelled only at night and secreted himself during the day, for the Indians were still prowling about everywhere in little parties, as they had been doing all summer. On the second night out, daylight overtook Cassidy as he reached the vicinity of Sheridan's Buttes, opposite the mouth of the Powder. He decided that the top of the buttes would be a safe place of concealment for the day and made his way there. From his vantage point he commanded a wide view over the country and not long after he had settled himself, he saw a large party of Indians come down to the Yellowstone about a mile below and cross over to the north side. They remained in the vicinity all day, Cassidy watching them and not daring to move from his elevated lookout. But at nightfall he crept away and, in obedience to his orders, which were to return at once to camp in case he saw Indians, hastened back to the Tongue and reported.

The information was of great value to General Miles, who promoted Cassidy on the spot, while General Terry was warned of the Indian movement and sent the 7th Cavalry post-haste up the Missouri to head them off. Cassidy had developed a strong attachment to Captain Marsh and the next year, when his term of enlistment expired, he went down to Yankton, where the captain lived, and there took up his residence, far from scenes of warfare.

The Yellowstone was falling so low now that even Captain Marsh hesitated to tempt fate by remaining longer, lest his boat be imprisoned until the next spring. About the middle of September, therefore, he bade farewell to his many friends of the army who were to remain and, turning his back on the scenes of that never-to-be-forgotten summer, hastened down to Buford and thence straight on south to Yankton, expecting to rejoin his family and put his steamer into winter harbour. But he had scarcely reached Dakota's capital before he was called upon again for active service, this time, however, in the cause of peace instead of war.

After the death of Custer, popular indignation against the Indians became so pronounced that great pressure was exerted upon the Government to compel them to relinquish their title to the Black Hills, long coveted by settlers. The demand was a hardship upon the many red men who had remained quietly at the agencies throughout the war in Montana, but they were made to suffer for the errors of their brethren. Such powerful chiefs as Spotted Tail and Red Cloud, recognized both by the whites and by their own people as leaders of the first magnitude, had steadfastly refused to be drawn into hostilities, and they, not the hostiles, were the ones actually in possession of the Black Hills.

But, in response to the popular outcry, a peace commission was appointed to treat with the principal chiefs of the tribes interested and secure their consent to the cession of the Black Hills as well as the buffalo country of Wyoming and Montana. Some money was to be paid for the territory, of course, but it was to be as little as the commission could induce the Indians to accept. The government representatives were, at the same time, to arrange with the tribes for new and definite reservation boundaries. The chiefs in arms against the government were, naturally, not to be consulted, the peaceable element among the tribes alone being considered.

The commission included among its members, ex-Governor Newton Edmunds, of Dakota, a man who, on several previous occasions, had distinguished himself as a successful negotiator with the Sioux; Hon. George W. Manypenny, of Ohio; Gen. H. H. Sibley, who was early compelled to leave the commission owing to illness, and Right Rev. Henry B. Whipple, Protestant Episcopal Bishop of Minnesota. It proceeded to work at once and late in September secured upon its proposed treaty, the signatures of Spotted Tail, Red Cloud, Man-Afraid-of-his-Horses, American Horse (the younger), and sixty-one other leading men of the Ogalalla, Northern Cheyenne, and Arapahoe tribes. There was not one among them who was not bitterly reluctant to thus sign away the choicest portion of their birthright for any consideration, but they were helpless and could do nothing but submit with as good grace as possible.[2]

Proceeding differently from previous peace commissions, this one did not call all the Indians into one great council, but itself went from one agency to another to meet them. After it had visited the Red Cloud Agency near Laramie, and the Spotted Tail Agency on the upper White River, the commission came around by Yankton on its way to the reservations along the Missouri. Here Captain Marsh was encountered and the government representatives insisted that he should take them on up the river. With reluctance he again left home and put the *Far West* in motion for the Yankton Agency, where the chiefs of the Lower Yanktonais, and also a number of Uncpapa and Blackfoot leaders, signed the treaty. The commission then went on to Cheyenne River, Crow Creek, and the Lower Brule Agencies, securing the signatures of Sans Arcs, Blackfoot, Two Kettle, Minneconjoux and Brule chiefs, and finally completed its labours at the Santee Agency, in northern Nebraska. Captain Marsh was able to return to Yankton before the river closed.

Throughout the trip his passengers were greatly pleased with the treatment accorded them by the master of the *Far West*, and the rapidity with which he conveyed them from point to point on their important mission. As a tribute, they adopted and presented to him the following resolutions:

---

2. *History of the Sioux Indians*, by Doane Robinson.

Resolved, that Captain Grant Marsh, commanding the Steamer *Far West,* for the skill and energy displayed in navigating his vessel and for his courteous attention during the passage from Yankton, merits the sincere thanks of this Commission.

Resolved, that we commend Captain Grant Marsh to the travelling public as a skillful officer and a gentleman ever worthy of their esteem and patronage.

 (Signed) Geo. W. Manypenny, Chairman.
       H. C. Beelis.
       Newton Edmunds.
       H. B. Whipple.
       Sam'l. D. Hinman.

Standing Rock, October 9, 1876.
 (Signed) C. M. Hendley, Secretary, Sioux Com'm'n.

After the captain left the theatre of war in the Yellowstone country, military movements, under the vigorous direction of General Miles, continued with little interruption throughout the winter. The cantonment on the Tongue, at first known as Tongue River Barracks, was completed as a base of operations. Difficulties without number were experienced in bringing up to the cantonment all the supplies left at Wolf Rapids and Glendive by the steamers. The wagons available were few and many tedious trips had to be made to and fro, attended with great labour and danger. Sitting Bull and Gall had again gathered their forces into some semblance of order and, though they were few in number compared with the horde of early summer, there were enough of them to render a strong escort necessary for the safety of every wagon train moving across country.

In October, a detachment of Colonel Otis's troops, accompanying a train bound for the cantonment from Glendive, was attacked and driven back to its starting point. Colonel Otis himself, with a larger escort, then assumed command and took the train through, though not without a two days' running fight. General Miles, sallying forth from the cantonment to meet the train, went on in pursuit of the Indians. He overtook and defeated them, forcing most of them to surrender, though Sitting Bull and Gall, with about four hundred people, escaped and made their way northward into British America, where they remained for several years. The surrendered Indians gave hostages for their return to the agencies in the spring, pledges which most of them redeemed.

Returning to the cantonment, Miles refitted his troops for a winter campaign and took the field again in December. Early in January, in a desperate battle at Wolf Mountain, on the upper Tongue River, he defeated Crazy Horse, capturing so much of the latter's camp equipage that the fierce Ogalalla became disheartened and surrendered in the spring. No other general who had ever fought against Crazy Horse had been able to subdue this most redoubtable of all the Sioux chiefs.

General Terry, meanwhile, had been actively engaged in another quarter. Early in October he sent the 7th Cavalry, accompanied by some infantry and artillery, from Fort Lincoln down to the Standing Rock and Cheyenne River agencies. Assisted by the local garrisons at these places, the regiment forcibly disarmed and dismounted all the Indians congregated there, among whom were many of those who had been on the warpath during the summer. The confiscated weapons and horses were sold and the proceeds applied to the purchase of cows and working oxen for the Indians. At Fort Peck, Montana, General Hazen's troops performed a similar duty, and by the 21st of November General Terry was able to report[3] that virtually all the Indians in his department had been deprived of their firearms and riding animals, rendered dependent upon the Government for food and clothing, and helpless to engage in further hostilities.

Thus the campaign which at one time had seemed doomed to a total and disastrous failure, under the skillful, tireless and courageous guidance of the men directing it, was brought to a successful conclusion. The names of Terry and Gibbon, Crook and Miles and Otis, will ever be associated with the subjugation of the great Sioux Nation, the most powerful confederation of aborigines on the continent, for, though the work was not quite completed, and after 1876 the warlike spirit of this proud people still manifested itself at times in bloody outbreaks, the Sioux never again undertook war against the whites as an united nation. But to the enlisted soldiers and the few civilians with them, who, through that long, eventful campaign had fought and suffered and worked uncomplainingly, belongs almost as much credit as to the officers who led them. Not the least deserving were the captain and crew of the *Far West,* who had rendered such valuable services with their steamer; services without which the army would have been crippled and the very success of the campaign jeopardized.

Years afterwards, when he had risen several grades in his profes-

---

3. General Terry's Annual Report, 1876-77.

sion, General Miles is said to have stated that Captain Marsh did not a little toward placing the first star on his shoulder. The captain and his sturdy vessel doubtless helped to place a coveted bar on many an officer's shoulder-strap that summer, and chevrons on the sleeves of many a man in the ranks.

But the rewards that he prized most highly for his season's work were not the glories gained for himself or for others. They were simply the added confidence and friendship he had earned from the army he loved and from its officers, and the satisfaction of having done his duty and merited his winter's rest. The gratification of such modest ambitions of conscience has always been his chief desire and, like most men who hold fast to simple and generous ideals rather than adopt craftiness and selfishness, life has brought him little of material wealth. But, in its stead, it has given him a capacity for enjoyment, a tranquillity of mind, and a faith in and love for, his fellow men which no earthly riches could ever purchase.

A pathetic fate eventually overtook the captain's gallant steamboat. After 1876 he never again commanded the *Far West,* and some years later she drifted into the lower river trade, running between St. Louis and Roche-port, Missouri. At last, one day in the autumn of 1883, October 20th,[4] to be exact, while downward bound with a trip for St. Louis, she struck a snag in Mullanphy Bend, seven miles below St. Charles, and sank, a total loss. Though it can hardly be said that, like Kipling's galley, "a craven-hearted pilot crammed her, crashing on the shore," yet her destruction was doubtless due to some error in navigation on the part of her lower river pilot.

It seems a pity that she could not have found her last resting place somewhere in the regions where her days of glory had been spent. But under the sands at the foot of the forest-clad Charbonnier Bluffs she lies, in view of the site of old Fort Bellefontaine, where long ago the flags of France and Spain floated over the infant territory of Louisiana. At least in the restless waters that wash her wasting bones are mingled many drops from those far-off torrents of the Northwest, the Big Horn and the Yellowstone, which once, in the days of battle, bore her sturdy timbers so faithfully through every danger that they carried her at last, the Missouri Valley's most famous steamboat, to an immortal place in history.

---

4. Capt. H. M. Chittenden, U. S. A., in Report of the Missouri River Commission, 1897.

CHAPTER 43

The "Rosebud" Carries the General of the Army

Through the period of cold weather while navigation was at a standstill, the Coulson Packet Company improved the time by building more boats to accommodate the increasing traffic. The military activity in the Northwest had given a great impetus to steamboating, for the profits were enormous from running vessels at $300.00 or $350.00 per diem, the prevailing rates for government service. Along the Missouri River, moreover, thousands of settlers were annually making new homes in regions as yet remote from railroads and their presence added constantly to the local business of the river steamers.

After the army had established itself there, even the Yellowstone Valley began to attract settlers, and hardy ranchmen and farmers were herding cattle and turning the prairies into cultivated fields even before the buffalo had vanished or the rifle of the hostile had ceased to be a menace.

Early in the spring of 1877 Captain Marsh went down to St. Louis to meet and take command of one of the Company's new boats which had been built at Pittsburg during the preceding winter. She was the *Rosebud*, a vessel very similar to the *Far West* in hull construction, capacity and draught. Upon receiving the boat, the captain started at once for Bismarck with her, doing a profitable local business from St. Louis on up the Missouri.

About forty miles below Sioux City, Iowa, the *Rosebud* passed the wreck of the unfortunate steamer, *J. Donald Cameron*, which had struck a snag and sunk on May 18th.

This boat, together with the *W. T. Sherman*, had been built by the Government for service between Bismarck and the posts on the Yellowstone. The two vessels had left Jeffersonville, Indiana, together and had taken on board at Fort Leavenworth, Kansas, the families and the personal property of the officers of the 5th Infantry, which were to be conveyed to Tongue River Barracks.

When the *Don Cameron* sunk she had on board about seventy-five passengers, principally women, including the wife of General Miles and her sister, Miss Lizzie Sherman, a niece of the general. The boat had gone down quickly in eighteen feet of water, but by heroic work the crew of the *Sherman,* which was close at hand, succeeded in rescuing them all. The *Sherman* had then taken them on to their destination, but all the private property of the regiment had been lost in the wreck and was never recovered.

The *Rosebud* reached Bismarck early in July and here Captain Marsh found a distinguished party awaiting his arrival. It included W. T. Sherman, general of the Army of the United States; Colonels Poe and Bacon of his staff; General Terry, Major Card, Department Quartermaster; and Captain Smith, *aide-de-camp*. General Sherman was making a tour of inspection of the western posts and had arrived at Bismarck on his way to the Yellowstone. Being met here by the Department commander, General Terry, the latter advised that they wait the arrival of Captain Marsh, who was expected soon, as he did not wish to entrust the safety of his distinguished visitor in the hands of a less experienced navigator. It was not a difficult matter to accommodate the party comfortably, for the cabin of the *Rosebud* was much more commodious than that of the *Far West,* and as soon as the details were arranged the northward journey began.

Brief halts were made at Fort Stevenson and Fort Buford and the boat then entered the Yellowstone on her way to the cantonment on the Tongue. Nothing of particular interest had as yet occurred, though many boats were passed, either carrying up supplies or returning for fresh cargoes. But at the mouth of Glendive Creek, General Miles was unexpectedly encountered. The indefatigable Indian fighter had just reached the Glendive on one of the almost unnumbered hard scouts which he was constantly making over his district in pursuit of the Sioux who were still avoiding surrender.

When the *Rosebud* arrived, he left the field for a brief space to accompany the commanding general to his own rude headquarters, which he seldom occupied during those troublous days. His scouting column, consisting of nine troops of the 7th Cavalry and six mounted companies of the 5th Infantry, he turned over temporarily to the

Steamer *Rosebud* on the Missouri River near Fort Benton.

command of Col. S. D. Sturgis, 7th Cavalry.[1] General Miles had left the cantonment for this scout on July 4th. It was now the 15th, and on the 11th the government steamer *Sherman* had reached the post with his wife on board. But he had not yet seen her, nor did he until the *Rosebud* came in at the Tongue, about four o'clock on the afternoon of July 16th.

In the isolated posts of the upper Missouri and the Yellowstone the monotony of daily life sometimes became almost unbearable. At each one of them the garrison was a world unto itself during at least eight months of the year. Each one had within it a little cluster of crude buildings sufficient to house the troops and their supplies, and without, a wilderness peopled only by prowling savages. Usually the only relief from the ceaseless round of garrison drudgery was found in occasional scouts, while the only evidence of "the pomp and circumstance of glorious war" was the brief burial ceremony now and then required over the grave of some comrade stricken down by a Sioux bullet. In such surroundings it is not surprising that many soldiers became restless and dissatisfied, nor that desertions were frequent.

At Tongue River Barracks in 1877 these conditions did not yet prevail to so great an extent as they did in later years, for the garrison was still chiefly occupied in active campaigning, which furnished a sufficiency of excitement. Nevertheless, it may be imagined that at such a post the advent of so important a personage as General Sherman was an event of great moment. As the *Rosebud* drew near on that July afternoon it was easily to be seen that the news of her approach had travelled ahead and that preparations had been made to give the commanding general a fitting reception.

At the landing, when the boat drew up, were assembled all the officers present in garrison, and as General Sherman and his attendants stepped ashore the regimental band of the 5th Infantry struck up a martial air, for the cantonment boasted no artillery and the customary salute had, perforce, to be dispensed with. Preceded by the band, the party walked up to the post, where General Miles was privileged to meet his wife after a year's separation, and General Sherman to greet

1. Though his name is seldom mentioned in this connection, Colonel and Brevet Maj.-Gen. S. D. Sturgis, a distinguished officer of the Union Army during the Rebellion, was the actual colonel of the 7th Cavalry during nearly all of the time that Lieut.-Col. G. A. Custer held active command of the regiment. General Sturgis was assigned to the colonelcy in 1869 and retained it until his retirement from the service in 1886. During a great part of the time he was on detached service, but after the death of Custer he assumed active command.—J. M. H.

both her and his other niece, Miss Lizzie Sherman.

It was a strange place for such a family reunion, out there on the banks of the Yellowstone, amid the alarms of border warfare, and the fact was brought home to them even while they were exchanging greetings by the appearance across the river of a mounted battalion of the 5th Infantry, which had been out on the scout with General Miles and was just returning. That night General Sherman accepted the hospitality of General Miles and remained on shore, but all the other visiting officers returned to sleep in their cabins on the steamer.

The following morning was spent by General Sherman in looking over the cantonment and reservation and in examining the new and permanent post then in course of construction about one mile and a half west from the old. The new post was to be called Fort Keogh, in memory of one of the gallant troop commanders of the 7th Cavalry who had fallen with Custer. It was being built by about 200 mechanics under the direction of Captain Heintzelman, assistant quartermaster. In the evening, General Sherman received the officers and their wives at General Miles' quarters.

At ten o'clock on the morning of the 18th the officers of the garrison appeared on board the *Rosebud* to pay their official respects to General Terry, who carried his headquarters there, and at six o'clock that evening a dress parade and review were held on the plain near the post. The troops participating were the band and eight companies of the 5th Infantry, four of the companies, comprising the battalion of Captain Snyder, being mounted on Indian ponies. It was an unusual event for the hard-worked soldiers, reminding them of earlier days they had spent in the pleasant stations of the East, where dress parade was a part of the daily routine. But the interest of this occasion was enhanced by an addition to the usual ceremonies which could have been made only before a body of troops engaged in active warfare, and that of the sort which breeds heroes.

While the companies were standing on parade previous to passing in review before General Sherman and the other officers and the ladies of the garrison, some thirty enlisted men were called by name from the ranks and marched to the front and centre, accompanied by the colours. Upon the breast of each General Sherman then pinned a Medal of Honour, awarded to the recipient for some specific act of gallantry during the hard-fought engagements with the Sioux in the preceding winter. It is not an easy matter to win a medal for bravery from Congress, and perhaps nowhere else than at the Tongue River cantonment could so many men have been found deserving of such recognition. During the north-western Indian Wars in the years 1876 and 1877, the ratio of loss of officers and men to the number engaged was equal to, if not greater than, the ratio of loss to the numbers engaged on either side during the Civil War.[2] The fact is hard to realize, but it is plain that under such circumstances there was no dearth of opportunities for gallantry in action.

At ten o'clock on the evening of the parade, Generals Sherman and Terry bade farewell to their hospitable hosts at Tongue River and the *Rosebud* resumed her journey. Following the course of his memorable trip of the year before, when the boat reached the mouth of the Big Horn, Captain Marsh turned her into that stream and steamed up to the Little Big Horn. But a different scene greeted his eyes from the desolate one he had looked upon thirteen months earlier, when lying at this spot waiting for Reno's wounded. Now, 600 yards above the mouth of the tributary were encamped four companies of the 11th Infantry under Major G. P. Buell.

On the high ground nearby, the framework of substantial buildings, corresponding in number and general design to the ones at Fort Abraham Lincoln, were rapidly rising under the hands of the one hundred mechanics who had been there since July 1st. Across the mouth of the Little Big Horn a boom was stretched with hundreds of logs floating behind it, which a saw-mill close to the bank was busily cutting into lumber. Up in the timbered valley beyond could be heard the ringing axes of wood-cutters felling yet more timber to go into the structures which ere long were to become the post of Fort Custer. At this point, General Sherman said goodbye to General Terry and to Captain Marsh and his steamer. Escorted by a troop of the 7th Cavalry, sent up from Tongue River Barracks for the purpose, he departed for Fort Ellis overland, passing around to view the Custer battleground on his way.

---

2. Official Report of Gen. P. H. Sheridan, 1877-78.

CHAPTER 44

The Bones of Heroes

The battlefield of the Little Big Horn when General Sherman looked upon it, was not in the condition in which it had remained for more than a year after the fight. Only a few weeks before the commanding general reached the historic scene of disaster, a detachment of troops had visited the spot for the express purpose of clearing the field of the debris of battle, properly interring the remains of the soldiers slain there, and recovering and taking away the bodies of the officers. The party detailed for the duty was Troop I of the 7th Cavalry, under Captain Nowlan. Col. Michael V. Sheridan, a brother of Gen. Philip H. Sheridan and a member of his staff, was in general charge of the burial party, while Sergeant M. C. Caddle, the non-commissioned officer who had served so faithfully on the *Far West* during the preceding year, was with Troop I.

Captain Marsh bore no personal share in the expedition of Colonel Sheridan, as the latter went to and returned from the battlefield on the steamer *Fletcher*. But he was naturally much interested in the results of the trip and became thoroughly acquainted with them through his friendship with Sergeant Caddle and other participants. It may therefore be excusable to mention here some facts concerning the work of the burial party which are vouched for by Sergeant Caddle, though they seem to have remained practically unknown until the present time, to everyone save the men who were in that party.

Troop I in the battle of the Little Big Horn had been under the command of Captain Myles W. Keogh, who, together with every man of the troop present on the field, had been killed. Later the troop was reorganized with recruits and the few survivors of the old organization who had been absent from the colours on the fatal 25th of June. Among the latter had been Sergeant Caddle. When Custer's column moved out on the campaign, Caddle had been detailed to remain at Powder River in charge of the 7th Cavalry's property which was left there. Owing to his intimate acquaintance with the officers and men of his regiment, particularly those of Keogh's troop, the Sergeant was able to be of much assistance in identifying the dead when Colonel Sheridan reached the field in July, 1877.

All the official reports published after the battle, all the personal narratives by survivors of Reno's and Gibbon's troops, and all the later histories which the author has had access to, state, if they mention the matter at all, that on Wednesday, June the 28th, 1876, Reno's and Gibbon's men, "buried the dead" of Custer's command. Sergeant Caddle,[1] on the other hand, declares that when Colonel Sheridan's burial party arrived at the field a year later, they found all the skeletons lying on top of the ground. This is accounted for, the sergeant says, by the fact that immediately after the battle the survivors and the relief column had no means of digging graves. There had been not a pick nor a shovel with Custer's command, and probably there were not a half-dozen such implements with Gibbon's troops. Both columns had set out on forced marches, and they were not carrying a pound of superfluous baggage. Under such circumstances and with the limited time at their disposal, the task of digging over 260 graves in the hard prairie soil was manifestly an impossible one. Nor does it seem to have been seriously attempted.

Colonel Sheridan and his men camped on the field for about ten days, interring the bones. Sergeant Caddle states that the bodies of all of the officers who had fallen, excepting two who were never found, were placed in coffins. Each body had a stake at its head marked with a number to correspond with the name in a list which had been prepared immediately after the fight. The sergeant says that when they came to the body marked Number One in the list and on the stake at its head, and supposed to be that of General Custer, it was placed in a coffin, and then on the ground was found a blouse on which it had been lying. An examination of the blouse revealed the name of the wearer in an inside pocket; it was that of a corporal. It was a disconcerting discovery to find that even the general could not be satisfactorily identified, but the sergeant goes on to state that later they "found another body and placed in coffin. I think we got right body the second time."

General Edward S. Godfrey, undoubtedly the best living authority

---
1. In personal letters to the author and to Captain Marsh.

on the campaign of the Little Big Horn in all its aspects, (as at time of first publication), throws further light on this distressing topic in a letter to the author, in which he says:

> What Sergeant Caddle says as to the burial of the greater number of the bodies is pretty correct. There were very few tools in the command. Each troop had a certain part of the ground to go over and bury the dead within its limits. But I feel quite sure that in the case of the officers greater care was exercised. Captain H. J. Nowlan, 7th Cavalry, told me that he marked the grave of each officer with a stake driven below the surface of the ground. The name of the officer was written, on a slip of paper, this paper was put in an empty cartridge shell, and this shell driven into the top of the stake. He made a sketch of the ground to show the location of the grave of each officer, and he went with General M.V. Sheridan when the bodies were removed. In some cases part of the bones were somewhat removed from the places of burial, but Captain Nowlan told me great care was taken in their collection.

On the field Sergeant Caddle picked up a shoe which he recognized as having belonged to Captain Keogh.[2] Most of his former comrades of Troop I he was able to identify by their clothing and other distinguishing marks which he found. All were lying as they had fallen, in skirmish line about nine feet apart. Before the burial party left, each grave was marked with a wooden headboard on which was painted the name and rank of the dead, if known. A number of them had to be marked "Unknown." A large monument was also put up on the spot where General Custer was supposed to have fallen. It was in the form of a pyramid and was constructed of cord-wood, the interior being filled with bones of the dead horses which were scattered all over the field. The head-boards have all since been replaced by stones, while a handsome monolith now stands instead of the first crude pile of timber, as sentinel over the field of glory.

Sergeant Caddle relates an incident of the battle itself which is not generally known. The stories have often been told of the troopers,

---

2. There seem to have been more relics of Captain Keogh recovered than of any other officer who fell with Custer. His horse, Comanche, was saved, as previously related, while among other booty of the 7th Cavalry recovered by General Crook on the battlefield of Slim Buttes, Dakota, was one of Captain Keogh's gauntlets, marked with his name.

Morton, Goldin and Kanipe, who were sent from Custer's column with orders to Reno and Benteen after the parting of the squadrons and who thus narrowly escaped with their lives. But there was yet another man who slipped through the jaws of death even later than they did, though perhaps the fact that he did so involuntarily deterred him from ever making a public statement of his adventure. Sergeant Caddle, in a letter to Captain Marsh, gives a brief account of the incident which may as well be given here in his own words, since it leaves nothing to be added:

.... There was one thing I forgot to mention about the Custer fight that very few know about. The company blacksmith of I Company, 7th Cavalry, Captain Keogh's company, was Gustave Korn. When the command was about a half mile from the Indian camp, he had to stop to cinch up his saddle. When he came up to the company again he could not stop his horse, which ran right through the Indians to where Colonel Reno was. His horse dropped dead just when about two rods from the breastworks. He was shot five times. The man did not get a scratch. This same Gustave Korn was one of the first men killed at Wounded Knee, S. D., 1890. The horse that Korn had killed was the first horse that was issued to me when I came to N. D., in 1873. I traded with Korn before starting out on trip, for another horse. . . .

After General Sherman had left the steamer *Rosebud* at the mouth of the Little Big Horn, the boat returned to Fort Keogh with General Terry still on board. She was met at the fort by General Miles, who informed Captain Marsh that he desired the boat to remain in the Yellowstone during the balance of the summer for the purpose of transporting supplies. General Terry therefore left the *Rosebud* and went on board the *Far West,* which was about departing for Fort Buford, while Captain Marsh began running his steamer in quartermaster's service between the Tongue and the Big Horn, continuing the work until the water became too low for navigation.

The sudden and remarkable dash of Chief Joseph and his nontreaty Nez Perce Indians from north-western Oregon across Idaho and Montana almost to the British line, furnished plenty of excitement for the soldiers during the late summer. General Miles, hurrying across country, intercepted the Nez Perce fugitives at the Bear Paw Mountains, nearly on the Line, and prevented them from forming the junction with Sitting Bull, which they contemplated. But the campaign was fought far from the Yellowstone regions where Captain Marsh was stationed and he had no part in it. Indeed, he seldom left his boat at all, for she was very busy all through the season in carrying to Fort Custer the supplies brought up to Fort Keogh by other boats which were of too deep draught to convey them further.

The round trip between the two posts usually occupied only a few days and it soon became customary on almost every trip for some of the ladies of the Fort Keogh garrison to make the journey for pleasure. It furnished a welcome break in the monotony of their life at the post, and since the danger of Indian attacks had ceased to be as great as formerly, Captain Marsh was glad to have them along. On one occasion Miss Lizzie Sherman and Mrs. C. E. Hargous, wife of the First Lieutenant commanding Company C, 5th Infantry, made the trip, escorted by Lieutenants O. F. Long and H. K. Bailey of the 5th. Both of the ladies, but especially Miss Sherman, speedily won the approval of Captain Marsh by their cheerful tempers and the uncomplaining spirit with which they bore the little inconveniences unavoidable to travellers in such a country.

As usual, the boat made frequent landings to obtain firewood, and when she did so it was the duty of her officers to take their guns and go out with the working party as guards against Indian attack. The ladies usually improved these opportunities to walk ashore and ramble along the bank near the boat with their escorts. Toward sunset one evening the *Rosebud* landed at the side of a bluff covered with good-sized pine trees, and the crew went out after logs, which they were to take on board and saw up under way. Captain Marsh accompanied the choppers and while standing near them at the crest of the bluff, rifle in hand, he heard his name called. He turned and saw Miss Sherman and Lieutenant Long a little way down the slope. The young lady was beckoning to him excitedly and calling:

"Come, quick, Captain! Bring your gun!"

He hastened down and as he reached her side she was looking with trepidation at a hollow log lying near, while Lieutenant Long was half-laughingly trying to quiet her alarm.

"Oh, Captain Marsh," exclaimed Miss Sherman, as he came up, "a big, striped snake just ran past me into that log. I saw it. Please shoot it quick, oh, please!"

The captain walked over and peered into the log, but he could see nothing. His action naturally increased Miss Sherman's agitation and she implored him to "shoot quick!" So, being anxious to display his gallantry in the presence of so pretty a girl, he thrust the muzzle of his gun into the hole and blazed away. Scarcely had the report of the shot sounded when something leaped forth from the log and, darting across the open space, disappeared in the bushes.

There was a moment of silence while each looked at the other in horrified surprise. Then everyone turned, and with significant speed fled to the boat and disappeared within their respective cabins. A few moments later, if someone had stepped to the stern of the *Rosebud*, he might have discovered, floating away on the swift current of the Yellowstone, some objects strongly resembling human wearing apparel. And such, in fact, they were. Miss Sherman's "big, striped snake" was striped, undoubtedly; her only error had been in mistaking a quadruped for a reptile, for the quarry was a polecat and he had left his pursuers with very positive evidence as to his identity.

When the *Rosebud* finally went out of the river in the fall, Miss Sherman was a passenger as far as Bismarck. On bidding Captain Marsh farewell, she gave him this solemn, parting injunction:

"Captain, beware of the snakes on the Yellowstone!" During the following winter Miss Sherman was married to Senator Don Cameron of Pennsylvania. Though Captain Marsh never saw his fair passenger again after she left his boat at Bismarck, her advice has not been forgotten.

CHAPTER 45

Rustlers

After lying dormant for seven years, the Northern Pacific Railroad, in the spring of 1879, at length began pushing construction work westward on its line from Bismarck. The first division on which actual operations were undertaken extended from the Missouri River due west about one hundred miles toward the Little Missouri. During the summer the surveyors, graders and track-layers were exposed to great danger from Indians, and four companies of infantry from Forts Buford and Lincoln remained constantly with them as they moved forward. The Indians who made such precautions necessary were chiefly from the camps of Sitting Bull in British America. Since his escape to alien territory three years before with his thirty wretched lodges, the haughty troublemaker of the Sioux had gained in strength and importance almost daily.

The restless elements in all the tribes of the Northwest naturally regarded him as the master-spirit of disaffection and it became the ambition of every unruly red man from the boundaries of Nebraska to the mountain valleys of Idaho to make his way to the camps of Sitting Bull. There he fondly imagined he would find again the old-time freedom and plenty which had vanished forever from the regions he had been wont to roam.

It was this vision of barbaric liberty to be found beyond the Line which gave Chief Joseph the impulse to lead his Nez Perce followers on their desperate northward dash in 1877; which impelled the Bannock tribesmen to essay the same adventure a twelve-month later, and which for years sent little parties straggling northward constantly from the great reservations along the Missouri. In 1879 General Miles estimated that the camps of Sitting Bull contained not less than 6,000, and possibly as many as 8,000 souls, and from 12,000 to 15,000 horses.[1] The Dominion authorities permitted this formidable body of hostiles to remain unmolested on their soil, gathering all the arms and ammunition necessary for frequent incursions into the United States. Such incursions became more numerous as time went on, for the Indians did not find the easy existence in their new abode which they anticipated. Game was becoming almost as scarce north of the Line as south of it and to keep themselves from starvation, Sitting Bull's followers resorted to raids into Montana, where many pioneer farmers and stock-raisers fell easy victims to their attacks.

In spite of the dangers they were compelled to encounter, settlers poured into the fertile valleys of the Missouri and the Yellowstone, most of them engaging in the herding of cattle, for which industry the country was peculiarly suited. In March, 1880, Lieutenant Maguire, an officer of the corps of Engineers who visited the country on surveying and scientific work, found 600 people in the new settlement of Miles City, under the shadow of Fort Keogh, fifty-four settlers between that place and Fort Buford, seventy-two ranchers along Tongue River, and 588 white people in the Yellowstone Valley above Fort Keogh, of whom seventy-seven were women, while over 23,000 cattle and 8,000 sheep were being grazed over the prairies from which the buffalo and other wild creatures were rapidly disappearing.[2]

But in protecting these infant settlements from Sitting Bull's warriors and those white outlaws of the border who were scarcely less ruthless, the garrisons of Forts Keogh and Custer, Ellis and Shaw and Buford, were kept busy night and day. Hardly a week passed that scouts were not out from one or more of the army posts in pursuit of marauders, red or white, who had been raiding ranches and farms and committing robbery and murder.

As in the early mining days of western Montana fifteen years before, Sheriff Plummer and his cut-throat confederates had long held the community in terror, so now in the new grazing country of eastern Montana a younger generation of *desperadoes* preyed on a people as yet too feeble to enforce the laws. Among the Bad-Lands back from the Yellowstone and in the remote fastnesses of the hills along the Little Missouri, the outlaws found safe havens whence they might sally forth to waylay travellers or swoop down by night upon the scattered cattle herds pasturing in the river bottoms. From their dual occupation the outlaws became equally well known as "cattle rustlers" and "road

---

1. General Terry's Official Report, 1879-80.
2. Report of the Chief of Engineers, 1880-81.

agents," and they gave the troops almost as much trouble as the Indians. When business became dull in their shady professions they would turn temporarily to the trap and the rifle and secure a few peltries for barter at the nearest post. Or, shouldering their axes, they would go down to a timber point and cut cord-wood for passing steamers. But while posing as industrious frontiersmen, eager to earn an honest dollar, they were ever on the alert for opportunities to practice their chosen vocations. Nor were they at any pains to conceal the fact, for they held the fragile law of the settlements in utter contempt, as one of Captain Marsh's experiences with them well illustrates.

After the season of 1877 the captain gave up the steamer *Rosebud* and, at the same time, his long connection with the Coulson Packet Company. The following spring he engaged himself to the firm of Leighton and Jordan, post traders at Forts Buford and Keogh and at Poplar River Agency, on the Fort Peck Indian Reservation. Leighton and Jordan were constantly receiving large quantities of freight from Bismarck during the open season, and they determined for the sake of economy to have a steamboat of their own. Accordingly, during the winter of 1877-78, a boat was built for them at Pittsburg, Pa., under the direction of an Eastern partner in their business, Captain C. W. Batchelor of Pittsburg. The new vessel was named the *F.Y. Batchelor*, in memory of a deceased brother of the captain. Early in the spring Captain Marsh entered into a contract with Leighton and Jordan to take command of the boat and he went East to bring her up to Bismarck.

On the 9th of May the *Batchelor* cleared from Pittsburg, carrying as passengers Captain Batchelor and several of his friends, bound for a sight-seeing tour in the far Northwest. An excellent way-landing business was done along the Ohio and Mississippi to St. Louis and thence up the Missouri to Yankton, where the boat arrived on June 3rd. At Ste. Genevieve, Missouri, the places of the two Ohio River engineers were taken by Missouri rivermen, one of whom was George Foulk, who had served the *Far West* so well two years before. Captain Marsh's partner at the wheel, Andy Johnson, left the *Batchelor* at Yankton to take charge of the *Nellie Peck,* downward bound. The river was high and rising and the *Batchelor* made a quick run to Bismarck, where she arrived on June 12th and discharged nearly all the cargo brought up from below, a new cargo of post traders' goods being taken on for the upper forts and for Miles City. At Bismarck one of the owners, Mr. Joseph Leighton, joined the boat and on the 12th she started up river.

When Fort Buford was reached, Mr. Leighton found bad news awaiting him. Among the government contracts held by his firm was one for keeping the garrison of Fort Buford supplied with fresh beef. The herd for this purpose was pastured opposite the fort in the point of land between the Missouri and the Yellowstone Rivers, where the heavy timber protected the cattle from inclement weather and good grazing was close at hand. But one night just previous to the arrival of the *Batchelor* a gang of "rustlers" had paid a visit to the herd and the next morning fifty fat steers were missing. When Mr. Leighton received this information, his anger knew no bounds, but as he had never met with a similar experience before and did not know how to proceed, it seemed that his resentment would probably have to waste itself without result.

The boat had not gone far on her way up the Yellowstone when she came to a newly established woodyard. She went to the bank to take on some fuel, and it was then found that the proprietors of the infant industry were four men well known in the country, whose reputations for honesty were exceedingly dubious. From certain of their remarks which he overheard, Captain Marsh soon became convinced that the seeming wood-hawks knew a great deal concerning the recent disappearance of the beef cattle from the Fort Buford herd. He quietly informed Mr. Leighton of his suspicions, but had no sooner done so than the latter, bursting with indignation, rushed over to the men and, after abusing them roundly, finished his tirade by announcing that if they did not immediately return the stolen stock he would inform Judge Strevell, at Miles City, and have them all arrested.

Mr. Leighton's dire threats had an effect upon his auditors which was painfully surprising to him. Not only did they fail to show any evidences of consternation, but, on the contrary, they laughed at him scornfully and walked away. His torrent of invective had burst forth before Captain Marsh could foresee or prevent it, and the captain had been obliged to stand by and listen to it in uncomfortable silence, well knowing that Mr. Leighton was merely making himself ridiculous. The captain had passed through long years of experience with men of the hardened class to which these rustlers belonged, and he was well aware that they no more feared the majestic name of Judge Strevell than they did that of the King of Siam. As soon as he could break in, he drew Mr. Leighton aside and exclaimed:

"Now, see here, Joe, you're making a bad break. These fellows don't care anything, for that sort of talk, and you'll get no cattle by raising such a disturbance."

"Well, then, how in h—— am I going to get them?" sputtered the irate trader.

"I'll tell you how if you'll do as I say," replied the captain. "The boys like to play a game of poker now and then."

Leighton was mystified. "Go on," he said, doubtfully.

"They've got to have money to play it with, haven't they? Give it to them. Make it $250; five dollars apiece for the cattle. Have somebody fix it up with the boys and give them fifty five-dollar bills, and the cattle will be back in the herd mighty soon."

"Oh, get out," cried Leighton. "That's throwing good money after bad. They'll keep the money and the cattle, too."

"No, they won't," answered the captain. "You do as I say and you'll get your cattle, and it's the only way you ever will get them."

Though sceptical, Mr. Leighton took his advice. "The boys" were invited on board and went up river some distance. While the boat was under way the financial arrangement was made and the $250 were quietly handed over to the rustlers. Then they went ashore, and a few days later Mr. Leighton received the comforting intelligence that the missing cattle had returned to the herd as suddenly and mysteriously as they had previously vanished from it.

When the *Batchelor* arrived at Fort Keogh on June 24th she was warmly welcomed, and during the evening the officers and ladies of the post gave a military hop on board, the music being furnished by the regimental band of the 5th Infantry. Next morning the boat entered the Big Horn on her way to Fort Custer. The incidents of her journey up the Big Horn and of her stay at Fort Custer are interestingly described in her log, which was kept by the clerk, S. J. Batchelor, writing from the dictation of Captain Marsh:

June 26.—The first buffalo was seen this morning. During the day a great many were seen, and many shots fired at them, but we failed to find any choice buffalo steaks served up for our meals. Didn't stop to pick them up. At 6 p. m. we arrived at the old Custer battleground (now Fort Pease) of 1873. At 8 p. m. we entered the Big Horn River and laid up for the night five miles above the mouth, having made the run from Tongue River in two daylights, being pronounced the quickest time ever made.

June 27.—All hands were called up this morning to see the

snow-capped Big Horn Mountains. To see the sun glistening on the snow, while we were sweltering with heat, was truly a sight to be witnessed. The distance to the mountains was estimated at seventy-five miles, but seen very distinctly with the naked eye. The Big Horn River is one of the most rapid and tortuous rivers that has ever been navigated by a steamboat. The current is terrific and at places it seems impossible for any boat to stem it. Have had no occasion to use a line on account of the current.

June 28.—Arrived at Fort Custer at 7 a. m., being the first and only boat that has arrived there this summer. Fort Custer is situated at the junction of the Little Big Horn and Big Horn Rivers. The fort stands at an elevation of one hundred and seventy-five feet above the river, and at an altitude of seven thousand feet above the ocean. Part of the 2nd Infantry and part of the 11th Cavalry, under command of General Buell, are stationed here. While lying here, something more than one hundred lodges of Crow Indians were busily engaged crossing the river with all their plunder and ponies, on their way to their new reservation on the Big Horn. It was a sight well worth seeing. We had many a '*how*' and shake during our stay. These Indians are a very honest tribe; won't steal unless they get a chance.

Captain Baldwin, adjutant general of General Miles' staff, sent an ambulance to the boat and took Captains C. W. Batchelor, Warner and Sharpe out to the Custer battlefield, where General Miles had gone that morning, with a company of infantry as escort, to make an examination of the battlefield. General Miles ordered horses and escorted the visitors around the entire field, a distance of not less than fifteen miles, pointing out and showing them all prominent places known in that terrible struggle against such odds in which more than three hundred brave men lost their lives.

The party crossed the Little Big Horn at the same ford where General Reno crossed in his retreat. Curley, the Crow scout, the only known living being saved from the Custer massacre, was interviewed through an interpreter on the boat, by General Miles. More details and correct information was obtained from him than had ever been given. Curley had never recovered from the fright of that memorable day. General Miles was accompanied over the battlefield by White Horse and Little Creek, two

Cheyenne Indians who were in the fight against Custer. The Indian village, where Custer made the attack, was five miles in length along the Little Big Horn, and said to number from five to seven thousand warriors. The plain where the Indians were encamped was a beautiful, wide prairie, covered with good grass. The Little Big Horn, where Reno crossed on his retreat, to-day contained water deep enough to come to the middle of the saddle-flaps of the horses.

General Miles and his party went down on the boat as far as Fort Keogh, where they disembarked while the *Batchelor* proceeded to Bismarck. Later in the season, having discovered that his boat was possessed of unusual speed and staying powers, Captain Marsh determined to try her for a record. How well she succeeded is shown in the log of the Steamer *F.Y. Batchelor*, trip No. 4, which reads:

August 10.—Left Bismarck at 4:30 p. m. Arrived at Turtle Creek at 10:30 p. m. Took 22¾ cords of wood. Met steamer *Josephine*.

August 11.—Arrived at Knife River 4:30 a. m. Met steamer *Eclipse*. Reached Stevenson 9 a. m., 16½ hours out. Arrived at old Berthold 12:25, 19 hours 55 minutes from Bismarck. Arrived 1½ miles below Little Missouri at 4:30 p. m., 24 hours out. Took 4 cords wood. Landed at Pleasant Point and took 25 cords. Met steamer *Big Horn* a little above Berthold.

August 12.—Arrived at Knife River No. 2 at 3 p. m., 34½ hours out from Bismarck. Met steamer *Helena* at 7:30 a. m. at Strawberry Island. Arrived at Tobacco Garden at 9:40 a. m.; at Lanning & Grinnell's wood-yard at 9:55; took 12½ cords wood. When 48 hours out were ten miles below the Big Muddy. Arrived at Big Muddy at 6 p. m., 49½ hours out. Arrived at Buford 11:55 p. m., 55 hours and 25 minutes out from Bismarck. We, the undersigned passengers on the steamer *Batchelor*, certify to the correctness of the above statement.

L. N. Sanger,
Captain, 11th Infantry.
Sig Hanauek,
J. E. Walker,
Bismarck, D. T.[3]

---

3. The above log of the steamer *F.Y. Batchelor*, as well as the extract from the log of her first trip, previously quoted, are taken from *Incidents in My Life*, by Charles William Batchelor.

STEAMER F.Y. *BATCHELOR* AT THE FORT BUFORD LANDING, 1878

(The photograph was taken on August 13, 1878, the morning after the Batchelor had reached Fort Buford from Bismarck, having made the quickerst run on record between the two points: 55 hours and 25 minutes).

Though the *Far West* had made over twice the distance in twenty-five minutes less time when bringing Reno's wounded to Fort Lincoln two years before, she had done it while steaming with the current. The *Batchelor*, on the other hand, made her record against the current, as speed records are customarily made. Her time for the upstream run between Bismarck and Fort Buford has never been equalled by another boat.

CHAPTER 46

With Kendrick to the Musselshell

It is noticeable in the history of all Western rivers that as railroads have become well established to points along their banks the steamboat industry below these points has languished and finally died. Before railroads had reached the Missouri River, St. Louis was the commercial centre for the entire valley of that stream and the starting place of all its steamboat lines. Then, as the railroads crept into Omaha and other towns above St. Louis, Sioux City became the base of navigation; then Yankton, and, at last, Bismarck. The changes were wrought quickly and positively. There was never a reaction to old conditions when once they had vanished.

One season the levee of a river town might be crowded with busy packets; the next, after the whistle of the locomotive had sounded somewhere along the shores above it, that levee would be deserted and grass-grown. The spirit of the age demands rapid transportation, and the speeding railroad train struck the knell of the leisurely river boat. Though in recent years the enormously increasing demands of commerce make it evident that a resort will soon have to be made to the rivers for the transportation of slow and heavy freight in order to relieve the overtaxed railroads, the revival of river commerce is still in the future and, when it comes, it will doubtless be conducted by methods differing radically from those formerly in vogue.

Though Yankton had not totally lost her river trade in 1878, 1879, and 1880, it was on the wane, and Bismarck, built up by the Northern Pacific Railroad, was profiting by the older city's loss. The steamer *F. Y. Batchelor,* going upriver in the spring of 1878, spoke but one boat between Yankton and Bismarck, while between Bismarck and Fort Keogh she spoke six. The prosperous boating days of even the Yellowstone were numbered, however, and every rail spiked down on the

294

westward-creeping line of the railroad brought nearer the time when the packets, their occupation gone, must be laid upon the bank to rust and decay. But a few years of life were still left to the trade of the extreme upper rivers, and Captain Marsh remained in it as long as he could profitably do so.

The season of 1879, and the early part of that of 1880, were uneventful to the captain. He continued on the *Batchelor,* plying between Bismarck and the Yellowstone. During the winter of 1879 he built at Sioux City for local ferry purposes a stern-wheel boat which he named the *Andrew S. Bennett,* in honour of his old friend, Captain Bennett of the 5th Infantry. This brave officer had fallen in a battle with the Bannock Indians on Clark's Fork, Montana, September 4, 1878,[1] and his death caused deep sorrow to Captain Marsh, who had come to know him intimately during their days together on the Yellowstone.

As soon as General Miles learned of the captain's action in naming his new ferry-boat after the deceased soldier, he and the other officers of the 5th Infantry engaged an artist in the East to paint a life-size portrait of Captain Bennett, which they presented to Captain Marsh. He hung it in the cabin of the vessel and, though the latter was cut down and sunk by the ice at Sioux City many years ago, the portrait was rescued and is still in the captain's possession.

While owning the *Andrew S. Bennett,* Captain Marsh did not himself operate her, but hired a master, as he did for the ferry-boat at Bismarck, which he had acquired several years earlier. He found it more profitable to remain on the *Batchelor* himself, where he could command a good salary during the open season.

Throughout the years ending with 1880, the Indians along the British line were becoming constantly more troublesome. The scarcity of game in Canada was not only forcing the followers of Sitting Bull back into Montana for subsistence, but was also driving the native Canadian Indians, of the Cree, Blood, Piegan, and other tribes, to indulge in similar forays. Such conditions naturally aroused great indignation among the agency Indians in northern Montana, whose reservations were invaded, and the United States troops were steadily engaged in pursuing the hostiles and in fighting dozens of insignificant engagements which must ever remain nameless in history, though they brought death to many a brave soldier.

In this desultory warfare Captain Marsh, quietly steaming back and

---

1. *The Army of the United States.*

forth along the Yellowstone, bore no part. But at length, late in the autumn of 1880, so late, indeed, that it was really winter, a situation arose in which the military authorities were glad to be able to turn again to the veteran boatman who had served the army so well in the past.

At such an inclement time of year General Miles was again contemplating one of those hard winter campaigns against the marauding Indians from Canada to which he so often resorted. In order to have supplies readily accessible to his troops when they should take the field, he had caused a depot to be established on the Missouri at the mouth of Musselshell River. To this point, on October 30th, he despatched a party of twelve soldiers, ten Indian scouts and an interpreter, under Lieutenant Kislingbury, 11th Infantry, to guard the supplies which were already there and others which were still to arrive.

The lieutenant and his detachment arrived at their destination on November 6th. Next morning, in that still hour just before dawn so often chosen by Indians for their attacks, the drowsy herd-guard suddenly found itself fighting for life with a war party of Sioux who rushed upon them like phantoms. As the rifle fire crackled out, the entire detachment hurried to the rescue and after an hour's contest the enemy was driven off, losing one warrior in the encounter. On their part, the assailants killed one horse of the herd and wounded three.[2] The Indians drew off but remained in the immediate vicinity, keeping a close watch on the party of soldiers and evidently intending to secure reinforcements and return to the attack.

According to Lieutenant Kislingbury's report, it was a perilous predicament in which he found himself, for unless assistance could reach him before the attacking force was increased, his entire command was in danger of destruction. Captain Marsh in the meantime, knowing nothing of the events going forward at the Musselshell, had come up to Fort Buford on the *F.Y. Batchelor* with a cargo from Bismarck, expecting that it would be his last trip for the season and anxious that it should be.

On the morning of the 4th of November he was unloading the last of his consignment of goods preparatory to leaving when Captain Woodruff, the Commissary of Subsistence at Fort Buford, came on board and inquired how much he would charge to carry a cargo of supplies to the depot at the Musselshell. Captain Marsh was surprised at the question, for the distance was 318 miles, the river was very low and the season so late that any boat which undertook the trip would

2. Annual Report of General Terry, 1880-81.

almost certainly be frozen in before she could return to Fort Buford, if, indeed, the ice did not prevent her even reaching the Musselshell. He was reluctant to accept the work at any price, but finally stated that he would go for $350 per day.

Captain Woodruff was a good friend of Captain Marsh, for he it was who had commanded the artillery in Major Moore's fight with the Indians at the mouth of Powder River. He was evidently desirous that Captain Marsh should take the supplies to the Musselshell, but one obstacle stood in the way. It happened that, beside the *Batchelor*, another boat was still lying at the Fort Buford levee, the *General Terry*, a vessel built after the model of the *Batchelor* and similar to her in all respects. Woodruff quietly informed Marsh that Captain Sims, of the *General Terry*, was anxious to secure the work at $160 per day.

Captain Marsh shrugged his shoulders at the information.

"Very well," he replied. "If Captain Sims wants to do it for that price he is welcome to, and you had better accept. I don't want to go, anyway, and I can't safely undertake it for less than the price I named."

"Well, I will telegraph General Terry at St. Paul and ask him for instructions," said the army officer, as he left the boat.

A few hours later he returned with a telegram from the General. The purport of the message was that there was a great difference in the prices asked by the two steamboat masters, but "the interests of the government" demanded that the *F.Y. Batchelor* should make the trip to the Musselshell. Captain Marsh consequently set to work loading the supplies which were to be carried up, the cargo consisting chiefly of oats. It did not take long to ship them and as soon as they were arranged Lieut. Frederick M. H. Kendrick, 7th Infantry, came on board and assumed military command and the *Batchelor* cast off her lines and started.

The voyage proved no less arduous than had been anticipated. Owing to the condition of the river the spars had frequently to be resorted to. Yet, considering the difficulties encountered, good time was made and on November 12th the boat arrived a short distance below the Musselshell, where she stuck on a bar. Of the events immediately following, Major, formerly Lieutenant Kendrick, speaks as follows:[3]

> Early on the morning of the day we reached the Musselshell, and while sparring over a bar, a mounted soldier from Lieut.

---

3. In a letter to the author.

Kislingbury's command hailed us from the bank. We took him on board, when he informed us that the night before[4] Lieut. Kislingbury's guard over his stock had been fired into by Indians, that his command turned out and drove them off, and that Fort Keogh being easier to communicate with, Lieut. K. had sent a courier to that post with his report.

We reached Musselshell early in the forenoon, unloaded, and pulled out that afternoon, fearing that as it was late in the season we might get frozen in before reaching Buford. From Lieut. K.'s conversation with me while unloading, I concluded that the attack came from a hunting party of Yanktonais returning to their reservation. We passed a party on the opposite bank of the river just before reaching the Musselshell. I thought their object was to cut out his herd, but, being discovered, they fired a few shots (and retired?).

Lieutenant Kislingbury and his men were glad to see the *Batchelor,* but the latter made haste to depart as soon as her cargo of grain, so indispensable to the success of General Miles' operations, had been put ashore. It did not appear that the presence of the steamer's crew was necessary to the safety of the depot guard. As stated by Major Kendrick, Lieutenant Kislingbury had already sent to Fort Keogh for assistance, and on November 12th, the same day the boat reached the Musselshell, Troops B and E, 2nd Cavalry, and Company H, 5th Infantry, left Keogh for that point, reaching their destination on the 19th. The Indians, probably aware that help was coming to the besieged, did not press their attack, though they remained in the neighbourhood until the re-enforcements appeared.

Before the *Batchelor* left the depot, Lieutenant Kislingbury presented to Captain Marsh the scalp of the Indian who had been killed in the skirmish a few days before; surely a sufficiently ghastly and realistic memento of the occasion. The captain retained it for some time and then, in turn, gave it to one of his friends.

Though Lieutenant Kislingbury came scathless through this characteristic bit of frontier campaigning, he was destined soon to lose his life under most unusual and distressing circumstances. In the following spring, 1881, he volunteered for service with the ill-fated expedition into the Arctic regions which was conducted by Lieutenant A.

---

4. The attack had taken place on the morning of November 7th, as previously noted.—J. M. H.

W. Greeley, 5th Cavalry, later Major-General Greeley. The party was in the Arctic for nearly three years. Toward the end of that period their supplies gave out and a majority of them perished miserably of starvation before relief came. Lieutenant Kislingbury's robust physique enabled him to survive until almost the end, but he at last succumbed, dying on June 1, 1884, only three weeks before the steamers *Bear* and *Thetis,* under Capt. Winfield S. Schley, U. S. N., rescued Lieutenant Greeley and the few remaining members of his party.

During the 13th, 14th and 15th, the weather remained fine and the *Batchelor,* fleeing through the shallow bends with speed accelerated by the fear of coming winter, made good progress. But on the next day it began to snow and blow, and it soon became evident that the steamer's course was run and that she must yield to the inevitable. Major Kendrick says:[5]

> I think it was the next morning, or the morning of the second day of our return, that slush ice began to form, and by noon our wheel was a solid mass of ice and we were at the mercy of the current. When we had drifted to a favourable looking place we tied up for the winter. The next morning, the ice being solid, I sent several of the crew[6] across to go to the nearest point where they could communicate with Buford and inform the C(ommanding) O(fficers) that we were frozen in.
>
> While these men were absent we built a log cabin for winter quarters for such of the crew as Grant Marsh might decide were sufficient to care for the boat till released in the spring. We stocked the cabin with stores from the boat. Captain Grant Marsh, myself, and such of the crew as was not required then left by transportation sent from Buford.

The point at which the *Batchelor* became imprisoned in the ice was near the mouth of Milk River, the upper boundary of the Fort Peck Indian Reservation, and 138 miles below the Musselshell. The cabin built on the bank, which was sonorously termed a *fort,* was rendered necessary by the fact that the lightly-built cabin of the boat could not be made habitable for the crew during the extremely cold winter weather of that region. All portable property was taken from the steamer and placed in the cabin, the *Batchelor* herself being tempo-

---
5. In the letter to the author previously quoted.
6. Captain Marsh states that two Fort Berthold Indian scouts who were on board carried the message.—J. M. H.

rarily abandoned. Captain Marsh placed his stout-hearted and level-headed engineer, George Foulk, in command of the ten men of the crew who were left as guards. They were plentifully supplied with food, weapons and ammunition, but when Kendrick, Marsh and the rest of the crew left them on November 25th and started for Fort Buford, it was a difficult if not a dangerous position in which the eleven men found themselves.

They were marooned in the midst of a howling wilderness, with no possibility of getting out for many months; a wilderness whose only human occupants were Indians from Sitting Bull's camps, ferocious with want and bitter in hatred of the white men. No one could tell at what hour of the day or night some of these enemies might pounce upon the lonely cabin on Milk River. But the plucky little garrison survived all the perils of Arctic climate and threatening foes, and springtime found them still at their post, unharmed.

CHAPTER 47

The Sioux Bend to Fate

Captain Marsh and his companions made their way down the Missouri as best they could, suffering not a little from the cold, and in a few days they reached Poplar River, where the agency of the Fort Peck Reservation was located. At the time of their arrival trouble of a serious nature was brewing here with some of the Sitting Bull Indians, which, in a few weeks, was to culminate in bloodshed. Strangely enough, the crisis had been produced by the efforts of the Government to bring about peace.

During the previous summer, Mr. E. H. Allison, post interpreter at Fort Buford, a man possessing great influence among the Indians, had been authorized by General Terry to visit the camps of Sitting Bull in Canada with the object of inducing that chief to come in with his followers and settle down on the reservations assigned to them. Suffering severely from lack of food and clothing and harassed whenever they ventured across the Line by General Miles and the other indefatigable guardians of the border, the remnant of irreconcilables had very nearly reached the limit of endurance. As a result of Mr. Allison's assurances that if they would surrender their previous misconduct would be forgiven and their necessities relieved by the government, numbers of them soon began coming in at Poplar River Agency.

At first their conduct was peaceable, but after their hunger had been appeased their confidence in themselves was restored, especially as their numbers were constantly being increased by new arrivals from Canada. They grew arrogant and began thinking more of plundering the agency and escaping once more to the north than they did of surrendering. The agent, Mr. Porter, becoming alarmed, appealed for troops and two companies of the 11th Infantry, under Capt. O. B. Read, were despatched to his assistance.

It was at about this time that Captain Marsh and his companions from the *Batchelor* reached the scene. The appearance of Captain Read's troops had not at all overawed the Indians assembled about the agency, who were still in such superior numbers that it had tended rather to increase than to diminish their arrogance. On the morning of Captain Marsh's arrival, he and his party spent some time at the post trader's store of Leighton and Jordan, the principal *loafing place* of the agency. A crowd of the hostile Indians were in the store, trading, and they were conducting themselves in so overbearing a manner that the clerks waiting upon them could not conceal their uneasiness. Presently one of the latter brought out a pouch full of mail which was to go to Fort Buford under escort. The clerk ran a leather strap through the iron staples at its top, locked it and set it down by the front door.

The Indians had been watching him intently and after he had finished, one of them stepped over to the pouch, set it up on end and, whipping out his knife, made motions as if cutting the pouch in two, contemptuously indicating that the staples and strap were *no good*. His companions assented with a chorus of hearty "hows," looking around defiantly at the white men in the store to see whether any would dare offer objections. Had anyone done so there would undoubtedly have been a fight at once, but the clerks were wise enough to keep still and the mail-sack was not damaged. Captain Marsh and his men left next day for Buford, and took part in none of the subsequent trouble with the Indians.

But a few days after their departure, another appeal for re-enforcements was sent from Poplar River to Fort Keogh, for the Indians were increasing so rapidly in numbers that Captain Read's detachment was not sufficient to cope with them. Though the wily Sitting Bull remained out on Milk River, in uncomfortable proximity to Engineer Foulk's *fort*, awaiting the result of events at the agency, Gall, The Crow, and other noted chieftains of his following had come in and were directing the action of the Indians. In response to the second call for help, Major Guido Ilges with five companies of the 5th Infantry from Fort Keogh and two troops of the 7th Cavalry from Fort Custer, was despatched to Poplar River.

The overland march of the troops, lasting nine days, was made through deep snows, in a temperature ranging from ten to thirty-five degrees below zero, and was attended with much suffering. On his arrival at the agency, Major Ilges entered into negotiations with the Indians, but after several days had been devoted to fruitless "talks",

The Crow, on the evening of January 2nd, 1881, put an abrupt period to the hope of a peaceful settlement by delivering the following remarkable ultimatum to Major Ilges:

> I and my people will not move until spring. I am tired of talking with you. The soldiers are cowards and afraid to fight. They cry in winter and cannot handle a gun. If you attempt to interfere with my people there will be trouble. I am ready to fight if you want fight.[1]

At the same time, The Crow sent word to the employees at Leighton and Jordan's store that if they wanted to save their lives they must escape at once, as he intended to attack and kill all the soldiers. "You people have been kind to me in the past," he said, "and I do not want to hurt you. Tomorrow we will fight and wipe out the soldiers and kill everybody at the soldier camp."

Major Ilges was quite ready to accept The Crow's challenge. Next morning, long before daylight, he marched out with his troops and several pieces of artillery and surrounded the main Indian camp in a timber point about two miles below the agency. After a desultory fight lasting several hours, during which considerable loss was inflicted on the hostiles, the greater part of the latter, some three hundred in number, were driven to the agency, where they surrendered at discretion.[2]

A few escaped and carried the news to Sitting Bull, who, taking the alarm, fled again to Canada before he could be intercepted. But one of his principal lieutenants, Crow King, disheartened by the defeat of Gall and The Crow, left him almost immediately with three hundred followers, made his way to Poplar River and surrendered, and soon after, together with the prisoners previously taken there, was transferred down river to the lower reservations. Sitting Bull, with a handful of adherents, remained in the British possessions until the following summer.

On reaching Fort Buford, Captain Marsh remained a few days with Mr. Jordan, one of the owners of the *F. Y. Batchelor,* and then resumed his journey to Bismarck in a lumber wagon. The weather grew constantly colder during the trip, until the mercury reached thirty-five degrees below zero. The low temperature was accompanied by a stinging wind and the captain suffered a great deal, his face

---

1. Official Report of Major Guido Ilges, 5th Infantry.
2. Official Report of Major Ilges.

being black with frost-bite when he arrived at Bismarck. He reached his home in Yankton safely, however, and remained there during the rest of that winter, which was one of the most bitter ever experienced in the Northwest. The snows were so deep that not a train moved on any railroad in northern Minnesota or Dakota between January 1st and April 1st, 1881.

When spring at last opened, it came so suddenly that great floods swept the Missouri Valley, doing millions of dollars worth of damage to agricultural interests, bringing destitution to thousands of settlers and wrecking a number of steamboats, especially at Yankton, where a huge ice-gorge below the city piled the levee with the wreckage of the packets which had been in winter harbour there.

None of Captain Marsh's personal interests suffered in the flood. When it occurred, he had already started from Yankton for Milk River, where he arrived in due season, extricated the *Batchelor* and released Engineer Foulk and his party from their unpleasant guard duty. The captain brought his boat down to Fort Buford and thence went up the Yellowstone to Fort Keogh after a cargo of furs which had been accumulated at Leighton and Jordan's trading-post there. He then went to Bismarck with his cargo, which was one of the most valuable ever carried down the Missouri. It consisted of beaver, otter, and wolf pelts and a few buffalo hides, and was valued at $106,000; a sufficient proof that at that time game was still plentiful in the upper country.

Upon arriving at Bismarck, the captain found that Leighton and Jordan had just purchased a new steamer, the *Eclipse*. She was placed under his command and he continued to operate her during the season of 1881. His first trip with her was to Fort Keogh, where he went, accompanied by four other steamers, to bring down to the lower reservations the several thousand Indians whom General Miles had been gathering together and holding near that post during the preceding few years. The *Eclipse* was the flag-ship of the fleet, which consisted of the *General Terry,* Captain W. H. Sims; the *Josephine,* Captain William Gould; the *Black Hills,* Captain Bob Wright, and the *Batchelor,* Captain T. D. Mariner, the latter the successor of Captain Marsh on his old boat.

There were about 3,000 Indians of both sexes and all ages to be taken down, many well known chiefs being among them, and the fleet presented an imposing appearance as it steamed down the river. At Bismarck and every other town along the route, the people came to the banks to look at the erstwhile hostiles and congratulate themselves that the border was at last safe from their depredations. Such a horde of Indians had never before been gathered as prisoners on the decks of steamboats and until the last had been put off at their destination they were the absorbing topic of discussion along the river.

In collecting such a large body of hostiles at Fort Keogh, General Miles had also come into possession of great quantities of the Indians' property, which he held as contraband of war. The most valuable portion of the booty consisted of several thousand head of horses. Shortly after the *Eclipse* and her consorts had taken the Indians down river, the captured horses at Fort Keogh were sold at auction. Before the sale, the officers of the 5th Infantry at the post looked over the herd and picked out the two finest animals it contained, a pair of beautiful bays, so equally matched in colour, size and manners that they could not be told apart. When the sale began, every officer in the regiment contributed his share to a sum of money sufficient to bid them in. When the next downward bound steamer left Fort Keogh, the team was shipped on her to Mrs. Grant Marsh, at Yankton, with the compliments of the 5th Infantry. Mrs. Marsh was deeply affected by the gift, testifying as it did so delicately to the friendship felt for her husband by the officers of the army, and the horses always remained among her most cherished possessions.

During the summer of 1881, the *Eclipse* was one day steaming away from the landing at Fort Berthold when the attention of everyone on board was attracted by an object of strange appearance floating rapidly down the river toward them. Conjecture was rife for a few moments and then, as the object drew abreast of the boat, the mystery was explained. It was Paul Boynton, the renowned long-distance swimmer, on his way to St. Louis from Glendive, where he had entered the Yellowstone. He was swimming, as was his habit, on his back, propelling himself with a short, two-bladed paddle, and towing behind him a little boat called the *Baby Mine*, which he held by a line fastened around his waist.

Oddly equipped as he was, his appearance in the water was enough to arouse the lively curiosity of any one, but it produced a violent sensation among the Fort Berthold Indians. Those who chanced to be along the shore when he came into view, watched him for a time as if fascinated, their astonishment and alarm growing as he drew nearer. At length they turned and ran at top speed to the camps, to summon their friends and relatives, shouting in their native tongues as they went that a beaver with two tails was coming down the river. Such was their explanation of Boynton's two-bladed paddle. The swimmer eventually reached his destination at St. Louis safely and since that time he has navigated, by his peculiar method, many other of the world's great watercourses.

It is probable, however, that had he undertaken his voyage on the Yellowstone and Missouri a few years earlier, while their banks were haunted by the hostiles of the Sioux, the latter, whatever their awe might have been for "the beaver with two tails," would not have permitted him to escape their rifle balls.

In the spring of 1882, Captain Marsh purchased on his own account the packet *W. J. Behan,* the last upper Missouri River boat with which he was to be identified for many years, for the river trade in that region was rapidly declining and steamboat men were finding it necessary to seek occupation elsewhere. While operating the *Behan,* the captain had an opportunity of meeting that last pillar of uncompromising Sioux hostility, Sitting Bull, under circumstances better calculated to make the acquaintance pleasurable, from a white man's standpoint, than any which could possibly have arisen during the fifteen preceding years, while the name of the famous chieftain was a terror along the border.

As has been previously stated, Sitting Bull held out in Canada until the summer of 1881, when, being in the last stages of destitution, and without the slightest hope of relief or re-enforcement, he came down to Fort Buford on July 19th and gave himself up, together with 187 men, women and children, all there were left of the non-treaty faction of the Sioux Nation. He and his followers were conveyed to Fort Yates, on the Standing Rock Reservation, where they were held as prisoners of war for a short time and then taken on to Fort Randall. Here they remained through the winter and in the spring of 1882 it was decided to take them back to Standing Rock and settle them permanently there.

Captain Marsh was called upon to take the Indians to Fort Yates and the *W. J. Behan* was chartered by the government to convey the much-travelled Sioux to their final location. The boat left Sioux City early in the spring and upon arriving at Fort Randall, took on board 171 Indians. Among them all, the ones who naturally attracted the most notice were Sitting Bull himself and his family, the latter consisting of two wives and a number of children. It was not uncommon among the "heathen" Indians for a man of consequence to have more than one wife.

Sitting Bull had been made the object of much attention during his winter's sojourn at Fort Randall. This had not tended to diminish his already abundant supply of self-esteem and during the northward voyage he gave himself the airs of royalty. The missionary priests in Canada had taught him to write his name and from the soldiers at Fort Randall he had learned the value of money. As the *Behan* steamed up the river, the inhabitants of the country for miles around flocked to the landing-places to catch a glimpse of the renowned medicine-man and hundreds of them were eager to secure his autograph. He was perfectly willing to write it any number of times, at the rate of one dollar per signature, and as nearly everyone was glad to get it for any price, he soon had more money than he knew what to do with. He wrote the name "Seitting Bull," but the peculiar spelling only added to its value as a curiosity.

At Chamberlain and Pierre the people came to the boat in such numbers that the escort, consisting of one company of the 15th Infantry, under Lieut. T. F. Davis, had difficulty in keeping the crowds in order. When Cheyenne River Agency was reached, a half-breed living there, by the name of Frank Chadron, presented Captain Marsh with a handsomely carved pipe-stem. The captain showed it to Sitting Bull and the latter took a fancy to it. Through the interpreter on board, Charles F. Picotte, a well-known and much respected character of the frontier, Sitting Bull told Captain Marsh that he wanted to buy the pipe-stem. As it had been a gift the captain did not wish to part with it, but the chief was so persistent that at last the captain said, jokingly, that he could have it for fifty dollars. Sitting Bull indignantly grunted that fifty dollars was too much money.

"Well," replied the captain, addressing the interpreter, "tell him he has kept me scared for twenty years along the river and he ought to give me something for that."

"I did not come on your land to scare you," retorted Sitting Bull, with dignity. "If you had not come on my land, you would not have been scared, either."

The reply was so convincing that Captain Marsh made no attempt to pursue the argument further, though the chief did not get the pipe-stem.

While not applying particularly to Sitting Bull, Captain Marsh noticed an amusing peculiarity of the wild Indians during this trip and the voyage of the preceding summer from Fort Keogh; a peculiarity which few white people have probably had occasion to notice. For some reason they were unable to walk up a stairway. Invariably when they tried to do so they would stumble and fall, making ludicrous attempts to right themselves. But they could only reach the top finally by going on their hands and knees and crawling up.

After reaching his new dwelling place, which was not far from the spot where he had been born, forty-three years before,[3] Sitting Bull settled down quietly and caused no further trouble until the beginning of the Messiah Craze, in 1890, when he threw his influence with the ghost dancers. On December 15th, 1890, he was killed by Indian police, men of his own blood, while resisting arrest at his home. Students of Indian history generally do not rate Sitting Bull very high, either as a soldier or as a statesman. But certain it is that, whatever his deficiencies, he succeeded in holding for himself throughout his life a position of great prominence among his people. His name will doubtless be a familiar one in American annals long after those of most of the other men who fought on the North-western frontier, both white and red, are forgotten, save by the historian.

With Sitting Bull's surrender had come, at last, a final conclusion to the long series of wars, which, beginning with the Minnesota outbreak in 1862, had lasted, almost without interruption, for nineteen years. The conflict for the subjugation of the Sioux was the most extensive, the most sanguinary and the most costly war ever fought with the aborigines of the North American continent. During its course, hundreds of gallant soldiers and thousands of brave warriors laid down their lives in the name of a patriotism whose purity could be as truly claimed by one as by the other, for the contest was between two utterly diverse modes of existence, one of which had inevitably to be blotted out in order that the other might live.

When it began, the vast region between the Mississippi and the Rocky Mountains was the undisputed empire of the Sioux Nation; when it ended, nothing of that empire remained to the Sioux save the comparatively insignificant patches of ground which the United States government had elected should be theirs. A proud, a patriotic and a fearless people, they had fought with desperate valour for all the human heart holds most dear, freedom and home and native land, pitting the naked breast and the untutored mind of savagery against the relentless skill of civilization.

The Baron de Jomini has truly said:

---

3. *History of the Sioux Indians*, Doane Robinson.

National Cemetery and present (1909) monument of the battlefield of the Little Big Horn.

National wars are the most formidable of all. This name can only be applied to such as are waged against a united people, or a great majority of them, filled with a noble ardour and determined to sustain their independence; then every step is disputed, the army holds only its camp-ground, its supplies can only be obtained at the point of the sword, and its convoys are everywhere threatened or captured.[4]

If the above definition was not applicable to the Sioux war, it never was applicable to any war. For, whatever, may be said of the Sioux for their failure to observe "the humanities of warfare," it cannot be denied that they were fighting for their unquestionable moral rights. They were vanquished, but the example which they set should be an inspiration in love of country to future generations of Americans if ever they should be called upon to defend against foreign invasion the lands won from the Indians. The memory of the fiery Sioux, when all is said, is an honour to the wide, wild prairies that bore them.

---

4. *The Art of War* by Antoine Henri Jomini also published by Leonaur.

CHAPTER 48

Turned Turtle

After having safely landed Sitting Bull at Fort Yates, Captain Marsh went on to Bismarck, where he unexpectedly found two men who were anxious to purchase his vessel at a good profit to himself. He made a bargain with them and then returned to Yankton, where he broke up his home and removed with his family to Memphis, Tennessee. His children, two sons and three daughters, had grown up in Yankton; the sons, John and Grant C, completing their education in the schools of that city. The captain was loath to leave the town where he had resided for so many years, but he foresaw better business opportunities on the Mississippi, and availed himself of them.

Though the lower river trade had diminished until its importance was insignificant compared with earlier years, at the same time so many steamboat men had left it for other fields of enterprise that there was still employment for the few good men who clung to the life. Several private companies were engaged in freight and passenger business on the Mississippi, while the United States Government kept a number of steamboats constantly employed in river improvement work. So for the next twenty-one years Captain Marsh found a satisfactory means of livelihood on the Father of Waters.

During 1884 and 1885, he operated the ferry-boat *P. H. Kelley* at Memphis. The next season he bought an interest in the tow-boat, *R. A. Speed,* and for the following four years acted as master of this vessel, towing lumber barges to St. Louis from Cairo, Illinois, and below. In 1890, Mr. T. T. Lewis, of the Eagle Packet Company of St. Louis, secured his services and the captain remained in his employment until 1896, commanding at different times the Cairo and St. Louis towboats *Jennie Gilchrist, Charlotte Brincker, Little Eagle No. 2, Jack Frost* and *Polar Wave.* In 1896, he went on the Pittsburg steamer *Harry Brown,* towing coal from Louisville to New Orleans.

Well and favourably known to the army as Captain Marsh was, the engineers in charge of the extensive National works along the river for the improvement of the channel and the protection of the banks, had long been anxious to obtain his services. After he had been in the tow-boat business for seven years, the opportunity came and he was placed in command of the United States steamer *Mississippi,* the vessel which was used by the Mississippi River Commission for their tours of inspection along the stream from St. Paul to the Head of the Passes, below New Orleans. For three years the captain remained with the government, then, receiving an attractive offer from Captain James Rees, of Memphis, in 1900 he assumed charge of the Memphis and Arkansas City mail packet, *Kate Adams.*

This vessel was the fastest and best equipped on the river. Her hull was built of steel, which afforded her protection against those constant menaces to steamboats—snags. While Captain Marsh was in command of the *Kate Adams,* he was accustomed to run her an average of 1,000 miles per week, three days and three nights of that time being spent in port. In 1902, he left the employment of Captain Rees to again enter that of the Government, this time as master of the Missouri River snag-boat *Choctaw.*

While the captain's life during all these years would have been most interesting if entered into by one unfamiliar with the river and its ways, it contained but few incidents of as stirring a nature as had his earlier career on the upper Missouri, and a recital of its material facts would be more fitting for a government report or a trade journal than for a chronicle of personal adventure and historical incident. One of his experiences during this period, however, by reason of its almost incredible nature, is worthy of mention.

During the summer of 1894, while he was in the employment of Mr. Lewis, the captain had the steamer *Little Eagle, No. 2.* As usual, she was towing lumber barges from points below Cairo to St. Louis. On the morning of September 17th, a day when the sky was cloudy above and the river oily beneath, the *Little Eagle* swung out from the St. Louis levee for a daylight run down river. She was pushing one large barge ahead, neither barge nor steamer carrying any cargo. At about eleven o'clock in the morning, when some seventy miles below St. Louis and just above the point where the Okaw River comes in on the Illinois side, the captain, who was in the pilot-house, steering, glanced to starboard.

The air was perfectly still, oppressively so, and in the western sky he noticed an ominous cloud rapidly gathering. His practised eye instantly comprehended that it was a cyclone. Turning to the speaking-tube, he shouted down to Charlie DeWitt, the engineer on duty, that a bad storm was coming but he would try to make a landing before the boat should be struck.

But in less than thirty seconds the storm was upon them. Under the terrific force of the wind the *Little Eagle* began to careen. Captain Marsh, standing by the wheel, again shouted to DeWitt for all hands to run for the barge. The men obeyed, but none too soon, for they had scarcely reached it when the capsizing steamer careened so far that the boilers broke loose from their fastenings and slid off into the river. The instant they struck the water, they exploded with tremendous force, shattering the forward hull and deck and tearing loose the hawsers which held the barge to the steamer.

The captain, still in the pilot-house, was now cut off from the barge and his only hope for life was to get aft and there seek some means of escape. Fortunately the furious wind had driven the scalding steam and the flying wreckage of the exploded boilers away from him, so that he was not injured. He climbed through the pilot-house window and, as the boat continued to careen, scrambled upward toward the highest point until in a moment the hull was on edge, with the captain clinging to the upturned side. A second later, with a great splash, the *Little Eagle* "turned turtle" completely, and the captain walked out on her flat bottom, dry-shod and unharmed.

The barge with the crew on board was drifting off downstream and presently the wind drove it into the bank at Fort Gage, just above Chester, Ill., where all hands landed safely. The *Little Eagle,* with her single passenger, floated down river for some distance, then some of her submerged upper works caught in the bottom and she grounded in the channel. The short-lived "twister" had now passed, and presently the tow-boat *Sidney Dillon,* Captain Nick Beaver, hove in sight, downward bound. She rescued Captain Marsh from his improvised raft and landed him at Chester, where he rejoined his crew.

All of the captain's possessions on board the *Little Eagle,* as well as those of his men, were, of course, lost, and the captain was even obliged to borrow money from John and Bill Rollins, the pilots of the *Sidney Dillon,* to take his crew back to St. Louis. It is said, and probably no one will arise to dispute the statement, that this is the only instance on record of a man walking from the pilothouse to the keel of a vessel without even getting his feet wet. An occurrence so startling might well be doubted, but there are a score of men today living in St. Louis and elsewhere who were eye-witnesses to it.

The captain had another cyclone experience, though not so disastrous a one, two years later, in the great storm which devastated St. Louis on May 27th, 1896. The river front as well as the city suffered a great deal and many steamboats were torn loose from their moorings and wrecked. Only four vessels remained at the levee and one of them was the Mississippi River Commission's big stern-wheeler, *Mississippi,* Grant Marsh, master. She sustained no damage and was as fit for service immediately after the storm as she was before it.

CHAPTER 49

The Garden Out of the Wilderness

After twenty years' absence from the scenes of his eventful earlier years, during all of which time he could not forget the subtle fascination of the Northwest, the thoughts and desires of Captain Marsh began to turn again almost irresistibly to the regions of the upper Missouri. He longed to look once more upon the vast reaches of prairie and the bald bluffs sweeping along the river, to feel the exhilaration of the keen, pure air borne down from the remote fastnesses of Canada. Nor were his longings impossible of gratification, for the energy and shrewdness of certain business men of the Northwest had been building up, during the years immediately preceding 1902, a new and prosperous river commerce on the waters of the upper Missouri, where, seemingly, it had long before died out for all time. Among these business men, General W. D. Washburn, of Minneapolis, ex-United States senator and flour-mill king, was a pioneer.

In the rich agricultural country bordering the Missouri above Bismarck, he saw an opportunity for the development of a promising river trade. There he purchased an immense tract of land, some 115,000 acres, and built a railroad through it to a point on the river about forty miles above Bismarck. The town which sprang up at the terminus of the railroad was christened Washburn in his honour. Near it, in one of the numberless veins underlying the country, he opened a coal mine which soon had a producing and shipping capacity of thirty carloads per day. On the river he placed some small, light-draught steamboats and barges to transport lumber and merchandise to the villages and farms up river and to bring down grain, the famous North Dakota wheat, to the Washburn elevators.

As soon as the steamboat line was started, General Washburn and his managers in North Dakota began importuning Captain Marsh to come up and enter their employ. Under the combined influence of their persuasions and his own inclinations he soon yielded and the summer of 1902 found him once more treading the deck of an upper river steamer and breathing with the delight of a returned wanderer the air of the land he loves so well. In the spring of 1904, General Washburn sold out his railroad and also his two steamboats and two barges, to the Minneapolis, St. Paul & Sault Ste. Marie Railroad Company. The latter immediately disposed of the floating property to Capt. Isaac P. Baker of Bismarck, who forthwith organized the Benton Packet Company. Under his management the fleet has been increased until today it embraces five steamboats, six barges and two ferryboats, the steamers being the *Washburn,* the *Expansion,* the *Bismarck,* the *Weston,* the *Imelda,* and one new boat. Even they are scarcely able to handle the business of the great stretch of country extending from Bismarck to Williston, thirty-seven miles below Fort Buford into which no railroad penetrates save at Washburn.

Captain Marsh has at different times commanded all the boats of the Benton Packet Company, but in the early autumn of 1905, while in charge of the *Weston,* he had a steamboating experience at Bismarck which was unique even in his varied career. One day, through some freak of the current, a sandbar suddenly began forming along the eastern bank of the Missouri, just below the Northern Pacific Railroad bridge. As is always the case on the Big Muddy, the bar built up rapidly and almost before its presence had been noticed, it had attained a height of eighteen inches above the surface of the water and a length of 200 feet along the bank, completely choking the intake pipe of the Bismarck water-works, which entered the river at this point. The water famine thus produced seriously affected not only the city but also the railroad, which depended upon the same source for the supply of its engines. Vigorous measures to reopen the intake pipe became imperative.

It happened that Mr. Nickerson, a constructing engineer of the Northern Pacific, was in Bismarck at the time, in charge of a large force of men who were remodelling the railroad bridge. He made an examination of the bar and then went to Captain Baker and asked him for his best captain and his best boat. Captain Baker instantly designated Grant Marsh as the navigator most thoroughly qualified for any difficult work to be done, and Mr. Nickerson chartered the *Weston* and sent for Captain Marsh. His instructions were brief.

"Captain," said he, "that bar has got to be cleared away at once so that the water-works can operate. I think you can do it with your boat. Ask for what you want, spare no cost, but *open the intake pipe!*"

"Well, I'll tell you, Mr. Nickerson," replied the Captain, doubtfully, "I never tried to run a steamboat through a 200-foot sandbar before, but I'll do my best if you will be responsible in case the boat is damaged or lost."

"I'll take the responsibility and help you all I can, too," answered the engineer. "You can do it and it must be done."

The next day was Sunday. At eleven o'clock in the morning, Captain Marsh backed the *Weston* down on the head of the bar, close in by the main bank, with her stern wheel resting against the sand. From the bow capstans he ran two long hawsers back past the stern, one on either side of the boat, and fastened the end of each to a large log, or *dead man*, buried some distance out on the bar. Then he started the wheel, which, as it revolved, dug out the sand and pushed it toward the bow, while the capstans slowly wound up the hawsers, keeping them taut and pulling the boat back as the wheel cut into the bar.

No current from the river, only slack water, followed the boat into the pocket she was making and presently the sand which was being thrown toward the bow began to settle in front of her, leaving her isolated in a small pool. It began to look as though she were going to imprison herself effectually in the heart of the bar, but her captain kept on with his work doggedly. Back on the bluffs, nearly the entire population of Bismarck had assembled to watch the interesting experiment, though not until afterwards did the captain know how many intent observers he had on that Sabbath afternoon. Mr. Nickerson had suspended operations on the bridge and put his entire force to work carrying coal to the *Weston* to keep her boilers going.

By mid-afternoon the boat had eaten half way through the bar and it became evident that, unless an accident occurred, her effort was going to be successful. Fortunately all went well and at half-past nine that night the pounding wheel broke through the last ridge of sand, and the steamer backed triumphantly out into the main channel. Once the way was cleared, the river current surged into the passage and by the following morning the bar had entirely disappeared, the intake pipe was clear and the water famine ended. Twelve hours after he had cut it through, Captain Marsh ran his boat down over the course she had followed on Sunday and, by sounding, found not less than eight feet of water at any point.

The undertaking had come out even more satisfactorily than Mr.

Nickerson had hoped, while both Captain Marsh and Captain Baker were gratified at its result. On first reaching Washburn in 1903, Captain Marsh was deeply impressed by the evidences on every hand of the rapid development which the country had undergone in the twenty-one years of his absence. When he had left it, it was a wilderness, broken only at wide intervals by a struggling hamlet or the half-subdued claim of an adventurous farmer. Now, its towns were many and flourishing and its rich prairies were either under the plough or furnishing pasturage for the flocks and herds of a prosperous people. The numerous improvements which he found in steamboating practice were also sources of surprise to him, especially when he reflected upon the crude and laborious methods of earlier years.

The Benton Packet Company conducts its business upon the most modern principles. When a load of lumber is to be shipped up river from Washburn, the boat which is to carry it drops down in front of the yard, where a chute leading from the railroad to the river in a few moments transfers a carload of lumber to the steamer's deck. In the same manner, a supply of native coal sufficient for an entire trip, the same coal which twenty-five years ago could not be made to burn by any means, is dumped in a moment upon the deck by merely raising the chute door of a storage bin on the bank. In only one respect did the captain see a chance for improvement in the company's methods.

On his first arrival he found the boats carrying their great loads of wheat down to the elevators in sacks. A great deal of labour was wasted in sacking and unsacking the grain and he began transporting it in bulk on a barge. His improvement was at once adopted by all the boats and now when a cargo arrives before the elevator, a marine leg is lowered into it which sucks up the grain at the rate of twelve hundred bushels per hour and deposits it in freight cars, ready to be hurried away to the markets of the East.

From Captain Baker's central office in Bismarck there radiates a system of telephones by means of which the movements of the boats can be directed for many miles up the river. The Washburn levee is equipped with a line of arc lights which change the darkest night to midday brilliancy and a boat arriving during any hour of the twenty-four suffers not a moment's delay in loading and unloading. Two or three hours are sufficient to discharge a cargo of grain, and two or three more to take on a trip of lumber and merchandise, so that a steamer coming in at midnight can clear again for up-river points before break of dawn. Near the levee is also located a machine-shop for the repair and construction of boats and barges, and a series of marine ways on which, when winter comes, the boats can be hauled up out of reach of the ice.

As soon as the ice goes out in the spring the steamers are ready to be slipped back into the river and set to work. Probably on no river in the United States is the business of steamboating today conducted more efficiently or with more satisfactory results than on that section of the Missouri lying between Bismarck and the mouth of the Yellowstone; an inland waterway long ago abandoned by the government in its river improvement work because it is alleged to be "unnavigable."

In the service of the Benton Packet Company, Captain Marsh has remained ever since his return to the Northwest, excepting for a short time in the fall of 1905, when he was employed by the Government to make an inspection of the Yellowstone. The snag-boat *Mandan,* Captain W. H. Gould, was placed at his disposal, and he examined the channel as far up as Glendive to learn whether it would be practicable to place one or more steamers in the river for the purpose of transporting building materials to the site of the reclamation dam which the government was projecting about twenty miles below Glendive. He found the river in good condition for navigation and the following spring construction work was begun on the dam, the object of which is to furnish water by means of irrigation ditches to a vast tract of partially arid lands in the vicinity.

Thousands of barrels of cement are required in the construction of the work which is to render fertile a section where, in former years, Captain Marsh was wont to encounter the Sioux and the buffalo. His steamer, the *Expansion,* was chartered by the government in the spring of 1906 and he was engaged through the summer in carrying cement from Glendive, on the Northern Pacific, to the site of the dam, which is almost on the dividing line between North Dakota and Montana, and at the western end of which a small town has been established, called Mondak. The dam was then but just begun and was not completed until the summer of 1908. Early in the fall, after he had brought down enough building material to complete the season's work on the dam, he took his steamer down to Washburn and engaged in the transportation of the wheat crop until the river froze over, about the middle of November.

During the early summer of 1906, the death of the captain's wife, his faithful companion for forty-six years, brought to him a sorrow from which he can never recover, though he has not allowed it to embitter him toward the world nor to hold him back while strength remains to him from performing the duties of life. His youngest daughter, Lillie, a beautiful girl hardly past twenty, died several years before her mother, whose own sad end was hastened by her loss. But the captain still has two sons and two daughters living, of whom both sons have worthily followed the vocation of their father, while one daughter, Mrs. Robert Gaines, is the wife of one of the most expert pilots of the lower Mississippi.

Thus draws to a conclusion the story of the more interesting events in the life of this navigator of the old-time steamboat era. At the age of seventy-four he is still physically and mentally unbroken, his eye keen, his hand steady, his memory so accurate that hardly one man in a thousand of any age possesses its equal. His recollection of the early steamboats which plied the waters of the Mississippi and its tributaries is phenomenal. If there chance to be mentioned in his presence some forgotten vessel which ran on the Ohio in 1853, he will almost certainly be able to detail, without a moment's hesitation, the names, including initials, of her captain, mate, pilots, engineers, steward and barkeeper, concluding probably with accurate information concerning her length and beam, the number and size of her boilers and the colour of her smokestacks.

Such a memory can belong only to one whose life has been sane and temperate throughout, and Captain Marsh stands today a perfect example, in mental and physical preservation, of the beneficent results of a vigorous, open-air existence, such as Nature designed man to live. Nor is there any reason for supposing that he may not have a long period of usefulness yet before him, for a number of men a dozen or more years his seniors are still navigating steamers on the Mississippi and doing it in a manner which cannot be rivalled by the younger generation. His greatest pride has always been in professional skill, and during his sixty-three years on the rivers of the West no boat under his command, save the *Little Eagle No. 2*, has ever been wrecked.

On neither the Missouri nor the Yellowstone has he ever lost one, even temporarily. Today, with public sentiment rapidly crystallizing in favour of deepening the channels and securing the banks of the nation's inland waterways, such a career may well be studied by those men who would withhold a share in the improvements from the great Missouri on the ground that it is only "a graveyard for steamboats." Grant Marsh never found it so, other men as skilful at the wheel would not, and, sooner or later, the Missouri will have to be prepared for carrying deeper draught vessels and made an avenue for helping to relieve the freight congestion of a territory whose railroad facilities cannot keep pace with its increasing productiveness.

But, after all, the greatest accomplishment of Grant Marsh's life has been the manner in which he has lived it, guiding it by conscience, sweetening it by domestic happiness and mellowing it by consideration for others. He never flinched at the call of duty, he never betrayed an employer, public or private, he never withheld help from the hand of need. Had he been in the habit of giving less generously of his substance he might have laid aside more material wealth for his later years, but he might have had, also, in forfeit, less peaceful contentment of soul. Today, (as at time of first publication), loved by his family, honoured by his many comrades, distinguished and obscure, of the old, valorous days of Indian warfare, and trusted by his associates of the present, he has little to regret in his works accomplished and little to covet in the years ahead, for the greatest rewards of life are already his: a calm mind and a clean heart.

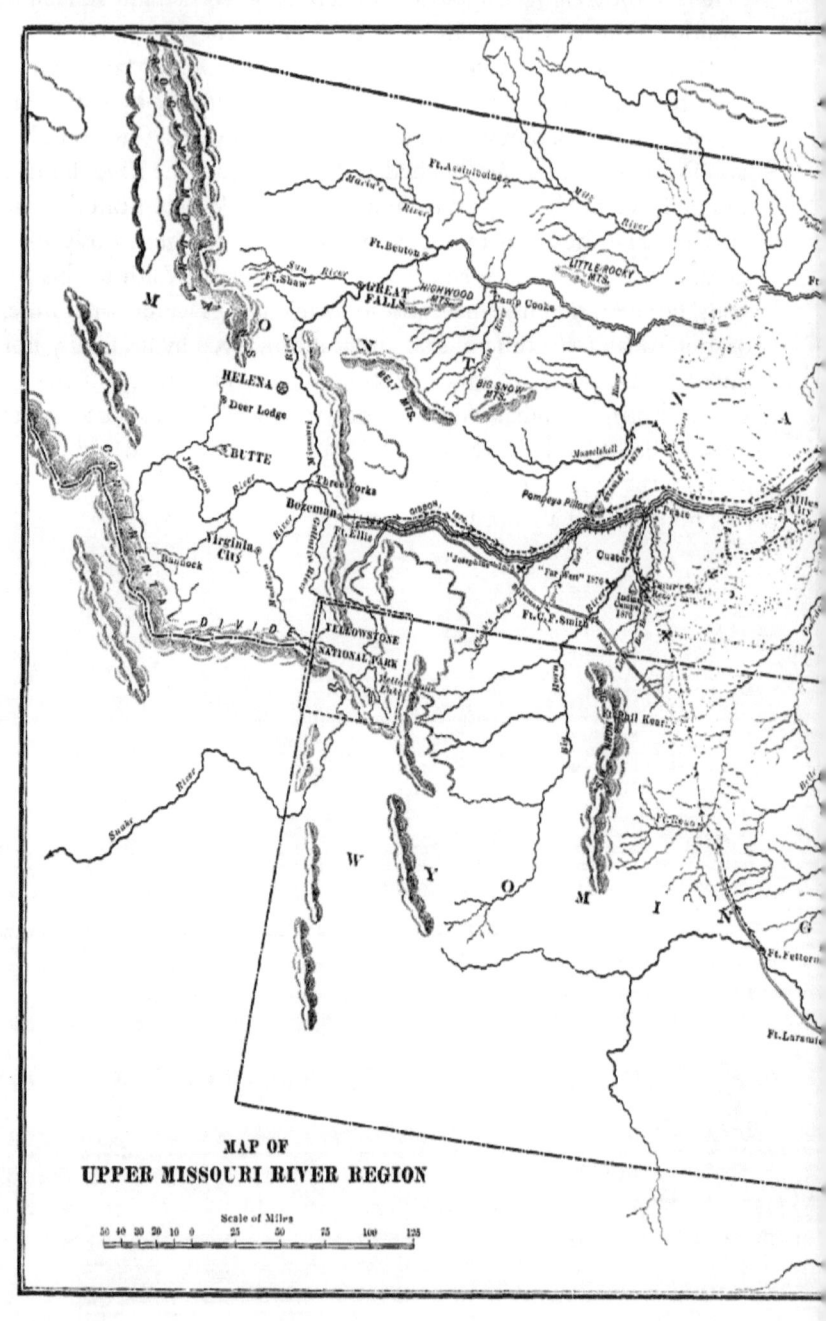

MAP OF
UPPER MISSOURI RIVER REGION

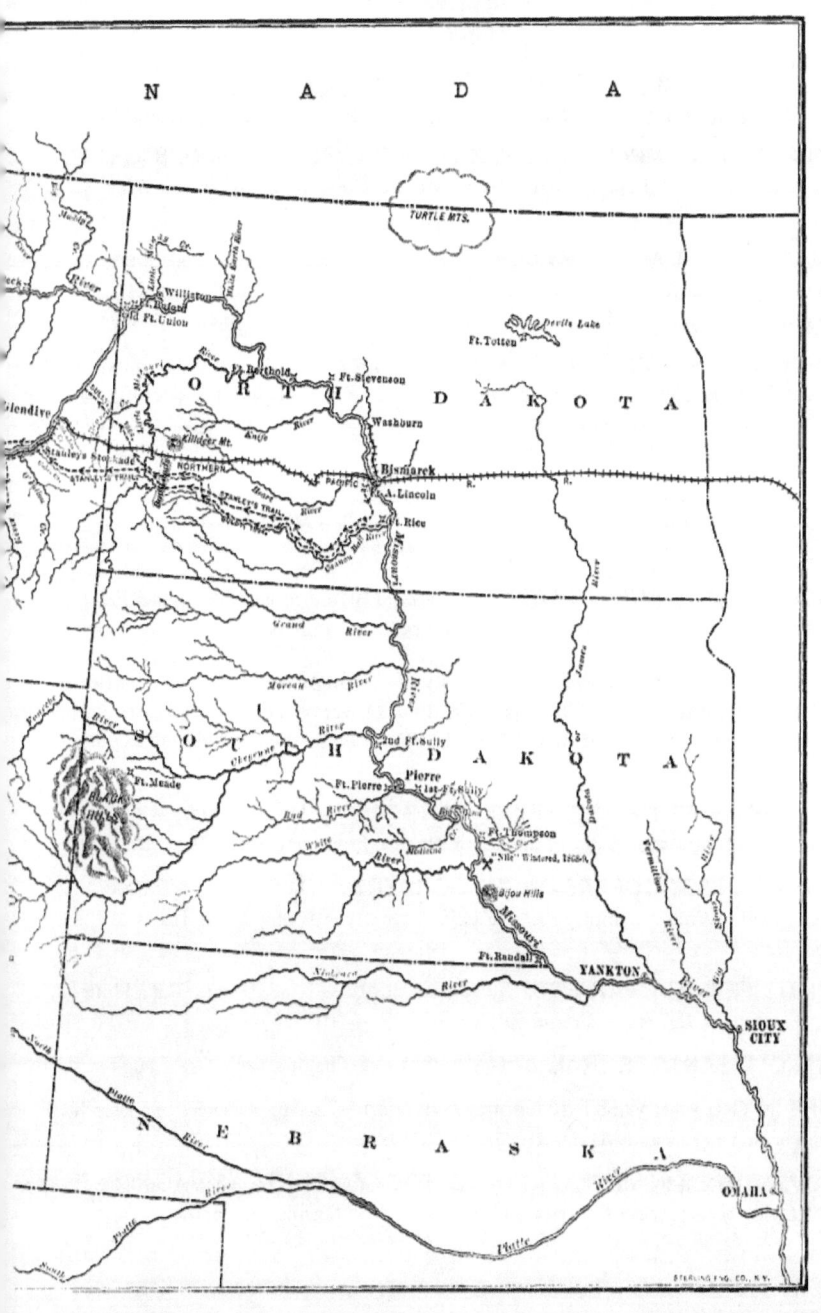

ALSO FROM LEONAUR
AVAILABLE IN SOFTCOVER OR HARDCOVER WITH DUST JACKET

AN APACHE CAMPAIGN IN THE SIERRA MADRE by *John G. Bourke*—An Account of the Expedition in Pursuit of the Chiricahua Apaches in Arizona, 1883.

BILLY DIXON & ADOBE WALLS by *Billy Dixon and Edward Campbell Little*—Scout, Plainsman & Buffalo Hunter, *Life and Adventures of "Billy" Dixon* by Billy Dixon and *The Battle of Adobe Walls* by Edward Campbell Little (*Pearson's Magazine*).

WITH THE CALIFORNIA COLUMN by *George H. Petis*—Against Confederates and Hostile Indians During the American Civil War on the South Western Frontier, *The California Column, Frontier Service During the Rebellion* and *Kit Carson's Fight With the Comanche and Kiowa Indians*.

THRILLING DAYS IN ARMY LIFE by *George Alexander Forsyth*—Experiences of the Beecher's Island Battle 1868, the Apache Campaign of 1882, and the American Civil War.

INDIAN FIGHTS AND FIGHTERS by *Cyrus Townsend Brady*—Indian Fights and Fighters of the American Western Frontier of the 19th Century.

THE NEZ PERCÉ CAMPAIGN, 1877 by *G. O. Shields & Edmond Stephen Meany*—Two Accounts of Chief Joseph and the Defeat of the Nez Percé, *The Battle of Big Hole* by G. O. Shields and *Chief Joseph, the Nez Percé* by Edmond Stephen Meany.

CAPTAIN JEFF OF THE TEXAS RANGERS by *W. J. Maltby*—Fighting Comanche & Kiowa Indians on the South Western Frontier 1863-1874.

SHERIDAN'S TROOPERS ON THE BORDERS by *De Benneville Randolph Keim*—The Winter Campaign of the U. S. Army Against the Indian Tribes of the Southern Plains, 1868-9.

WILD LIFE IN THE FAR WEST by *James Hobbs*—The Adventures of a Hunter, Trapper, Guide, Prospector and Soldier.

THE OLD SANTA FE TRAIL by *Henry Inman*—The Story of a Great Highway.

LIFE IN THE FAR WEST by *George F. Ruxton*—The Experiences of a British Officer in America and Mexico During the 1840's.

ADVENTURES IN MEXICO AND THE ROCKY MOUNTAINS by *George F. Ruxton*—Experiences of Mexico and the South West During the 1840's.

AVAILABLE ONLINE AT **www.leonaur.com**
AND FROM ALL GOOD BOOK STORES

ALSO FROM LEONAUR
AVAILABLE IN SOFTCOVER OR HARDCOVER WITH DUST JACKET

FARAWAY CAMPAIGN *by F. James*—Experiences of an Indian Army Cavalry Officer in Persia & Russia During the Great War.

REVOLT IN THE DESERT *by T. E. Lawrence*—An account of the experiences of one remarkable British officer's war from his own perspective.

MACHINE-GUN SQUADRON *by A. M. G.*—The 20th Machine Gunners from British Yeomanry Regiments in the Middle East Campaign of the First World War.

A GUNNER'S CRUSADE *by Antony Bluett*—The Campaign in the Desert, Palestine & Syria as Experienced by the Honourable Artillery Company During the Great War.

DESPATCH RIDER *by W. H. L. Watson*—The Experiences of a British Army Motorcycle Despatch Rider During the Opening Battles of the Great War in Europe.

TIGERS ALONG THE TIGRIS *by E. J. Thompson*—The Leicestershire Regiment in Mesopotamia During the First World War.

HEARTS & DRAGONS *by Charles R. M. F. Crutwell*—The 4th Royal Berkshire Regiment in France and Italy During the Great War, 1914-1918.

INFANTRY BRIGADE: 1914 *by John Ward*—The Diary of a Commander of the 15th Infantry Brigade, 5th Division, British Army, During the Retreat from Mons.

DOING OUR 'BIT' *by Ian Hay*—Two Classic Accounts of the Men of Kitchener's 'New Army' During the Great War including *The First 100,000* & *All In It*.

AN EYE IN THE STORM *by Arthur Ruhl*—An American War Correspondent's Experiences of the First World War from the Western Front to Gallipoli-and Beyond.

STAND & FALL *by Joe Cassells*—With the Middlesex Regiment Against the Bolsheviks 1918-19.

RIFLEMAN MACGILL'S WAR *by Patrick MacGill*—A Soldier of the London Irish During the Great War in Europe including *The Amateur Army*, *The Red Horizon* & *The Great Push*.

WITH THE GUNS *by C. A. Rose & Hugh Dalton*—Two First Hand Accounts of British Gunners at War in Europe During World War 1- Three Years in France with the Guns and With the British Guns in Italy.

THE BUSH WAR DOCTOR *by Robert V. Dolbey*—The Experiences of a British Army Doctor During the East African Campaign of the First World War.

AVAILABLE ONLINE AT **www.leonaur.com**
AND FROM ALL GOOD BOOK STORES

ALSO FROM LEONAUR
AVAILABLE IN SOFTCOVER OR HARDCOVER WITH DUST JACKET

THE 9TH—THE KING'S (LIVERPOOL REGIMENT) IN THE GREAT WAR 1914 - 1918 by Enos H. G. Roberts—Mersey to mud—war and Liverpool men.

THE GAMBARDIER by Mark Severn—The experiences of a battery of Heavy artillery on the Western Front during the First World War.

FROM MESSINES TO THIRD YPRES by Thomas Floyd—A personal account of the First World War on the Western front by a 2/5th Lancashire Fusilier.

THE IRISH GUARDS IN THE GREAT WAR - VOLUME 1 by Rudyard Kipling—Edited and Compiled from Their Diaries and Papers—The First Battalion.

THE IRISH GUARDS IN THE GREAT WAR - VOLUME 1 by Rudyard Kipling—Edited and Compiled from Their Diaries and Papers—The Second Battalion.

ARMOURED CARS IN EDEN by K. Roosevelt—An American President's son serving in Rolls Royce armoured cars with the British in Mesopotamia & with the American Artillery in France during the First World War.

CHASSEUR OF 1914 by Marcel Dupont—Experiences of the twilight of the French Light Cavalry by a young officer during the early battles of the great war in Europe.

TROOP HORSE & TRENCH by R.A. Lloyd—The experiences of a British Lifeguardsman of the household cavalry fighting on the western front during the First World War 1914-18.

THE EAST AFRICAN MOUNTED RIFLES by C.J. Wilson—Experiences of the campaign in the East African bush during the First World War.

THE LONG PATROL by George Berrie—A Novel of Light Horsemen from Gallipoli to the Palestine campaign of the First World War.

THE FIGHTING CAMELIERS by Frank Reid—The exploits of the Imperial Camel Corps in the desert and Palestine campaigns of the First World War.

STEEL CHARIOTS IN THE DESERT by S. C. Rolls—The first world war experiences of a Rolls Royce armoured car driver with the Duke of Westminster in Libya and in Arabia with T.E. Lawrence.

WITH THE IMPERIAL CAMEL CORPS IN THE GREAT WAR by Geoffrey Inchbald—The story of a serving officer with the British 2nd battalion against the Senussi and during the Palestine campaign.

AVAILABLE ONLINE AT www.leonaur.com
AND FROM ALL GOOD BOOK STORES

www.ingramcontent.com/pod-product-compliance
Lightning Source LLC
Chambersburg PA
CBHW030229170426
43201CB00006B/162